C

Distant Horizons

BY

Gian J. Quasar

Brodwyn-Moor
&
Doane

2011

Cataloguing-in-Publication Data

Quasar, Gian Julius

Distant Horizons

ISBN 978-1-105-19252-4

1ˢᵗ Edition

Distant
Horizons

Distant Horizon

There is a continent on this planet that remains dark, hidden and foreboding. Its foliage is lush and exotic, though it is unseen. It grows on its high mountains. They rise miles high. Yet they too remain unseen. Its ground is desert, yet it is covered by water. It is the largest continent on this planet. It is not far away nor is there any map of its scenic wonders. Those who travel it, travel over it. They are hydronauts, forever on the top of its atmosphere. The oceans of this Earth cover a vast world. It is the opposite of our world as that mad world which pulled

Alice through the looking glass. Yet as night is to day, so is the world of the oceans the partner of our world of the land. As night is the opposite, is the madcap and unpredictable sibling of the day, so is the sea the alter ego of the land.

Storms unleash their impudence over both. But the sea picks up its heels and runs on its hind legs. It dashes to and fro. It's a mad tea party and its tempo is set by a fickle host. Its table-cloth plunges and surges forth. It yanks down and thrusts up-ward. Heller madness! Then it is calm. A flat lifeless desert. Hot, languid, boring.

The sea is not a world that beckons us. The land opposite beckons us, and we chance the world of the seven seas. Ever since mankind began to sail we have used the sea as a highway to rush over to another of our destinations. Other than this we remained by the coasts and cast our nets, never sure exactly what new thing may come with our catch of the day. We didn't know where the fish bred, how they lived or how they migrat-ed. Until the last hundred years we did not even bother to chance the sea's depths. We now know they are miles deep. They cover mountains and valleys, gorges and cliffs. In many places there are mementos of mankind. The skeletons of trage-dy cry out 'shipwreck!' But for some there is no trace. They sailed the top of this vast hydrosphere and have found no peaceful grave on this Dark Continent.

What is that distant horizon but the place that none of us in-tends to go and yet unexpectedly we find ourselves there? That distant horizon is the dwelling place of mystery: the final abode of a taunting fate. It is to those, those who found that distant horizon, that this book is dedicated.

Three quarters of this planet is covered by water and three fifths of it is congregated in the great oceans of this sphere. Thousands have set sail over it and yet never made their port of call. They met only that uncharted destination. Many did not perish by any conventional sense of the term. They vanished utterly and completely. That distant horizon must have taken them completely by surprise. In some cases they even abandoned their ship, their only island of safety in the vast world of the sea, and entered that doorway to this distant horizon by this most unlikely means.

This is not just a book of the unexplained: this is a book of the unexpected. Sea mysteries have captured mankind's attention for centuries because there is no parallel in sea travel that can be found on land. At sea dozens, even hundreds, of people are journeying to the same place, existing in the same element, experiencing the same collective moment, and faced with the same problems of voyagers. When they utterly vanish and leave their ship behind, or when the entire ship vanishes, a collective fate has overwhelmed dozens to hundreds and yet has left no calling card.

Trains are not found abandoned on land. Hundreds have not vanished without clue. Buses do not disappear and their full complement of passengers never seen again. The sea is a shrew, this is true. She cannot be tamed, and she has played a hand in the misery and mystery to those who challenge her realm. But for as many tragedies that left debris to testify to the gambols of her whim there are as many mysteries where no trace is found, though it should have been.

Distant Horizons is not just a compendium of tales of the sea; nor is it the product of mystery magazine reading. Every story in here is based on official accident reports, investigations, and eyewitness accounts. It proves a massive dossier of the unexplained, of the macabre and of the tragic— a dossier of lawless seas and brutal piracy; a ledger of mystery, a chapter in the annals of the inexplicable, a testimony to mankind's audacity, courage and foolishness. Some of these incidents have become quite famous, like the derelicts *Mary Celeste* and *Carroll A. Deering*, but this is the first time they are told with official documentation and, more critically, analyzed on all the evidence.

Thousands of pages of archival papers form the foundation for *Distant Horizons*. These transform these popular stories with hard facts, often making them startlingly different than they have ever been presented before. Pulp renditions have often followed legends and sensationalized angles. Truth is eventually obscured by folklore. But I strive to present the real evidence here. Sometimes this explodes myth. Sometimes it reveals myth to be anemic when compared to the actual mystery the truth provides.

True mysteries of the sea are not just idle tales good for nothing more than whiling away the time. They represent a challenge to our preconceived ideas. The disappearance of large freighters should not be happening; the desertion of a dozen people from a sound and stable ship has no reason. Modern freighters should not have to carry arms and repel boarders. And yet these things do occur. . .and yet only over the sea. Only at sea is mankind so far from civilization, so far from help, so alone. Only there do we realize there is no century of progress. Only there do we realize it is survive or die. . .or meet that distant horizon.

PART I

Uncharted Destinations

CHAPTER ONE

Lo and Behold!

Far out at sea is an uncanny place to be. The curve of the Earth is very apparent. Wherever you are you feel you are on top of the world, sliding on top of a huge dome. How many have said the sea is like the face of a clock that has stopped? Time is recorded only by the passing of a ship. First the mast appears, then the entire vessel. It mounts the dome with skillful ease and soon sails upon even seas. Passing by it sails on and eventually disappears beyond, once again sinking over the horizon. The last tip of the mast falls over and you are left all alone. Here on the top of the world is a lonely place to be.

Landlubbers, which most of us be, very often are surprised at what the greatest part of our planet really looks like beyond the span of our land bound gaze. We would also be surprised by its sound. There is, in fact, very little, if any. The sounds are provided by wind in the sails or the lapping of the waves against the hull. But if the ship was not there, the voice of the sea would only be an occasional whisper of the wind.

Not only is the sea a vast desert, it is the smooth plain between antagonizing foes. The sky can tear with lightning and the wind can mischievously churn this plain into a tumultuous caldron. The Deep can burst open with flame and smoke and push waves up by hundreds of feet. Scars on the ocean bottom testify to an horrendous past. The Marianas Trench in the Pacific, for example, goes down a staggering 7 miles. When it ripped open at some ancient date the ocean levels must have noticeably plunged.

From the point of view of its bottom, a ship sailing over it would look as tiny and as faint as a big jumbo jet does at 36,000 feet to a ground observer's eyes. As far as that might sound, if this was a distance on land the average person could walk from surface to bottom in a couple of hours. The world is really not so big. Since the Trench goes down several miles from the regular sea bottom, the distance from sea surface to sea bottom is only a couple of miles— 40 or so minutes' brisk walk.

The sea really is but a thin blanket on this planet. But it is an impenetrable veil for the human being. We have, however, probed it by remote submersible and sidescan to know that much of what has been lost over it has not been found. Where do all the relics of mankind's passing finally end up?

Of the many mysteries of the Deep which have caused us to ponder, there is no greater mystery than that of derelict ships. Ships disappear and we shrug. We assume they sank. Or "Pirates, Captain Flint!" But missing crews are a problem indeed. How to explain them? How to explain a perfectly sound ship with no crew? It is so eerie that it fascinates seafarers and land-lubbers alike. In fact, the whole concept of a deserted ship is so intriguing that legends have become fantastic to the point they are unbelievable. These legends may have obscured the real cases or laced them with embellishments, but this does not minimize the fact that the real thing has happened far more than we think. Legends are inspired by genuine cases of mystery. The unnatural aura of a drifter strikes a chord in our inner being. With time we may embellish, but the mind does not embellish the mundane or the easily explained. Embellishment only thrives from enigma. The kernel of truth is often more interesting than legend, for the kernel represents a fact not yet understood and legend often represents a mere mythicized example of its potential.

The kernel of fact is that deserted vessels and missing crews used to be commonplace, especially in the North Atlantic Ocean. Legends may have stolen thunder, and it is these that enter the myths of we landlubbers, but these myths were spun (or begun) by seamen more than a little inspired by the real thing.

A case in point is that of the British ship *Marlborough*. She's a proud unearthly story of a ghost ship. According to the legend, which was even endorsed by Robert Ripley, the *Marlborough* was first sighted in 1913 by the *Johnson* while off Chile. The strange bark was drifting with her sails set but dangling limply. Both the sails and the masts were covered with green mold. When a boarding party came upon the deck, one member fell through because the timbers were so rotted. Rushing to his aid, his mates discovered a floating morgue. Under the helm was a skeleton. Three more were discovered near a panel, 10 in their quarters and 6 on the bridge. Everything about the ship confirmed it was the *Marlborough* of Glasgow. But. . .but. . .she had left Lyttelton, New Zealand, as long ago as January 1890. Her cargo was frozen mutton and wool. Her captain was W.

Hird, and he took on this voyage several passengers. Investigation revealed that the *Marlborough* was last spoken in the Straits of Magellan. She had been searched for as overdue in April 1890 and never found. Now 23 years later she was finally found, with a crew of the dead. All this time she had been a drifter, floating idly with the indifferent currents. Only a mute skeleton manned her ghostly helm.

The story of the *Marlborough* first appeared in the Wellington *Evening Post* on November 13, 1913, so that it had the air of being a newly reported story. On November 26, the official French news agency *Havas* even picked up the story. Ripley would put it in his 1929 book *Believe It or Not Omnibus*.

When I began investigating sea mysteries some 21 years ago this was the first case I examined. Sadly, there was little mystery. Miss J.M. Wraight of Guildhall Library, Aldermanbury, London, where Lloyd's of London's wreck reports and shipping lists are kept, searched the registers. She included the extract of Lloyd's List from October 8, 1913: "London, October 7— The published accounts of the discovery off Cape Horn of the remains of the Glasgow ship Marlborough, which left Lyttelton for London in 1890 and has not been heard of since, are stated to be inaccurate. They appear to have had their origin in a statement made early last year by a pilot to the effect that some twenty-two years ago, when shipwrecked, he came upon the relics of a vessel which he took to be the Marlborough. The statement became known in London some four months ago and after full investigation was considered to be mistaken."

Not much to chew on, but obviously Lloyd's knew about the matter before the *Evening Post* created the lurid story on November 13. Lloyd's not only discounts the new published stories but also the idea that the marooned seaman could have come across the rotting timbers of the old ship. But from this account sprang the legend of the cursed, perpetual drifter, a floating morgue sailing the thin twilight between common existence and supernatural curse.

There is little need to investigate beyond the Lloyd's report. The picturesque scene created by the imaginative writer in Wellington is enough to discount the actual story. Abandoned ships drift at sea, often for a long time. They shift directions and it is therefore unlikely that moss or mold is going to grow appreciably on any part of the vessel. Also, the winds play havoc on sails. After 23 years not one would have been in place; all would have been ripped free.

But that is not to say that most anything else about the *Marlborough* story is impossible. The legend is probably partially based on the actual drift of the tern *Fannie E. Wolston.* She was first reported derelict on October 15, 1891, west of Bermuda in the Gulf Stream, and last reported, as of the publishing of the Hydrographic Office's 1894 wreck report, on February 20, 1894, just a little southwest of that position. But from reports by other ships in those intervening years it was clear that the tern had drifted in the currents around the Sargasso Sea and had come back to the place where she was first abandoned. The author of the report, Commander C.D. Sigsbee, writes: "She has, therefore, been a derelict for 850 days, during which she drifted 7,025 miles, the longest track of the kind on record; and, as she is supposed to be afloat yet, her track will probably be still further extended." Published reports, such as the aforementioned Hydrographic Office report (*Wrecks and Derelicts of the North Atlantic, 1887 to 1893 Inclusive*) were few and far between. How many times was the ghostly tern sighted thereafter? How many years did she continue to haunt the Atlantic? Did she make yet another complete orbit of the huge Sargasso Sea? Was she in limbo for many more years?

The legend of the *Marlborough* is quite real it seems. Wrong name, wrong ship perhaps. But in substance such things are possible. Maybe the *Fannie Wolston* is not so dramatic, but she is a worthy inspiration for eerie elaboration. Three and half, perhaps four or more, years drifting at sea being sighted by countless ships (34 ships by the time of the report) is enough to inspire a great and substantive sea yarn. As her legend grew, as more and more ships reported the vessel still miraculously afloat and never re-boarded or hauled to port, how many ships started to give her a wide berth? She earned the reputation as a damned ship, and for this reason she was never towed to port so that any master might dine from her bones in the court of salvage. She continued on until. . .until judgment day buried her and her clues.

No discussion of mysteriously missing crews and haunting drifters can avoid mention of the Sargasso Sea. This sea is essentially ovoid or elliptical in shape and occupies the central North Atlantic Ocean between 20° to 35° North Latitude and 30° to 72° West Longitude— roughly starting a few hundred miles off the US east coast and extending into the eastern Atlantic. Its position places it in the midst of the busiest sea lanes between Europe and America. Ever since the Spanish treasure armadas, ships have used the surrounding powerful Gulf Stream and its associated currents— The North Atlantic Drift, Canary Current, North Equatorial Current, and Antilles Current— to hasten their journey back to Spain or Europe (Gulf Stream, North Atlantic Drift) and back again to the New World (North Equatorial Current, Antilles Current). Experience, however, taught them to avoid the Sargasso Sea, for it was a place of unexplained calms and weak, indolent currents. This area is still called the Horse Latitudes because the Spanish conquistadores, becalmed for weeks, cast over their war horses in order to conserve water as they prayed for the wind to return and guide them out. These seas are also called the Doldrums, from which we developed the word for an inert, heavy depression.

The Sargasso Sea indeed remains one of nature's greatest oddities, for while the North Atlantic is cold and tempestuous the Sargasso Sea is largely an immobile body of warm water. Its relative calmness may largely be the result of the above inter-

The Sargasso Sea in relation to the strong surrounding currents. They completely interlock, forming this ovoid sea within the North Atlantic Ocean.

locking currents. But these currents have not created the Sargasso Sea's most visible oddity. A unique form of seaweed grows over its surface called *sargassum*, from which this sea gets its name. In no other place in the world does this particular seaweed grow. It floats because of little grape-like pods or bladders on its stems, and it feeds upon the sea and all that floats into it. Bunches float idly with the soulful stillness of the lazy swells. Huge mats can cover acres. It doesn't venture oft into the conveyor belt of currents around the sea. Rarely are clumps of it found in other parts of the ocean or washed upon windward shores. It grows here and remains in its native environment.

Nothing, in fact, seems to float out of this sea. Things drift in. But once here they've entered a limbo. The strong surrounding currents funnel most anything in and then greedily clutch them here.

The Sargasso Sea is an odd contrast not only to its surrounding currents but also to all other seas within our great oceans. Almost all currents of the world are circuitous and interlock large ovoid seas in the middle of the oceans. For example, there are the South Pacific and Mentor currents which form the cradle of the South Pacific, and the Benguela and Brazil currents which do the same in the South Atlantic. Charted though they may be, and frequently traveled besides, neither have a peculiar history of calm seas and strange indigenous growth so thick and unaccounted for. Yet the Sargasso Sea is a strange, stagnant abyss of sea and sky with its own floating forest.

Picturesque stories tell us of deserted ships found idling throughout its realm. Becalmed, their fate was to forever remain in its limbo until the crew died and rotted and the vessels became eternal ghost ships. Paintings show ancient galleons next to rusted old steamers. Such paintings are wonderful metaphors, but they are not entirely false. They are artistic distillations. They condense the Sargasso Sea's enduring aura into one powerful image. Doubtless galleons did not remain until the days of steam, but it is not fancy that every form of ship known to us has been found drifting in the Sargasso Sea's eerie solitudes.

As famous as the Sargasso Sea has become in sea lore, much of its mythos is actually stolen. Derelict vessels, especially during the heyday of sail, were actually more common outside of it. In fact, during the 7 years which *Wrecks and Derelicts of the North Atlantic* was compiled by Commander Sigsbee, 1,146 unidentified derelicts were reported and 482 identified vessels. The sum total for only those 7 years was 1,628. In noting the location of these vessels, Sigsbee uncovered an interesting coincidence. "Pilot Charts show that most of the derelicts are sighted in the Gulf Stream off the United States coast, north of 30 degrees north latitude, and west of 60 degrees west longitude. The number gradually decreases to the eastward along the transatlantic steamer routes. A number of those which remain afloat the longest time make the circuit of the Sargasso Sea. The majority of the derelicts were vessels which were abandoned near the United States coasts."

Today, this area is the heart of what perhaps is better known by the infamous name The Bermuda Triangle. Ironically, this modern reputation grew out of journalistic embellishment of only 50 or so missing ships and about 20 missing aircraft. This number, paltry compared to actual statistics, was enough to excite the world on the prospects of an eerie area of ocean where unexplained disappearances predominated. We have conceived theories of alien abductions and wistfully contemplated supernatural explanations. But the Bermuda Triangle, if defined solely as a place where more disappearances and derelicts occur, has a legend whose origins are quite definitely in fact.

For the Bermuda Triangle the 19th century stats on derelicts alone justify its famous and mythic aura. Even if the vast majority of these 1,628 derelicts have a known cause, where crew and captain escaped to tell their tale, it is still amazing that it is here where seamen forgot their senses and abandoned a sound ship more than any other place in the North Atlantic. Out of all the vast North Atlantic it is here where crews leapt from their vessels or mysteriously vanished. Either they flung caution and experience to the wind here more than other places or some mysterious fate befell them. It is interesting to note that Sigsbee's breakdown of derelicts by flag reveals that although American and British ships were the higher percentage (160 and 134 respectively) some 95 Norwegian ships, 24 German, 20 Italian, 11 French, 10 Swedish and even 9 Russian ships, among other nationalities, join the list of vessels where their crews fled safe ship for treacherous waters.

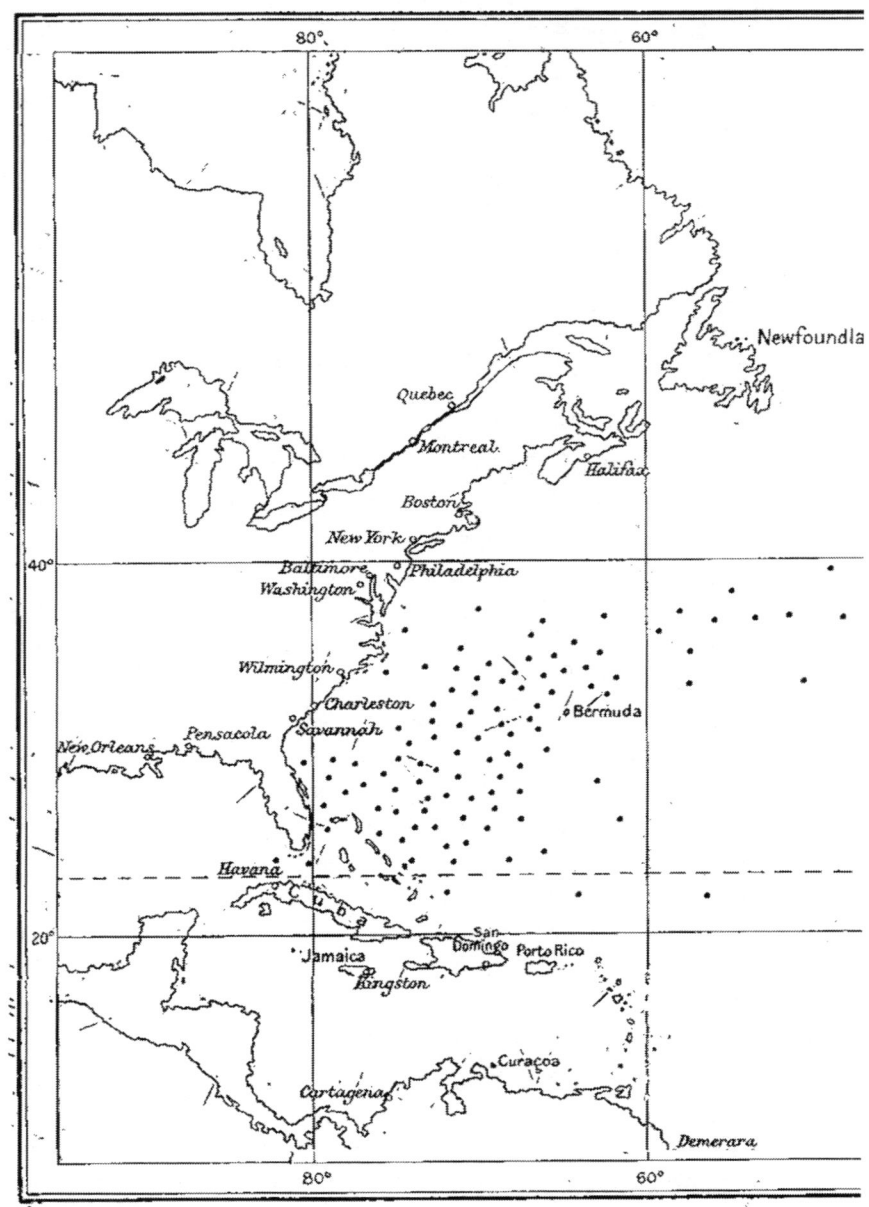

Charting only about 100 of the 1,628 derelicts in Sigsbee's study is

enough to illustrate the drift around the Sargasso Sea.

Even if only 5 percent of these derelicts are completely mysterious— without hint of crews' fate— that would leave a tall
number of 80 vessels for those 7 years of Sigsbee's studies.
Since some 316 were reported floating keel over, we can tenta-
tively reduce the number of ghostly sailing ships. However, we
cannot be sure if some of these capsized hulks were derelicts
keeled-over by storm. Therefore it is not certain whether the
ships were abandoned and drifted sometime before storm later
capsized them.

Sigsbee notes that the number of derelicts increased over the
7 years of research. "This increase is probably not so much the
increased number of derelicts, but it is due to the fact that this
office has gradually increased the efficiency of its ocean patrol
through its constantly increasing number of voluntary cooperat-
ing observers. This feature is exemplified by the fact that in
1893 there were 312 unidentified and 106 known derelicts; or a
total of 418, and an average of 35 per month; and since the average length of time a derelict remains afloat is one month, it is
evidence that there must be 19 derelicts constantly afloat on
the North Atlantic. Prior to 1893 this was estimated at 16, but
fuller reports are received now than in former years."

This minor increase indicates that Sigsbee's work is fairly re-
flective of the actual, routine number of derelicts for those decades before and after. This stable continuity also indicates that
many times the crews must never have been heard from again,
else reports would have been more consistently recorded and
obtainable from some source regardless of the Hydrographic Office's personal network of observers.

An example of how accurately Sigsbee's calculations must
extend backward in time can be found in the transatlantic encounters of the bark *Abd-el-Kader.* On March 8, 1873, just
north of the Sargasso Sea, she came upon the abandoned *Robert C. Winthrop.* Captain Sparrow boarded with a prize crew
and discovered all sails set except the main topsail, which had
been blown away. Four feet of water was in the keel (deter-

mined by sounding the ship) and the boats were gone. Yet Sparrow reported the ship was perfectly fine and manageable. Before he could determine whether he wanted to put a prize crew on board and sail her to their destination (Boston) a gale arose and they returned to the *Kader*, leaving the *Winthrop* to her ghostly fate in the storm. Nearing Boston, the *Abd-el-Kader* then encountered the tern (three-masted schooner) *Kate Brigham*, perfectly sound but deserted. She was bound from New York to La Havre with a cargo of petroleum. Sparrow docked on the 24th, reporting two mysteries of the sea.

So exasperated by such abandonments, the New York *Times* reporter denounced them on March 31. "What can be the matter with the crews of American vessels that they thus abandon their ships and vanish into the unknown? Their vessels were not abandoned because they could no longer protect their crews from the elements. Neither could the motive of their abandonment have been the desire to defraud the insurance companies, for in that case the vessels would have been scuttled. Can it be that the *Flying Dutchman* has crossed the equator in search of forced recruits for his venerable crew?"[1]

A far more eerie encounter supposedly befell the *Ellen Austin* in 1881, when she came upon the same derelict *twice*. The first time she encountered the nameless vessel she was north of the Sargasso Sea. Her master placed a prize crew aboard and in tandem both vessels sailed on to New York. About 2 days later the *Ellen Austin* and the nameless schooner were parted by a squall. When the squall dissipated, the schooner had vanished along with the *Ellen Austin's* prize crew. No trace was ever found of the vessel, and the *Ellen Austin* crew, teeming with superstition, sailed on for New York. Another retelling has the *Austin* indeed finding the nameless schooner again. When next the *Ellen Austin* came across the schooner the vessel was sailing erratically. When the master and crew boarded her again, they

---

[1] The crews from both vessels were actually saved according to Lloyd's.

found the prize crew had also vanished as had the original crew. There they left the cursed drifter to rot at sea. The vessel floated away, a ghostly portal to another world.

Either of the above probably has more truth to it than yet another retelling. In this version the captain once again forced another prize crew aboard and this time the vessel completely vanished with the second prize crew.

The story of the *Ellen Austin* and the "nameless schooner" has gained the status of popular maritime lore, but I was apparently the first to actually try and uncover the facts. Yet all Lloyd's of London was able to confirm for me was that the vessel truly had existed and was sailing in 1881 under the command of Captain A.J. Griffin. She was a big ship, of 1,812 tons, 210 feet in length, built of white oak at Damariscotta, Maine, in 1854. She was one of Grinnell, Minturn & Co. Blue Swallowtail Line of London to New York packets, and by 1881 she was quite an elderly ship. This was actually her last sailing for that line. This voyage ended uneventful in New York on February 11, 1881. She had left London on December 5, 1880.[2] The company decided to sell her this year to Germany, where she was renamed the *Meta*. Did the encounter actually happen to her later that year under this new name? Alas, it was impossible to discover. Some 18 vessels were named *Meta*, and Lloyd's was unable to search all of them.

The story of the *Ellen Austin* was first told by Rupert T. Gould, a retired British naval officer who collected many stories about mysteries of the sea. It made its debut on his short evening radio broadcast from London on October 9, 1935. *The Stargazer Talks* was a popular show, and through this Gould introduced oddities and enigmas into the public mind for 15 minutes. Gould was noted to be very careful and reliable, but his story of the *Ellen Austin* has proven so far untraceable. As it

---

[2] One notes this is an unusually long voyage. If the event did occur at this time, her delay in arriving New York may have been from searching for the vessel and prize crew.

stands, it is also quite flawed. He considers the *Ellen Austin* to be a British ship sailing to St. John's, Newfoundland. Gould also mentions two encounters. "The two ships parted company in foggy weather— but a few days later they met again. And the strange derelict was once more deserted. Like her predecessors, the prize-crew had vanished— for ever."

Gould's many inaccuracies cause one to wonder if even the year of the encounter is a mistake. As we've seen in retrospect there were an incredible number of derelict vessels floating about the Atlantic at this time. It would have been easy to confuse the year. Gould had no doubt picked up a genuine story from a seaman. But much must have been confused by the time it reached Gould. Old mariners also frequently recognized a ship by the unique figurehead regardless if there had been a name change. The old sailor who told Gould the story may have heard the tale and knew some of the men on the vessel but hadn't noticed that the name had been changed to *Meta*.

It is also very possible that the publicized affair of the *Abd-el-Kader* influenced the story's evolution from one encounter to two. Yet as we know, it would not have been impossible, even unlikely, for a ship to have encountered 2 derelicts on this route, much less the same one twice. As a London to New York packet, the *Ellen Austin* most definitely sailed the sea lanes attributed to her in the legend, and was frequently in a position north of the Sargasso Sea to encounter the many derelicts that drifted out of the Bermuda Triangle.

Proof still lies somewhere. Gould rationally courted mysteries. He mentioned a ship long dead and forgotten which I had to uncover through letters to Guildhall Library in England, where Lloyd's Lists are maintained, and to the New York State Historical Society, both of which revealed the particulars of the ship and her last sailing under the American flag. The *Ellen Austin*, whether under that name or *Meta*, might indeed have encountered a schooner and lost its prize-crew to mystery and to a foggy sea.

Had the American Hydrographic Office been in operation for those decades prior to the precision it developed at the end of 1893 we would doubtless have the details on this incident and perhaps dozens more that sailed into that distant horizon and never re-emerged.

In the 19th century the Sargasso Sea's reputation essentially only fed off the crumbs of the as-yet-unnamed Bermuda Triangle. A fraction of many of these derelicts had funneled into its stagnant clutches after drifting in the surrounding currents. There they sat, some perhaps for years, helping to build the legend of a "Sea of Lost Ships" or "Port of Missing Vessels."

Few ghost ships ever drifted out of the Sargasso Sea or its currents to make a real port on their own. But this is the case with the bark *Vincenzo Perotta*. She was first spotted northeast of Bermuda on September 17, 1887. She thereafter drifted 2,950 miles over 536 days to finally end up at Watling Island in the Bahamas. In that time 27 ships reported her, and each carried a tale of mystery to some foreign port.

One alarming incident gives us an idea of what might frighten men from a sound ship in the seas west of Bermuda. It was off the Carolinas in 1904 that the British ship *Mohican* had a bizarre encounter. It was reported by the New York *Times* and the Philadelphia *Enquirer*, July 31, 1904. Here is the story.

ELECTRIC CLOUD ENVELOPED SHIP

Caused Mohicans's Sailors to Become like Animated Magnets

Compass Was Set A-Spinning and Iron Chains Could Not Be Lifted From the Deck

When the British steamer *Mohican*, from Ibraila, Roumania, which reached this port on Saturday, was making for the Delaware Breakwater, it had a most remarkable experience which terrorized the crew, played havoc with the ship's compass and brought the vessel to a standstill for nearly a half hour.

For that length of time the vessel was enshrouded in a strange metallic vapor, which glowed like phosphorus. The entire vessel looked as if it were afire and the sailors flitted about the deck like glowing phantoms. The cloud had a strange magnetic effect on the vessel, for the needle of the compass revolved with the speed of an electric motor and the sailors were unable to raise pieces of steel from the magnetized decks. Captain Urquhart described the thrilling experience and his story is vouched for by every man of the crew.

"It was shortly after the sun had gone," he said, "and we were in latitude 37 degrees 16 minutes and longitude 72 degrees 48 minutes. The sea was almost as level as a parlor carpet and scarcely a breeze ruffled the water. It was slowly growing dark when the lookout saw a strange gray cloud in the southeast. At first it appeared as a speck on the horizon, but it rapidly came nearer and was soon as large as [a] balloon."

Ship in Shining Cloud

"It had a peculiar gray tinge, and as it bore down upon us, we saw bright glowing spots in its mass. A mile away we perceived that it rose several hundred feet above the level of the sea and was almost that broad. It rolled over the sea toward us, the glowing spots becoming more and more vivid. Suddenly the cloud enveloped the ship, and the most remarkable phenomena took place. The Mohican suddenly blazed forth like a ship on fire, and from stem to stern and topmast to keel everything was tinged with the strange glow. The seamen were in terror when they found themselves looking as if they had been immersed in hell fire. Their hair stood straight on end, not from the fright so much as from the magnetic power of the cloud.

"They rushed about the deck in consternation, and the more they rushed about, the more excited they became. I tried to calm them, but the situation was beyond me. I looked at the [compass] needle and it was flying around like an electric fan. I ordered several of the crew to move some iron chains that were lying on the deck, thinking that it would distract their attention. But what was the surprise to find that the sailors could not budge the chains, although they did not weigh more than seventy five pounds each. Everything was magnetized, and chains, bolts, spikes and bars were as tight on the deck as if they had been riveted there."

Hair on Heads Stood Out

"The cloud was so dense that it was impossible for the vessel to proceed. I could not see beyond the decks, and it appeared as if the whole world was a mass of glowing fire. The frightened sailors fell on the decks and prayed. I never saw anything so terrifying in the years I have been at sea. The hair on our heads and in our beards stuck out like bristles on a pig. After we had been in the cloud for about ten minutes, we noticed that it became difficult to move our arms and legs, in fact, all the joints of the body seemed to stiffen.

"Then it was that my sea legs began to fail me for the first time. I've heard of phantom ships and stories about the needle running wild, but shiver me if I had ever seen the like of that. For a half hour we were enveloped in that mysterious vapor. And for nearly all that time, after the sailors' first cries of fright had subsided, there was a great silence over everything that only added to the terror. I tried to talk, but the words refused to leave my lips. The density of the cloud was so great that it would not carry sound.

"Suddenly the cloud began to lift. The phosphorescent glow of the ship and the crew began to fade. It gradually died away and, at the same time, the stiffness left the hair. In a few minutes the cloud had passed over the vessel and we saw it moving off over the sea. It loomed above the water as a great, gray mass, spotted like a leopard's back with the bright, glowing patches.

"The crew gradually regained their composure and whispered to one another. I went among them, telling that all danger was past and they slowly went about their work. When I ordered them to move the iron chains for the second time, the men had no trouble in lifting them from the deck and tossing them about. Then I took a look at the needle and it was pointing steadily toward the north, as it (sic— if) nothing had occurred. I have sailed the seas for many years, but I never encountered a cloud like that. It must have been composed of some magnetized substance, which at the same time was combined with phosphorus."

Lest the reader think this pure fancy (though perhaps literary license has occurred), this report remained long buried and did not see the light of day until the New York *Times* put its archives on the World Wide Web. In the early 21st century the *Mohican* account continued to gain recognition. It did so because for years the survivors of unusual encounters in the Bermuda Triangle had spoken out about encountering weird "electronic fog," strange lenticular clouds with magnetic properties, and unexplained periods where compass needles went haywire and "crazy." These stories were first published in the 1970s during the heyday of world interest on the topic of the Triangle. Long before the many books, including this author's, similar encounters had clearly been had in the same general seas.

Other retrospective discoveries include Charles Lindbergh's flight in 1927. In his 1976 book *Autobiography of Values* he writes of his encounter with a gray mist he took to be a fogbank which caused his navigation equipment to become erratic. He had just left Havana for America and was flying in the area later so frequently dubbed the Bermuda Triangle.

Lindbergh's and the *Mohican*'s encounter are just two coincidences that overlap those seas famous as the epicenter of disappearances and derelict vessels. Even though the majority of crews may survive the high seas to be picked up, it remains an odd coincidence that it is here where more men flee from a sound and stable ship, where their trained and seasoned minds forsake them for a dark and abiding Deep.

Sigsbee noted that although derelicts were concentrated west of Bermuda, many subsequently drifted in the swift North Atlantic Drift, that powerful Gulf Stream current that forms the northern boundary of the Sargasso Sea. The derelicts with the longest track records are those that remained clutched within this current.

Among the *Fannie Wolston* there is the schooner *Manantico*. She drifted in this current for 206 days, traveling 2,600 miles, being spotted 8 times along her ghostly course. Joining her ranks is the *W.L. White*, which drifted 5,910 miles; the *Ethel M. Davis* drifted for over a year, racking up 4,400 miles. The *David W. Hunt* was derelict at the same time, drifting south of her, and making better speed. She covered 4,800 miles during the same period November 1888 to November 1889. The *May Gibbon* did 2,940 miles between August 1892 and July 1893.

In light of these (and dozens more) I include one of the lesser famous tales of sea mysteries here. The *James B. Chester* has been mentioned by a number of credible writers, including Edward Rowe Snow and Rupert T. Gould. Although they give some very intriguing details, Lloyd's was unable to find such a vessel with that name sailing in 1855, the year she was supposedly found derelict southwest of the Azores in the same currents in which those and hundreds more lazily traveled around the Sargasso Sea. According to Snow, it was the last day of February 1855 when the British ship *Marathon* came upon the *Ches-*

ter yawing back and forth as though no one was at the helm. Through the spyglass the captain wasn't able to spot anyone aboard her deck. So he sent Chief Mate Thomas and a crew over to board her. There they discovered the bark in a state of confusion. She had apparently been abandoned in a hurry. "Amidships below they found the cabins evidently ransacked, desks and chairs overturned, and clothing and books scattered seemingly without order or reason," wrote Rowe Snow. "The ship's papers and compass," he continued, "were missing, but the cargo of wool and provisions appeared to be unmolested."

Marathon supposedly towed her to Albert Docks in London, where the *Chester* became the object of much "curious speculation." Theories ran the gamut from the crew having mutinied and robbed the ship to the attack of the giant squid. "Evidently," concludes Snow, "the crew had fled the ship in terror, but what sort of terror it was and what happened to the crew afterwards will probably never be explained satisfactorily."

As we've seen, there isn't even evidence that this incident happened. It certainly didn't happen to a ship with that name in 1855. Had such a vessel been towed to Albert Docks, Lloyds would have been agog with reports. Due to the location of where the vessel was supposedly found, there is probably truth to some of the tale. It's too coincidental that a legend should be set in motion by someone unfamiliar with the pattern of drifting derelicts in the currents south of the Azores (due to the North Atlantic Drift). Perhaps the ship's captain was named James B. Chester and with time this was confused for the name of the vessel.

Such is the case with the famous ghost ship of Block Island off Rhode Island. Since the 18th century witnesses have come to see the burning apparition of the *Palatine*, a ship that went aground, supposedly lured to the rocky coast by murderous wreckers who set up false warning lights. There, according to the legend, they killed the passengers and looted the vessel. It is further said that one woman remained locked in her cabin and refused to come out. Thus when the seas pulled the vessel back out, she could be heard screaming in terror. Battered and rocked by the stormy sea, the *Palatine* slipped below, taking its lone, shrieking passenger to the depths. It is this spectral ghost, striding the glowing, flaming *Palatine* deck, which many have claimed to see thereafter.

Even into the 20th century many Block Islanders were offended that they were often regarded as the descendants of murdering wreckers. They denied their ancestors did this, and insisted in the case of the *Palatine* that their ancestors saved the passengers and treated them very well. One of the islanders, Elizabeth Dickens, was sufficiently irked to actually dig into the matter. She discovered that the ship's name had actually been *Princess Augusta* and that it was carrying German Palatines from the Palatinate State in Germany en route to Pennsylvania to settle. Many of the passengers were rescued and sent on their way to Philadelphia; two settled on the island. Tragically, one woman did stay aboard the vessel. A Mrs. Mary Vanderline owned several gold boxes and silver plate and in her madness refused to leave the ship. The rest is actually true. Battered by the waves and yanked by the winds, the *Augusta* was dragged to sea with her still locked in her cabin. Thus one of New England's most famous nautical ghost stories has far more than a kernel of truth behind the legend.

But what about the *James B. Chester?* As with the *Augusta*, the facts are no doubt waiting to be found. They reside in some dusty maritime annals amidst thousands of other derelicts. Perhaps her crew was later picked up and there is no mystery at all. This is far more frequently the case than not. Yet this does not dispel the chilling aura that the Sargasso Sea and its surrounding currents have inspired for centuries. Crews of passing ships seldom knew what happened to the crew of a deserted ship. They reached port and told of their eerie encounters with a ghostly enigma. And, obviously, they had many encounters to relate. With some 19 derelicts afloat in the area per month, almost every voyage was likely to cross one on the horizon.

Imagining oneself in the situation of finding a derelict ship may evoke the sensation of *angst* captured in this quotation of the short story *Jenny Hanaver*. Reflecting back to the first moment he saw the ship, the author says:

Never shall I seek to experience again, what I experienced that awful hour. An unanswered call, merely the fact of no sound a'tal, ran a cold finger, a lifeless bony finger up my spine.

There she lay becalmed, a three-masted schooner, big sleek and tall. Nothing was out of place in her rigging; her masts were tall in canvas, every line taught and fitting.

So too was the day, the hour in which I found her. She was a point off my beam, dazzled in the reflections of the sunlight. I yawed to catch her with all my might.

Yet when I caught her only the slightest breeze did stir her gaunt sails; a puff and a billow and they dangled limp again.

She was a sleeping phantom, making only the narrowest of creaks from her planks wedging her nails.

At a moment, when upon her deck, I could see at once. All was shipshape; yet there was no master, there was no mate.

The sails slatted in a sudden gust of watchful wind. The shadow of the shrouds swung gently back and forth over the deck; a creak and a groan, and I looked from side to side.

The greatest mystery now faced me, face me all around. Time had seemed to stop, stop at a moment, at an instance, freezing all things, recording a routine moment. The hours, the minutes, seemed little important. They ticked away to the rhythm of her methodically rocking helm.

Like a pendulum the wheel tipped to one side, then to the other. Gently, gently, it recorded the passing being, like the ticking hand of a clock. Yet time seemed to move in no direction; it simply took up space.

A fearful sensation now gripped me. I beckoned to the squeak of a pulley; the barest detectable noise as if an invisible hand had just slightly nudged it.

It was the lifeboat pulley; the lifeboats dangled in place. That was not all: children had left their toys on deck.

The gangway hatch was slid open. Out wafted the smell of a decaying lunch.

This ship coasted on, Jenny Hanaver by name, coasted on in a sea of space. Lifeless, Lifeless, everything was left in its place.

The fearful sensation that gripped me, at once grew greater, over powering it was, increasing an hundred fold as I descended the stairs to the deck below.

The shadows of her lazily swinging cabin doors moved across the corridor floors. Haunting every fiber of my being, I walked silently through their beckoning shadows. They played across my face and shoulders as I passed the cabins by. They seemed to jeer and mock me, pestering me to go. I called for no one, for I wanted no reply.

But alas and anon I gathered the courage: Ahoy, is anyone there?

The loud sound of my call returned to me void, upsetting me the more for its boisterous and rude contrast, for upsetting the gaunt and melancholy silence the lazily creaking ship seemed to covet.

I will never forget that heavy silence, parting before me like a swirling mist. It carried with it a hundred daggers, a thousand piercing and angry eyes, as though to disturb it meant to threaten a secret it guarded, a plaything it shielded.

There was no one left to see me, to hear me, yet I felt a spying eye, an animated conscience, a malevolent pressure. It haunted my back. Between my shoulders I felt it crawling to my neck.

Call it anxiety, if you will. But when I turned, it haunted only where I couldn't see. Yet where my eyes were cast, with a blink it was vanquished. But where they were not, there it brooded, there it considered me.

What had walked within these walls, I felt still stalked between her decks. Would I go where the others had gone? Where could this be? A perfect sea, a sound ship, the lifeboats still hung atop, the ship surrounded by a landless horizon. Where indeed? Where can where be?

A fleeting shadow made me to cringe, as a tiger waiting, hearing, watching for the thrashing of the brush. Though I listened keen for any sound, any faint recognizable sound of a human being, I heard only my pulsating heart. It pressed and pumped in my ear, confusing every frenetic sound . . . Was that a dash? A scurry? A singsong giggle? I could not tell. It was silent again. A terrible vaulting loneliness came over me.

Truth be known, I feared nothing aboard but that which I had brought. I feared not phantoms, spooks, and shadows. I feared what I could not know, what I could only suppose. I dreaded what I could not explain.

Wonder, ponder, and curiosity fill me now. But never, never, no never again, shall I seek to feel the greatest fear of all— not fearing what I cannot know . . . but fearing what might possibly be.

Out of the thousands that have for whatever reason drifted lifeless and crewless on these legendary waters, dozens await rescue from the musty pages of old registers. These dozens are the true mysteries of the sea of lost ships. They have been buried by such vast number of derelicts that they did not even enter legend like the *Marlborough* or *James B. Chester*. And yet, paradoxically, they may be genuinely more mysterious than those few muddled accounts that have been brought to land and bred with ill-gotten fancies over the last three centuries. To expose one legend is little comforting, for perhaps hundreds of real incidents wait to take its place. Whether we ever uncover these incidents or not, it doesn't change the fact that the cause that sent them to that distant horizon still awaits us all.

But there are some cases of drifters so well-documented that volumes exist wherein fact and speculation intertwine to give us disturbing examples of what may have happened in many other cases.

CHAPTER TWO

High Seas Drifter

The most famous derelict to haunt the dusty annals of the sea is the American brig *Mary Celeste*. No other name has come to possess the quality of mystery as that euphonious name carries. It strikes an ominous chord whenever it is spoken, and all around bend an ear to hear the tale recited yet again. Somewhere between her departure point of New York, November 7, 1872, and her destination of Genoa, Italy, her entire compliment of 10 people disappeared. Yet the *Mary Celeste* sailed on until she was discovered, lifeless but shipshape, on 5 December 1872, by the Nova Scotian brigantine *Dei Gratia*. Her master,

Captain David Morehouse, recorded in his ship's log the day's event:

> Begins with fresh breeze & clear, sea still running heavy but wind moderating. Saw a sail to the E 2 p.m. Saw she was under very short canvas, steering very wild and evidently in distress. Hauled up to speak her & render assistance if necessary. At 3 p.m. hailed her & getting no answer & seeing no one on deck on board, sent the mate & 2 men on board. Sea running high at the time. He boarded her without accident and returned in about an hour and reported her to be the "Mary Celeste" of & from New York for Genoa abandoned with 3 feet of water in hold.

To walk through a deserted, creaking ship and there to gaze upon the mementos of interrupted life is a rare experience. It fills one with curiosity and it stimulates the mind with questions and overpowers the senses with mystery. Despite pundits to the opposite, the human mind is a very logical device. We all think quickly. We analyze and we deduce rapidly, more than any computer can. It is utterly ridiculous to think that a crew is going to abandon a perfectly stable ship, for the alternative is to head into a very small lifeboat to brave a very inhospitable and temperamental ocean. Therefore no derelict vessel that has been found has ever been written-off lightly, either by those who found them or by those that have investigated them. And the *Mary Celeste* has become world famous for more than just this reason. She was found where she could not have drifted, sailed to the area without a crew, and she had some very suspicious evidence found aboard.

Now, I have had my share of humbugs drop their monocles in my mashed potatoes just from an introduction like this. So it is best that I put some facts in order here before we delve into this strange case. I'm not speaking of axe marks in the top gallant rail or rust on an old Italian sword blade that was promoted as blood. Renditions of the *Mary Celeste* that seriously contain those clues are a hundred years old, and they don't need regurgitating anymore. I'm speaking about a ship on the starboard tack. This setting of her sails was made to catch a wind from the *south*. Yet the wind had consistently been from the *north* since November 25, the last day there was an entry in her daily log. On such a tack it seems impossible that she could have drifted 9 days and some 500 miles and yet remained *on course* with a wind blowing in from an unfavorable direction.

The best explanation for the setting of the sails is that she suddenly hove to and came about and headed back over her course, either to avoid something or to reach another destination. With a wind from the north, a ship intentionally heading westward would indeed be on the starboard tack. And, indeed, she was fallen-in-with heading west and not east, though her course had been eastward to Gibraltar. Her jib was set to the port, but her foremast sails to the starboard tack. That means whatever happened happened before the crew had finished changing her tack. But this would mean that she had not drifted but had *sailed* intentionally to this area some 400 miles off Portugal first. Yet if that was the case, why was there no entry in her log since the 25th of November 500 miles away in the Azores?

We can dispense with the hundred year old rubbish of pirates, gay swordplay and mutiny. But we can also dispense with the bland rubbish that continues today as fact. There was no line attached to the stern of the vessel and leading back to a frayed end. The implication is made that this obviously means that the crew got into the lifeboat and attached it to the ship. Her cargo of raw alcohol is given as the excuse. This theory speculates that it was agitated by a rough sea and began to rumble. This made her master, Benjamin Spooner Briggs, fear a sudden explosion. Thus they took to the lifeboat and stood off, attached to her by a line, waiting to see what would happen. This theory has it that the line ripped free and the *Mary Ce-*

leste sailed on leaving her crew to be swamped in an unforgiving sea.

There was no line. The peak halyard, a long line of the running rigging, was supposedly found "broke." This bit of rigging, about 300 feet long, adjusts the gaff to the mainmast. Translated from nautical terms: the gaff is the top boom on a 4 cornered gaff-rigged sail. The peak halyard is a long rope that adjusts the end (or peak) of that top boom's position. Since it was said to have been discovered broken, it has been theorized that it had been used as a towline that conveniently broke free at the ship's end and thus left no trace of a towline.

Over one hundred years of theorizing has obscured fact with accepted assumptions and doctrinaire conclusions. This dominant theory remains, however, a sincere attempt to explain a very mysterious incident. Its weakest link, however, is that it ignores the fact that other running rigging was found "broke and gone" in the same manner as the peak halyard and yet this other rigging could never have been used as a towline.

But what the endurance of this theory really reveals to us is the extent to which stereotype and formulaic renditions have come to embody the substance of any retelling or speculating about the mystery of the *Mary Celeste.* They survive in the face of the impossible and render the actual evidence mute. This blinds us to examining the case afresh rather than simply fitting it into accepted parameters of economic storytelling.

For the *Mary Celeste* the result is that our popular impressions are hard to change, and these tick-tock between the outrageously sensational to the monstrously mundane. The incident has been written about so much that facts are mingled with conjecture. They no longer stand alone to be influenced by other facts in the chain of evidence. Unfortunately, even the actual testimony in the Vice Admiralty Court Proceedings at Gibraltar has been rendered mute amidst the stereotypes that had arisen within the 42 year time span between the incident and their initial release in 1930.

Writers have referred to the existence of the stenographic Minutes. George S. Bryan was the first in an admirable work, *Mystery Ship* (1942). But in that very year and almost to the month Charles Edey Fay's *Odyssey of an Abandoned Ship* came out and overshadowed it. Bryan quotes the Minutes with great paucity and little skepticism. Although Edey Fay reproduces large portions of testimony, they are not from the actual Proceedings but, once again, from the Minutes. The Minutes completely remove the actual questions posed by the Attorney General, other attorneys and even the Judge. The answers given are thus frequently and literally only one side of the coin. The motivations for the questions, and with this the intent of those asking, is completely void, and this is a deep void which takes away some of the context of the answers given. Edey Fay and Bryan's intent was to present facts that contradicted the overblown legend of half-cooked meals, mysterious survivors, preternatural causes and all the legend that had built up prior to their time. They wrote wonderful biographies of the case, but not investigative theses.

Large excerpts of the Vice Admiralty Court Proceedings were first published by Harold T. Wilkins, who had the genuine English bulldog grip of the old school. He first got the paperwork in 1930 after quite an ordeal with British officials. But his account of the *Mary Celeste* is paradoxically largely obscure. It first appeared as "Light on the Mary Celeste" in the London *Quarterly Review*, 1931. Soon thereafter credit for "rescuing from oblivion" the stenographic copies of the Proceedings was usurped by a man from Liverpool, who took this unfair credit in a New England historical publication (No. 74 Old Darthmouth Historical Sketches). He had actually secured them from Wilkins, paying only half what it cost Wilkins to get the records. It may be from this source that both Bryan and Edey Fay obtained what they did. If both did study the actual Record of

Proceedings at Gibraltar, they made very little critical use of them (although Edey Fay thought Wilkins' article interesting).

At the same time as their limited edition books hit the stands, Wilkins published a short book by a small publisher *New Light on the Mary Celeste*. It is this monograph that was placed within his later compendium *Strange Mysteries of Time and Space*, 1959, published by Citadel Press of New York, a publisher known for its offbeat topics.

Perhaps that's why Wilkins' contributions to the topic are ignored. He also liked to research and write about old South American Indian stories, UFOs, and other Fortean things. But unlike Charles Fort, Wilkins did not just repeat newspaper stories. He was a tenacious researcher for the facts. For the *Mary Celeste* he has preserved for us some very vital evidence.

For 20 years, hin and wieder, I have tried to locate the same documents. I have used, to no avail, a professional researcher who was sure they must still be in Gibraltar. I have contacted Gibraltar and received no aid. In the early 1990s, I asked for all that exists at the American National Archives, receiving much paperwork, but no Minutes. Solly Flood, the British Attorney General and Proctor for Gibraltar, had actually given copies to Horatio J. Sprague, the US Consul at Gibraltar. But he presented them as proof of his efforts on behalf of the USA in the case, asking for payment for all the costs the Proctor encountered during the investigation. Sprague was taken aback. He didn't know what to do. British officials with the Board of Trade then told him to give them back and refuse to pay. Alas, this Sprague did. His cover letter, along with Flood's, remains in the National Archives, but the special stenographic copy Flood had scribes transcribe for him is not there. Thus Wilkins' success of 81 years ago is revealed as doubly valuable.

Although I disagree with Wilkins' conclusions, his extracts of the Minutes and/or Proceedings must be relied on here. They are supported by his use and quotation of many ancillary documents which the US National Archives also has. I have obtained all of these and cross-referenced that Wilkins quoted exactly. The testimony of key witnesses is also identical with those quoted in detail by Edey Fay. The accuracy of his quotation of the V.A. Court Proceedings should not be suspect. I am disappointed, however, that he did not reproduce all the testimony in context. Yet what he does provide, plus the documents I have uncovered, gives us a very accurate accounting. And this gives us far more to mull over when it comes time later to try and assess this mysterious case.

It is best now to go back and start over again and begin to recount the strange case of the *Mary Celeste*.

It was about a week after passing the Azores that Morehouse sighted a sail on the horizon. The vessel was yawing erratically. He decided to close. It took about 2 hours to come around and stand-off. There was no sign of life aboard. There was no lifeboat and the gangplanks had been removed from the railing. The vessel was in a strange state of desertion. Only the jib and the fore top staysail were set. Another sail hung loosely by its corners. But in coming closer it was apparent that a couple other sails had been set, but they had been ripped away. The main stay sail had been lowered and shrouded the forward deck house. The others were furled. The entire ship had a forlorn, unkempt appearance. The tattered sails fluttered with the wind. Those set distended as the vessel's bow came into the wind and then fell back (yawing). Then the sails went flat again.

In the pitching seas it was hard for Morehouse to get a steady sight on the ship's name. The vessel was a brigantine similar to the *Mary Celeste*, but she should have been at Gibraltar by now. And she would not be heading west anyway, and this ship was bearing down on them. Morehouse was well acquainted with Briggs. Seeing what could be his ship like this was distressing. He told his First Mate, Oliver Deveau, to take a couple men and row over in the boat to investigate.

Once there, Deveau's hails of "ahoy" met with no answer. The sails fluttered. Doors to the forward house swayed open and closed. Rigging sulked upon the deck. There were creaks and groans, but no answer except the prying of the boards and the wind moaning plaintively over the open hatches. The wheel was unlashed. The crew hadn't even bothered to tether it. It gently rocked as the sea played with the rudder.

Deveau and one of the crewmen, John Wright (the other, John Johnson, remained alongside in the boat), started to investigate. The first thing Deveau did was sound the bilge. He had noticed one of the pumps had been disassembled to allow a sounding rod down to check how much water was in the bilge. It showed about 3 and a half feet.

At first Deveau didn't know what to make of it. But a quick inspection about the main deck and between decks revealed a possible cause. Her fore-hold and lazarette hold (aft hold) hatches were open, and there was a lot of water between decks. Since the ship seemed sound, he deduced that the water had come in through the open hatches and doorways. Water kegs on the main deck seemed to confirm this. They had been jolted from their chocks, as if hit by a big wave. The stove in the forward deckhouse had also been jolted a couple feet from its place. The condition of the binnacle proved surprising. This is the wood podium upon which is set the compass. It had been knocked over and the compass was smashed. Deveau had never seen a wave come so far up to the stern that it could dislodge the binnacle.

Looking down into the fore hold, however, revealed a utopian find. Hundreds, perhaps close to 2,000, of barrels of raw alcohol were neatly stowed. The cargo was worth a fortune, and it was simply sitting there, firmly racked, while the ship rolled and drifted onward. Something dire truly must have happened to inspire a crew to leave this.

Deveau took a closer look. The main cabin also suggested

heavy weather had been encountered. The 6 windows had been battened up. Canvas and wood had been nailed over them. Descending further into the darkness he found the crew's possessions in their sea chests. Razors had not been tainted yet by rust despite the dampness in the vessel. Cutlery was in its place in the galley.

Then Deveau found the Captain's cabin and the Mate's. Both cabins shared a skylight overhead. The skylight was raised and opened on both ends, allowing the cabins to air out. This was significant. This suggested the vessel had come through the heavy weather and was now airing itself out.

The condition of the *Mary Celeste* when first boarded. Only two sails were set, one was hanging and 2 others had ripped away. One had been lowered. The rest were furled.

The Captain's bed was damp, and the room was wet, apparently from rain coming in the open skylight. There was an impression on the bed. It appeared as if a child had lain there. A couple of open charts were also lying on the bed.

Deveau was looking at the eeriest thing possible: an interrupted moment. The child must have been taken from the bed while another person— the Captain no doubt— pulled out the charts and selected the right one. Is that the case? Was the ship airing itself out after a storm and something else happened that drove them quickly from the vessel?

It was hard to say. There were things that contradicted this. There was a rosewood melodium (like a small piano), for example, under the skylight. Yet it was not touched by water. How could it have not been dampened if the ship had been left open after being deserted? There was nothing else to indicate any dire emergency. Lanterns rocked back and forth, but there was no hint of fire.

Then Deveau noticed the log on the desk. The last entry was dated November 24. The vessel's position was given as 36° 56 minutes North Latitude and 27° 20 minutes West Longitude; in other words, passing through the Azores. Then he found the slate log in the Mate's room. He read the last entry: they had sighted St. Mary's Island, Azores. Since the last entry was at 8 a.m. November 25, and the log had no further entry, it seemed logical to deduce that the vessel was abandoned sometime on the 25th before the ship's daily log could be updated.

It also seemed logical to deduce the *Mary Celeste* had been abandoned while perfectly shipshape, and the sea had had her way with her thereafter. She had drifted for 9 days with her holds and skylight open. The derelict no doubt encountered more heavy weather. It had, in fact, rained that very morning. With her wheel unlashed she was at the mercy of every wave, bounding about and reeling like a newborn colt as the sea slapped her rudder this way and that. This would also explain the water kegs sprung from their position, and it also explained how the heavy cast iron stove was found jolted a couple feet from its place in the galley.

Continuing investigation indicated the vessel was abandoned in a hurry. The seamen's pipes were found. Deveau was surprised, for these are articles a seaman would normally take with him. There was no Bill of Lading for the cargo. The chronometer (to determine longitude), sextant and ship's register were missing. There was indication on the deck that a lifeboat had been secured over the main hatch and had been removed. The gangplanks had been removed from the rail. It seemed the boat had been launched and the gangplanks removed first because they were in the way.

But *why* did the crew leave?

All Deveau knew was that they had a derelict ship with a very valuable cargo. They rowed back to the *Dei Gratia* and he told the captain that from the log it was the *Mary Celeste*.

Morehouse was genuinely surprised. Before he had left on this voyage, he had dinner with Briggs. He knew that he had taken with him his wife, Sarah, their baby daughter Sophie, and what was thought to be a very reliable German crew. Briggs was also part owner of the vessel with James Winchester, a well-known name in New England shipping. Winchester's nephew, Albert Richardson, was also First Mate on the *Celeste*.

Deveau had no explanation. But no matter what had happened, the vessel was sound. He could sail it on to Gibraltar, but he'd need at least 2 men with him. Morehouse was interested in the salvage alright, so true, but he didn't fancy splitting his crew. Yet Deveau's enthusiasm caused him to relent.

By that late afternoon Deveau was headed back over to the vessel, with Augustus Anderson and Charles Lund. They took their things and what food their cook had prepared. For about 2 days his men worked about getting the vessel trim for sail. They pumped her out, repaired the sails they needed, re-secured the hatches, re-erected the binnacle and placed in their own compass.

All this time *Dei Gratia* stood off just in case Deveau would need assistance. Every day thereafter he sighted *Dei Gratia*, sailing in tandem, until the last two days. Heavy weather had hit on December 12 and Deveau set in by land and cast anchor. On the 13th he arrived at Gibraltar, there to see the *Dei Gratia* at anchor, Morehouse awaiting him.

It was required that they report in, and Morehouse had to formally claim salvage. This brought into the equation both the US Consul, Horatio Sprague, and the Vice Admiralty Court, the duty of which is to adjudicate on the matter of restitution after an investigation.

Within 2 hours T. J. Vecchio, Marshal of the Court, had "arrested" the vessel in order to determine the actual salvage rights and make assessments of value. This naturally required him to personally investigate. After his first visit he came back to the court with surprising information. The brig seemed completely seaworthy. Moreover, her cargo, 1,700 barrels of raw alcohol, was valuable, possibly worth over $36,000 dollars, far more than the value of the ship. This information excited the ears of no less than the Queen's Proctor and Attorney General for Gibraltar, Frederick Solly Flood.

Later writers have come to attach onus to Flood's name, so that one must give a lengthy preamble defending themselves if they wish to agree with him on even an insignificant point. Thus I bend a little to that urge here. Stereotype and those ghastly economic renditions of the story have locked Flood into the typecast part of pompous jackanapes, knave and incompetent grandstander. None are accurate. Flood was a flood himself. He could be overwhelming and overbearing. Contemporarily even Horatio Sprague referred to him as a "fussy little man." This may indeed be the case, but there is the old French proverb: "Even the blind sow that roots around long enough will find the acorn." Flood wasn't the most adept theorist, but the evidence indicated there was an acorn somewhere. His problem was that he was a noisy rooter. He did not initially jump to the conclusions that have mired his name with later biographers. But after he found said acorn he snuffled loudly on his way to find the oak.

What stuck in the Hon. Flood's craw the most was how

sound the ship was reported to be, how valuable was her cargo, and that strange location where she was found 500 miles from her last reported position. This motivated Flood's questions throughout the drawn-out Hearing to follow. The reader must keep this in mind as we now delve into testimony.

On the 18th of December, 1872, Oliver Deveau was sworn in before His Worship Judge Sir James Cochrane to give his full account *viva voce* in open court. Flood sat quietly.

Deveau began:

I left New York on 15 November, bound for Gibraltar for orders, Captain Morehouse master. On 5 December, about 1:30 p.m. sea time,[3] being my watch below, the captain called me and said there was a strange sail on the windward bow, apparently in distress, requiring help. By my reckoning, we were 38° 20 North Latitude, 17° 15 West Longitude. We hauled up, hailed the vessel, but found no one aboard. I cannot say whether the master or I proposed to lower the boat, but one of us did, and I and two men went in her to board the vessel. The sea was running high, the weather having been stormy, though then the wind was moderating.

I boarded the vessel and the first thing I did was to sound the pumps which were in good order. I found no one on board the vessel, which had three and a half feet of water in the pumps. The pump gear was good, but one of the pumps was drawn to let the sounding rod down. There was no place to let the rod down without drawing the box, as is often the case in a small vessel. I cannot say how long it would take to draw the pump— it depends on the circumstances. I only used the other pump on my way here, and the first pump I left in the same state as I found it.

I found the fore-hatch and the lazarett-hatch both off. The binnacle was stove in. There was a great deal of water between the decks, the forward house was full of water up to the coaming and is on the upper deck. I found everything wet in the cabin, in which there had been a great deal of water. The clock was spoilt by the water. The sky light in the cabin was open and raised, and the

---

[3] 4 December civil time. Thus the drift of the vessel from Nov. 25 to Dec. 5 was only 9 days.

compass in the binnacle was destroyed. I found all the captain's effects had been left— his clothing and furniture. The bed was just as they had left it, and that and the other clothes were wet. I judged there had been a woman on board. I found the captain's charts and books in the cabin— some were in two bags under the bed and two or three loose charts lay over the bed. I found no charts on the table. I found a log book in the mate's cabin on his desk. The long slate I found on the captain's table. There was an entry in the log book up to 24 November, and an entry on the log slate, dated 25 November, showing that they had made the island of St. Mary. I did not observe the entry on the slate, the first day, and made some entries of my own on it, and so unintentionally rubbed out the entry when I came to use the slate, at least I thought so. I did not find the ship's register, or other papers concerning the ship, but only some letters and account books.

I found the mate's notebook in which were entered receipts for cargo, etc. The book now shown to me is the book I found, also the Mate's Chart. In his cabin hanging over the mate's bed showing the track of the vessel up to the 24th there were two charts— one under the Mate's bed and one, as I have said, hanging over it. I'm not positive whether the chart with the ship's track marked on it was found above or below the mate's bed. There seemed to be everything left behind in the cabin as if left in a great hurry, but everything in its place. I noticed the impression of the captain's bed, as of a child having lain there. The whole of the vessel appeared in good condition and nearly new. There were a great many other things in the cabin, but impossible for me to mention all. The things were all wet. The sky light was not off, but open. The hatches were off, cabin was wet but had no water in it, as the water had naturally run out of it. The masts were good, and the spars, but the rigging was in very bad order and some carried away. The foresail and upper fore topsail had apparently blown from the yards, and the lower fore topsail was hanging by the four corners. The main staysail was hauled down and lying on the forward house as if it had been let run down. Jib and foretop staysail set. All the rest of the sails were furled.

Edward Rowe Snow's 1948 book *Mysteries and Adventures Along the Atlantic Coast* proved very influential on later writers. He suggested that no self-respecting New-England housewife would have an unmade bed past 8 a.m. Therefore the abandonment must have happened about this time. This, however, presupposes that one of the Briggs was not sick, especially the child, since it is a child's impression which was clearest to Deveau. By this reckoning, it could have been a couple of hours after 8 a.m.

In answer to Cochrane's question about how she was rigged, Deveau replied that the vessel was rigged a brigantine of over 200 tons. "I should say she was seaworthy and almost a new vessel. Anchors and chain were all right." He continued with the appearance of the deck.

There were no boats and no davits at the side. It appeared as if she carried her boat on deck; for there was a spar lashed across the stern davits; so that no boat had been there. I went back to my own vessel and reported the state of the brigantine to the captain. I proposed taking her in. He told me well to consider the matter as there was great risk and danger to our lives as well as to our own vessel. We consulted among ourselves and the crew and resolved to bring her in the distance I estimate at six to seven hundred miles, but have not made out the exact distance.

The captain gave me two men, a small boat, a barometer, compass and a watch. I took with me my own nautical instruments, and whatever food our steward had prepared. I went on board the same afternoon, and about the 5th hour afterwards, hoisted the boat on deck, pumped her out and took charge of her. Augustus Anderson and Charles Lund are the names of the two men I took with me. They are not the same men as I took with me when I first boarded the brigantine, whose names were John Wright and John Johnson. We arrived in Gibraltar on the morning of 13 December.

When we first went on board we had a great deal to do to get the ship into order. I found a spare trysail which I used as a foresail. It took me two days to set things to rights as to proceed on the voyage and make any headway. We had fine weather at first and until we got into the Straits when it came on a storm; so that I dare not make the Bay but lay to under Ceuta, and afterwards on the Spanish coast to the east. When I arrived at Gibraltar I found "Dei Gratia" already there. I had seen her almost every day during the voyage and spake her three or four times. We kept company with her until the night of the storm when I lost sight of her. I saw between decks the nature of the cargo— barrels marked 'alcohol' on the head of them— and likewise in the note of the mate of the "Celeste"; whereby it appeared he had given receipts for so many barrels of alcohol at a time. I forgot to state that the cabin, which was a deck cabin, had all its windows battened up. I also found the sounding-rod on deck alongside the pump.

Solly Flood: Would you call the "Mary Celeste" a good sailor?

Deveau: I call both the "Dei Gratia" and the "Mary Celeste" fair sailors. . .Supposing both vessels to have been equally well found and manned and sailed, she would have been faster than our own ship.

Solly Flood: Did you pass any other ship on your voyage before you sighted the "Mary Celeste"?

Deveau: We spoke one other brigantine on our voyage, bound to Boston; we did not pass or see any other vessel of a similar class on our outward voyage. So the first time we could have seen a ship was the day we found her as we did, deserted. I cannot say, without referring to my log where our ship was on the 24th or 25th. I do know we were to the north of the vessel from seeing her track traced on her chart. We were between latitudes 40 and 42. We did not sight St. Mary's at all. I do not know the latitude and longitude of St. Mary's without seeing a chart. I have made only one voyage from New York to Gibraltar before, and we did not sight St. Mary's then. I never was at St. Mary's— never have seen it. . . From 15 to 24 November, we had stormy weather. Most time of our passage the weather was very heavy. During that time we never took off our fore hatch since we sailed. . . The "Mary Celeste" has only two hatches, fore and main, besides the lazarett. . . .

. . .Her head was westward when we first saw her. She was on the starboard tack, but the wheel was not lashed. The wheel gear was good, and with her foresails set she would not come up to the wind and fall off again. With the sails she had set when I first saw her she might come up and fall away a little, but not very much. She would always keep those sails full. The wind was blowing from the north, but not strongly then, though blowing heavily in the morning. We allow for a current running easterly, but the currents there depend very much on the winds. The first point I made when I could take my bearings was Cape St. Vincent. . . .The vessel's sheet was fast on the port side, and she was found on the starboard tack. The wind would entirely govern the tack she was on at the time. Both vessels going one-way might be on the port tack, the other on starboard tack on the same day . . . .

The way in which Deveau gratuitously gave some information can be disturbing, such as how he harped on never seeing St. Mary's or how he tries to clarify, with the obvious intent to minimize, why it isn't necessarily suspicious that the *Celeste* was on the starboard tack and yet found where she was found. It is probably better to be gracious and say that this reflects the extent that Gibraltar was already abuzz with rumors about possible foul play. An uneducated (even an educated) man under oath and under these circumstances might be apt to ramble and let his nerves do the talking.

But, *but*, there is no denying that Morehouse wanted the salvage case sped through the process as quietly as possible. He had even been naïve enough to ask that Court be avoided. Indeed, on the very day the *Mary Celeste* was brought into port Horatio Sprague quickly wrote the State Department in Washington that "the Master of the 'Dei Gratia' claims salvage and would prefer settling this matter out of court if possible, to avoid formalities and other expenses." The last thing Morehouse wanted was a complex, publicized case. The result would be anything but a case sped through the system.

Examples of minimizing can be amply found. One curious bit of testimony concerns the supposed last log entry. Why did

Deveau make a point of clarifying he thought he had rubbed it out when he really hadn't? The only logical conclusion is that at one point after they had docked, perhaps even casually, he must have said that he rubbed it out and this rumor went through Gibraltar's small community and large ears until it reached Vecchio's. Behind the scenes this might have become quite a controversy. The implication would have been he concealed some explanatory or sensational entry. He now tries to make it sound as though there was nothing to it. Did he truly rub out the genuine last entry?

Another curious contradiction is the position of the sounding rod. Deveau said he found it conveniently by the pump. This position naturally tends to support the theory which Deveau had already expressed publicly: that the crew merely misread the reading and thought the ship was sinking, so they quickly abandoned her. Yet he describes a deck swept by heavy seas, and even speculated the heavy sea damage happened after the vessel was abandoned. How then did the sounding rod— but a small metal pin on the end of a line— not get washed away?

When it came to the sounding rod, Augustus Anderson even seemed nervous. He belabored his ignorance to Cochrane: "I was present when the pump was sounded. It was sounded with a piece of line and a bolt six or seven inches long. The line and bolt were found in the cabin. The bolt was about 1 ¼ inches thick, the line was fastened to the bolt 'round the end. There was no hole in it. It had no head to it— it was a piece of iron fastened by having a cord tied round it. We used the same bolt and line to sound with during our voyage to Gibraltar. The mate found the sounding rod on deck, but I did not see him find it. It was all wet and could not be used. I did not see it— the mate saw it. I never took notice of the sounding rod myself. I did not see it when I first went on board. I never saw any other sounding rod than the iron bolt and string. The mate told me that there was a sounding rod lying on deck but that it was all wet and could not be used. He did not tell me what he did with it."

In other words, Anderson wasn't sure if the rod they used was the real one or the one Deveau made because the original was no good. Supposedly, the original was a metal ball on the end of a line. If he initially used the original and yet it was too wet to be worth anything, what weight does his reading of 3.5 feet of water in the bilge carry? Aside from Anderson's skittishness causing us to wonder, the entire sounding becomes very unreliable if we are not sure what line was initially used and if it was actually capable of giving an accurate reading.

Minimizing the whole affair or, as in Anderson's case, distancing themselves from sensitive points, wasn't speeding the case through. It was raising many contradictions. For example, Deveau testified that the log line was missing. This is the long rope, rod and heavy spool used every hour to determine the ship's speed. Yet the flimsy, by comparison, sounding line and metal rod was supposedly still beside the pump. How could one be washed over and not the other?— and indeed not even washed from its place beside the pump?

Consternation over the vessel's sails being set to the starboard tack was definitely one aspect of the mystery that was considered suspicious to the Attorney General's office. It was a sensitive issue because no one, especially the Honourable Freddie Flood, could believe that the *Celeste* could have been abandoned off the Azores and drifted to where she was found in those 9 days. Moreover, the Azores Current in the area is a cross-current. It runs south to southeasterly. The *Mary Celeste* was found slightly *north* of her last position, so that she not only drifted 500 miles eastward but also drifted across the Azores Current and instead of drifting southeast with it she cut across northeast. It was hard not to think that she had been intentionally sailed to this area and abandoned shortly before the *Dei Gratia* came across her.

Much of this evidence is genuinely curious, and further testimony from the *Dei Gratia* prize crew didn't really help to set-

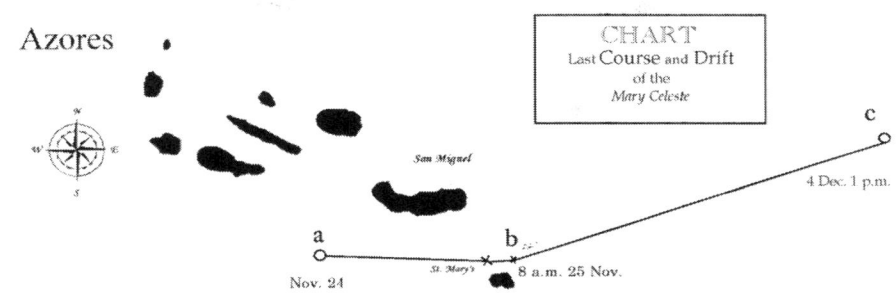

The greatest mystery of the *Mary Celeste*. *a.* position given in log annotation on November 24. *b.* last log entry off St. Mary's, Azores. *c.* Where she was found abandoned by the *Dei Gratia* on December 5 sea time 1872. How did she drift northeast across the current from the place of her last log entry?

tle the matter. Deveau also said too much when it came to the question of the *Mary Celeste*'s lifeboat. He said there was no evidence that the boat had been lashed to the main hatch, meaning not even the ropes that had lashed it to the fenders were present anymore. In this case, we should assume the ropes had been later washed overboard in the heavy weather the drifter encountered. Yet if that is the case, the mystery of the convenient sounding rod is raised yet again. How did but a 6 inch metal pin (or ball) and line not get washed at least down the deck?

Deveau's testimony continues:

> The way down into her hold is through the hatchways, which is quite different from the cabin. Into the cabin, the entrance is through the companion way, down steps. I went into the cabin within a few minutes of sounding the pumps. On the table there was the log slate, but I cannot say what else might have been on the table. I do not know whether there were any knives. I saw no preparations made for eating in the cabin. There was plenty to eat, but all the knives and forks were in the pantry. The rack was on the table, but no eatables. There was nothing to eat or drink, in the cabin, set out on the table.

But preserved meats were in the pantry. I examined the state of the ship's galley. It was in the corner of the forward house, and all things, pots, kettles, etc., were washed up. Water in the house was a foot or so deep. I cannot say how the water got in, but the door was opened and the scuttle hatch off. The windows were shut. There were no cooked provisions in the galley. I never saw the water come over the topmast of a vessel. There was a barrel of flour in the galley, one third gone. We used the provisions found on board the Mary Celeste. We used potatoes and meat, and she had, I should say, six months' provision on board.

Solly Flood: What else did you notice about the ship when you boarded her?

Deveau: The binnacle was injured when I went aboard. I fixed it and used it on our way here. Its glass was broken and the binnacle was washed away from its place. It is lashed on the top of the cabin above the deck, being a wooden one, the lashings had given way, and a cleat was gone. The second time I went aboard I found the cabin compass in the mate's room. There were two quadrants in the second mate's room. The cargo seemed to be in good condition, well stowed and had not shifted. As far as I could judge the cargo was not injured. I found no wine, beer, or spirits whatever in the ship.

Sir James Cochrane: Did you see anything to make you conclude that the Mary Celeste had been overset by a storm or heavy waves and had been thrown onto her beam ends?

Deveau: The vessel was perfectly upright while I was on board and I saw no signs whatever to suggest that she had been on her beam ends at any time. . .If she had been thrown on her beam ends, her hatches would have been washed off. But if she had been thrown on her beam ends, and her hatches had been all close, she might have righted again without her cargo shifting, or without showing any indication.

Sir James Cochrane: Can you form any idea why the officers and crew so mysteriously abandoned the Mary Celeste?

Deveau: My idea is that the crew got alarmed, and, by the sounding rod being found lying alongside the pumps, that they had sounded the pumps and found perhaps a quantity of water in the pumps at the moment, and thinking she would go down, abandoned her.

Again that sounding rod conveniently comes into play. Despite Deveau saying the heavy binnacle was knocked over and "washed away from its place" that sounding rod remained next to the open pump. Perhaps that raised a skeptical brow in the court, too. When John Wright testified later, he gave the sounding rod a little more room to have wandered. He said that it was "found lying on the deck near the cabin."

Deveau seems to have come to his simple theory early-on. Perhaps it was Morehouse's own suggestion in order to minimize the whole affair. Whichever, Deveau stuck with it and yet he could not see how his accurate description of other parts of the deck completely rendered his theory untenable. This theory also presupposes another crewman would not re-check the reading. It also never takes into consideration what inspired the crewman to check the pumps. Deveau's actual testimony, however, prefaces the crew checking the pump *after* getting "alarmed." This might put an entirely different slant on it, but he is often not very clear. His actual wording suggests that perhaps the *Celeste* had some encounter, such as ramming something, and naturally they checked the pumps. A misreading in this circumstance might cause a crew to hastily abandon a sound vessel.

This interpretation of Deveau's statement helps, but only superficially. It doesn't seem very well-founded in light of other factors. For one, when John Wright was called he testified that it would "take about 15 minutes to remove the box, etc., from the pump so as to be able to sound through it." To add injury to insult, there's no experienced mariner who cannot tell if his ship is sinking quickly. It slows drastically, becomes sluggish at the helm and takes the waves in a slow founder. He can feel it under his feet. At sea the ship and the mariner become one person tied together by the sinews of experience. Moreover, the *Celeste*'s holds were by weight only half full. A rapid ingress of water would have been easily felt. Put together, it seems the open pump cannot indicate anything too dire and sudden. A misreading inspired by a routine check would have been disbelieved and rechecked. Something truly imminent would not have left time to sound the pumps.

Yet there is no question that the pump had been drawn out. It is more likely that whatever happened to the *Mary Celeste* happened at the moment the crewman was going about his regular inspection, which included sounding the pumps, and this had nothing to do with why the vessel was abandoned. Deveau clarified that the "pumps would be sounded perhaps every two or four hours. In order to make entry in the long of 'pumps carefully attended to,' the pumps should be sounded every watch of four hours— if the vessel were leaky, more often."

Because Deveau found less than 4 feet of water in the bilge, he was right to assume most of the water had run into the ship after it had been abandoned. The trip to Gibraltar confirmed this. They had to pump the vessel's bilge very little. Deveau testified that "she made little or no water, about an inch in 24 hours. Therefore I conclude that all the water found in her went down through her hatches into her cabin."

If Deveau is right (and his sounding legit), the 3.5 feet of water in the bilge came there through the open hatches after the *Mary Celeste* was abandoned. Thus it is hard to imagine a crewman misread what must have been a miniscule amount of water in the bilge. Whatever the amount, it most likely wasn't much, since the vessel was not a leaky ship. She had been to sea about two weeks when she made the Azores, not enough time for even one and a half feet of water in the bilge. And this assumes they never pumped her daily as Lund did on the voyage to Gibraltar.

In short, the pump being drawn and the sounding rod lying by it probably means nothing. . .unless the ship had hit something. These thoughts, I dare say, were probably going through the Proctor's mind. At the end of that day he prepared a list of things upon which to follow up. One of them was to have

Cochrane issue Vecchio an order to make a thorough inspection of the ship. He quickly retained Richard Portunato, a diver, to make an inspection of the vessel's hull. This would tell whether the *Celeste* had actually hit something that would cause a crew to sound the vessel and, in a panic, suddenly flee a stable ship.

While this was being prepared, two days later, December 20, Solly Flood put Deveau back on the stand. For the first time, Flood showed his suspicion that there was more afoot here. He asked Deveau to state in detail the condition of the Captain's cabin. He went over it in detail yet again. Then the *Mary Celeste*'s chart was produced and placed before him.

> *Deveau*: I found that chart on board the Mary Celeste with the ship's course marked on it. I used it afterwards for our track here. The words written 'Mary Celeste abandoned 5 December, 1872,' are in my handwriting. I put it down merely by guess as the place where I supposed we found the vessel as nearly as I could. The arrows shown on the chart show the way the currents are supposed to run, but they often practically run just in the contrary direction. The chart was found in the mate's cabin.

—Another bit of gratuitous minimizing, just like his earlier comments about how a ship might be on the starboard tack even with a wind from the north.

Deveau wasn't taking into account the big picture, which Cochrane and especially Flood had already considered. He was probably more motivated by Flood and or Cochrane's skeptical faces (or in their tone/demeanor). But whether the currents could behave so in the immediate vicinity was irrelevant to the bigger picture and overriding suspicion. And, indeed, the learned judge now asked:

> *Sir James Cochrane*: How do you account for the fact that, as you say, the Mary Celeste ran 500 or 600 miles with no one aboard, and the sails set as you found them?

Deveau: I cannot give an opinion as to whether the derelict could have run the distance where we found her, in the intervals with the sails she had set. We passed to the north of the group while the Mary Celeste passed to the south. Between the 24 November, and 5 December, the wind was blowing from the north to the southwest.

She was going steadily from one and a half to two knots when we saw her with the wind off her beam. She might have had more sails set at first, but she would not run steadily before the wind with her rudder unlashed. She had two head sails set, her lower foretop sail was hanging by the four corners. The wind was North, her head was to the West. She was on the starboard tack, going in the opposite direction to ourselves when we met her. She probably had changed her course more than once. She was going backwards. It is impossible, therefore, to say how long or often she had changed her course. . .

In other words, once again to belabor a point, the *Celeste* had drifted cross the southeasterly current yet went slightly north, against the northwesterly wind, which was a headwind, and nevertheless maintained her course for 9 days. Now she was turned around, heading westward. John Wright said she was headed northwest by north, exactly opposite them (they were headed southeast by south). There is some debate on what Deveau meant by "backwards." The *Celeste* could have been facing them but drifting backwards toward Portugal. If not, the image their testimony paints is that of a ghost ship sailing on, bearing down on them defying the wind and currents. At the very least, this is truly odd.

When John Wright was called, Flood re-asked some of the same questions. He wanted as many details set in order from the beginning. He was particularly interested in the first thing Wright did after boarding her. He asked: "What did you see when you went down into her cabin?

Wright: I went down into the cabin after assisting to sound her pumps. . . .There is a door to the companion stairs. The door was open. The top of the cabin is above the deck, about ten inches. . . The windows were nailed up on the starboard side with plank, but not on the port side. The windows on that side were shut, but would let the light in. I could not say whether the windows were fastened up for the voyage, or had been fastened during the voyage. On the starboard side the planking was nailed outside the glass. On the port side the windows were shut with glass only, and were not broken. When below in the cabin there was plenty of light to see what was on the table. I did not see any of the sky light glass broken. I saw that the binnacle had been knocked off its stand and was lying on deck alongside the wheel, which was not lashed. There was nothing the matter with the binnacle. It had not been destroyed. But the compass was destroyed and its glass cover knocked off.

The door was open, it was in a bad state. The stove was knocked out of place. That could have been done by a sea striking the galley and the stove through the door. . .The main hatch was fastened and lashed with two rough spars. Why they were put there I can't say.

Flood now had more contradictions before him. Major discrepancies between Wright and Deveau include the latter saying that all the windows were battened down whereas Wright said only those on one side of the main cabin. Deveau had also said he removed one batten from the mate's window, making it seem as if he removed it from within the cabin. But Wright had said the windows were nailed from the outside. There was also disagreement on the state of the rigging. Deveau said the standing rigging was okay. Wright said it was in bad shape. Wright specially said he never noticed the peak halyard, which seems a hard thing to miss if it was snaking over the deck and broken.

By the 20th of December, the 2nd day of the hearings, the *Mary Celeste* case had interested Gibraltar for 7 days. Solly Flood had cross-examined the salvors for two full days. Few Vice Admiralty Courts had seen the intensity of the questioning as in this case. Although he had revealed some suspicion, Flood was not yet sure what to think. He was both Proctor of the Vice Admiralty Court and Attorney General, and he was now mixing the duties of both offices. As AG for Gibraltar he was responsible for criminal matters, which the VA Court is not.

At this time Flood either felt the *Dei Gratia*'s crew was so feckless that they had muddied up clues or they were intentionally lying to cover up clues of violence or mystery in order speed the salvage process. Vecchio's actions subsequent to his orders indicate that Flood must have confided much suspicion in him. As a part of his investigation he requested John Austin, Surveyor of Shipping for Gibraltar, to also get involved and make a full survey. Both began their investigation while Flood, on the 21st, continued to cross-examine other members of the *Dei Gratia*'s crew, in particular Augustus Anderson and Charles Lund.

This revealed more contradictions, especially about the peak halyard. Lund's and Anderson's testimony was more significant than Wright's because they were on board the vessel for days and were the ones who had to repair much of the damage in order to get the ship sailworthy again. Of her standing rigging, Lund said it was "old but taut." The peak halyard "was broke and gone" whereas Anderson said of the standing rigging "was all to pieces; the ratlines were all to pieces." He even said that the ropes of the running rigging (which includes the peak halyard) were "coiled on the deck," not possible if it was "broke and gone."

Each also testified that the first thing he did. Anderson said: "The first thing I did was to sound the pumps. I did not go into the Cabin until I had been on board half an hour." Lund said "I went down into the cabin perhaps in a quarter of an hour or ten minutes after I was on board. . . .The first time I went into the cabin was for the sounding line. I sounded the well of the Celeste— . . .I found it and the line in the cabin. The chief Mate [Deveau] sounded the pump with my assistance." This means everybody sounded the pump first, though it obviously was impossible.

On top of these contradictions, Flood now discovered that Vecchio and Austin considered their discoveries disturbing enough to enlist him to come along and accompany them on their final joint day of inspection. The need for Flood's presence was essential. He was the only one in court all those days. He alone could tell them exactly what had been claimed by the witnesses in contrast to what they had discovered. Vecchio had told him that Portunato had found no indication the ship had hit anything. Moreover, Vecchio could find no real indication the vessel had encountered heavy weather. The barrels of alcohol were well-stowed and had shown no signs of shifting or damage. Austin's findings corroborated this. There was no indication of storm damage.

John Austin's discoveries excited Flood the most. His presence, no doubt hanging moon-like over Austin's shoulder for 5 hours, influenced most of Austin's explanatory comments. His report is several pages long. In it he covers over 60 points, each in its own paragraph, in which he details everything he saw in contrast to what Flood was telling him about the *Dei Gratia*'s crew's testimony. It is safe to say that this document proved the greatest influence on Flood. Not only must he have come back from the *Mary Celeste* that night agog with questions and lurid possible solutions, he must have read and re-read this document. In it Austin contradicts Deveau's testimony in a number of significant places. It is best to quote the report in full.

The Queen in her Office of Admiralty

I John Austin, of the City of Gibraltar, surveyor of shipping, make oath and say:

That by desire of Thomas Joseph Vecchio Esq., Marshal of this Honourable Court, in company with him and Frederick Solly Flood Esq., her Majesty's Advocate General for Gibraltar and Proctor for the Queen in her Office of Admiralty, on Monday the 23rd day of December last, went on board a vessel rigged as a Brigantine name unknown supposed to be the "Mary Celeste" then moored in the port of Gibraltar and under arrest in pursuance of the warrant of this Honourable Court as having been found derelict on the high seas; and I then carefully and minutely surveyed and examined the state and condition of the said vessel and was occupied therein for a period of five hours.

2— On approaching the vessel I found on the bow between two and three feet above the water line, on the port side, a long narrow strip of the edge of one of her outer planks under the cathead, cut away to a depth of about three eighths of an inch and about one inch and a quarter wide for a length of about 6 or 7 feet. This injury had been sustained very recently and could not have been affected by the weather and was apparently done by a sharp cutting instrument continuously applied through this whole length of the injury.

3— I found on the starboard bow but a little further from the stem of the vessel a precisely similar injury, but perhaps an eighth or a tenth of an inch wider, which in my opinion had been affected at the same time by the same means and not otherwise.

4— The whole of the hull, masts, yards and other spars were in their proper places and in good condition and exhibited no appearances whatever that the vessel since she had undergone her last repairs or during her last voyage had encountered any seriously heavy weather. Some of her rigging was old but some of her ropes appeared to have been new at the commencement of her last voyage.

5— The peak halyards and throat halyards appeared to be the same with which she had been rigged during her last and more than once previous voyage. None of them had been recently spliced, and they were all in good working condition. If the peak halyard had been carried over during her last voyage they must have been subsequently spliced which was not the case.

6— If the peak halyard had been carried away while the vessel was under sail and the vessel had been abandoned hurriedly, and without letting go the throat halyards, the Gaff would have been carried backwards and forwards by the wind; the jaws of the gaff would thereby have been destroyed and the mainmast would have been cut into [sic]— but the jaws of the gaff exhibited no signs of any recent injury and the mainmast was undamaged— in such a case also the Gaff would have ripped the mainsail to pieces.

7— Moreover the main boom would have swayed backwards and forwards and in the event of there being any strong wind either the sheets would have been carried away or the bolts would have been torn out of their deck, but they were all uninjured.

8— Upon examining the deck, I found the butts and waterways in good condition. The pitch in the Water ways had nowhere started which it must have done extensively if the vessel had encountered seriously bad weather.

9— The vessel had not bulwarks but was provided with a top gallant rail supported by wooden stanchions, the whole of which were uninjured, but there was a single stanchion displaced. The water barrels on deck were in their proper places and secured in the normary manner but lade that if the vessel had ever been thrown on her beam and or encountered a very serious gale they would have gone adrift and carried away some of the stanchions of the top gallant rail.

10— Returning to the bow of the vessel I removed the forehatch immediately under which was a new hawser which had never been used and was perfectly dry. If any quantity of water found its way into this hatch the hawser would have exhibited signs of having been wetted. It exhibited none nor did any other of the articles which I observed there.

11— I found a forward deck house thirteen feet square and about 6 feet in height above the deck.

12— The deck house was made of thin planking painted white. The seam between it and the deck being filled in with pitch; a very violent sea would have swept this deck house away. A sea of less than very great violence would have cracked the paneling and cracked or started the pitch throughout or at least in some parts of the deck.

13— It had not suffered the slightest injury whatever. There was not a crack in the planking or even in the paint nor in the pitch of the deck seam.

14— The port side of the deck house was divided into two cabins; the forward one extended between nine feet, six inches and ten feet across the deck and about six feet nine inches fore and aft; the after cabin being on the same side was about six feet nine inches. The forward cabin entered by a sliding wooden door facing the bow of the ship.

15— Close in front of the door of the forward port cabin was a seaman's chest unlocked; and in the side of the door opposite to it was another, also unlocked. Both were quite full of seamen's effects of a superior description and mostly quite new. They were perfectly dry and not had the slightest contact with water.

16— Amongst the articles I observed in one of them was a new cigar case with metal clasp not in the slightest degree rusty. It contained nothing but 3 gold studs set with precious stones and a razor also equally unaffected by water. I also particularly noticed a pair of new instep boots and a pair of new high foul weather boots, both perfectly clean; a quadrant in its case together with a piece of chamois leather, all perfectly dry and uninjured and unaffected by water.

17— I also carefully searched for marks of mildew on all the articles, particularly on the boots and the rest of the clothing, but could not discover any or any other marks of water which I believe I must have discovered if the vessel had encountered any very bad weather.

18— I then examined the after cabin on the port side which I believe to have been the Second Mate's, and it contained a seaman's chest similar to those in the forward port cabin and containing clothes which I carefully examined but none of which exhibited the slightest appearance of having been subjected to water.

19— The sills of the doors of these cabins rise to the height of about a foot above the deck. If water had come into either of them to an extent to have flooded them an inch in-depth a great part of the clothing I observed would have shown signs of the water, and none of which were to be seen.

20— The starboard side of the deck house to the extent of about six and a half feet in width and about 3 1/4 feet forward comprise the ship's galley and was entered by a sliding door on the after side.

21— The stove and cooking utensils were in good order and exhibited no appearance of having suffered from exposure to water. Had any quantity of water found its way into the galley it would have immediately passed out thro' a scuttle hole on a level with the deck near the stove or thro' a hole which I found in the deck near the hearth into the hold.

22— The forward deck house was lighted by two windows on each side; those on the port side were covered by a thin sliding shutter; the after window on the starboard side was uncovered.

23— None of the shutters or of the windows were injured in the slightest degree. Some of them must have been greatly injured or wholly destroyed if the vessel had experienced very bad weather.

24— On the upper deck of the deck house I found the remains of two sails which apparently had been split sometime or another in a gale and afterword cut up as large lengths had been cut off with a knife or other sharp instrument, and I subsequently found what I believe to be portions of those sails.

25— On going aft I examined the skylight which lights both the main cabin and the Captain's cabin. It consisted of six panes of glass on each side, the whole of which had a small piece wanting. Had the ship experienced very bad weather the skylight, unless it had been covered which it was not when I surveyed the vessel, would have been greatly damaged.

26 —The height of the cabin is increased by means of a fake deck raised about 15 inches above the deck of the vessel.

27 —The entrance to the cabin is by means of a companion through a door in the forward side and a sliding hatch.

28— On descending into the main cabin I found at the foot of the companion an oblong piece of canvas which I believe to have formed part of one of the sails which had been split and which I had noticed on the forward house. It had been cut and fitted as a lining for a small recess to which it was carefully fastened with nail or screws into a small brass hook apparently intended for the purpose of hanging a towel on; had been carefully driven into one of the uprights.

29— This piece of canvas had evidently been fixed there before the vessel had sailed on her last voyage. The port side of the main cabin was the pantry; entered by a door, the sill of which was about an inch and a half above the level of the lower deck or floor of the cabin. On the floor of the cabin I found among other things an open box containing moist sugar, a bag containing two or 3 pounds of tea, an open barrel containing flour, an open box containing dry herrings, also some rice and nutmeg, some kidney beans together with several pots of preserved fruits and other provisions in tins covered with paper.

The whole of these articles were perfectly dry and had not been in the slightest degree injured or affected by weather.

30— On the plate rack was another piece of canvas apparently cut from off the sails which I had observed on the forward house. It was cut into the shape of a towel for which it was apparently used. On the starboard side of the main cabin was the chief mate's cabin; on a little bracket in which I found a small phial of oil for a sewing machine in its proper perpendicular position, a reel of cotton for such a machine and a thimble. If they had been there in bad weather they would have been thrown down or carried away.

31— The chief mate's bedding was perfectly dry and had not been wetted or affected by water. Underneath his bed place were the vessel's ensign and her private signal WT . The latter had been altered since it had been used. The letter W having been quite recently sewn on.

I also found under the mate's bed place a pair of heavy seaman' boots for storm weather, greased, cleaned and apparently unused, and also two drawers containing various articles.

33— In the lower drawer were a quantity of loose pieces of iron and two unbroken panes of glass which would have been broken to pieces had the vessel encountered any seriously bad weather.

34— In the lower drawer were, among other things, a pair of log sand glasses and a new log reel without any log line.

35— The whole of the furniture and effects in the cabin were perfectly dry and in good condition. None of the articles had been or were injured or affected by water.

36— In the cabin was a clock without hands and fastened upside down by two screws or nails fixed in woodwork of the partition, apparently some considerable time previously.

37— On entering the Captain's cabin, which is abaft the main cabin, I observed and examined a large quantity of personal effects.

38— In the center of the cabin against the partition was a harmonium in very good condition and near to it a quantity of books, mostly of a religious mind and which with the exception of a few which I was informed by the Marshal had been removed by him out of the lowest drawer underneath the Captain's bed place and which were damaged by water, were in excellently good condition.

39— I found also on the floor of the cabin a little child's help chair in perfectly good condition, a medicine chest containing bottles and various medical preparations in good condition.

40— The whole of which articles were uninjured and unaffected by water.

41— The bedding and other effects were perfectly dry. They had not been affected by water and were in good condition.

42— I am of opinion that some [illegible] quantity of water had fallen on the floor of the cabin through the sky light and found its way into the bottom drawer under the Captain's bed place.

43 —In the cabin I found one of the vessel's compasses belonging to the binnacle. The card of it had been damaged by water.

44— I also observed in this cabin a sword in its scabbard which the Marshal informed me he had noticed when he came on board for the purpose of arresting the vessel. It had not affected by water but on drawing out the blade it appeared to me as it had been smeared with blood and afterward wiped. Both the cabins were provided with lamps to be lighted by means of petroleum. They and their glass were uninjured.

45— On the port side of the Captain's cabin was a water closet; near the door of which, opposite to a window imperfectly covered on the outside, was hanging a bag which was damp and had evidently been much wetted by rain or spray or both coming in at the window.

46— I was informed by the Marshal that upon his going on board the vessel for the purpose of arresting her he had found this bag full of clothes, mostly belonging to a lady, and extremely wet.

47— On the starboard side of the cabins were three windows, two of which intended to light the Captain's cabin were covered with canvas similar to that of which the torn sales were made and apparently cut from it, the canvas being secured by pieces of plank nailed into the framework of the cabin. The third window intended to light the chief mate's cabin; no appearance of having ever been covered and the glass was injured. On the side of the cabin facing the bow of the vessel was another window, secured in the same manner, and with the same materials as those intended to light the Captain's cabin.

48— On the port side there was a window which lighted the water closet. It was partially covered in the same manner as that last mentioned. There was a port for another window to light the pantry, but it had been effectually closed up by a wood made to fit into it.

49— Returning to the deck I found one of the pumps in good order, the valve of the other had been removed for the purpose of the passing a sounding apparatus into the well.

50— A sounding apparatus which consisted of a metal ball attached to a line was lying near and was in good order.

51— I then carefully examined the binnacle which I found secured to the deck of the cabin between two battens, the original batten on the starboard side had been replaced by another roughly made. It was further secured by cleats on each side.

52— The binnacle was constructed to hold two compasses and the lamp between them with a pane of glass separating the lamp from each compass. Both their panes of glass were cracked perpendicularly and apparently from the heat of the lamp only.

53— One of the compasses was in good working condition and did not appear to have been otherwise during the voyage. The other was missing, being the one which I found in the Captain's cabin.

54— The binnacle itself did not appear to have sustained any damage.

55— In my opinion it never could have been carried away by a sea which would not have destroyed it and washed overboard.

56— Such a sea would also have swept the decks and carried away the sky light off the cabin, the top gallant sail [sic] and stanchions and besides doing other damage; probably have thrown the vessel on her beam ends.

57— The whole appearance of the vessel shows that the vessel never encountered any such violence.

58— I have examined the after or lazarette hatch, which is secured by an iron bar, and went into the after hold.

59— I found the barrels of stores and other provisions in good order and condition and in their proper places. The whole of these would have been capsized if the vessel had been thrown on her beam ends or encountered any very violent weather.

60— I also saw there a barrel of Stockholm tar standing in its proper position with the head of the barrel off; none of it appeared to have been used. Had the vessel encountered any very heavy weather this barrel would have been capsized or at all events some of the tar would have been spilt, but not a drop of it had escaped.

61— I found no wine or beer or spirits on board. I made the most careful and minute examination through every part of the vessel to which I had access to discover whether there had been any explosion on board and whether there had been any fire, or any accident calculated to create an alarm of an explosion or a fire, and did not discover the slightest trace of there having been any explosion or any fire or of anything calculated to excite an alarm of an explosion or a fire.

62 —The vessel was thoroughly sound, staunch and strong, and not leaking water to any appreciable extent.

63— I gave directions to Richardo Portunato, an experienced diver, minutely and carefully to examine the whole of the hull and bottom of the said vessel— her stern, keel, sternpost and rudder while I was engaged on board in surveying her, and he remained underwater for that purpose for a time amply sufficient for that purpose.

64— I have now perused and considered the paper writing Marked A produced and shown to me at the time of the swearing this my affidavit, and which purports to be an affidavit by said Ricardo Portunato in this cause on the 7th day at January now instant.

65— Having carefully weighed and considered the contents thereof and all and singular the matter aforesaid, I am wholly unable to discover any reason whatever why the said vessel should have been abandoned.

Once on deck, Austin obviously bee-lined it for the peak halyard, for this is the first item he discusses in depth. Deveau had said that the halyard had been carried away and (we must assume) that the re-rigging of same is partly why it took so long to get the brig in order to sail to Gibraltar. Austin's survey completely contradicts Deveau at this point. The peak halyard had *not* been re-spliced.

Those who cavalierly dismiss Austin's report as too influenced by Flood presume anachronistically that Flood wanted to find evidence of foul play. On the contrary, it is Austin's report that influenced Flood to his new attitudes and subsequent actions, which soon would be to try and embroil the US Attorney General in the case as well, not a tack one takes lightly. It seems undeniable that Flood took all this seriously and now implacably suspected Deveau of doctoring his testimony. The *Mary Celeste* had *not* been ravaged by storm. No reason for abandonment meant only one answer: mutiny and murder.

The logical and convenient thing for Flood to do would be to recall Deveau and re-ask him some questions to see how much he lied. Obviously, that was his intention. Thus one of Captain Morehouse's actions came back to haunt Flood yet again. The very thought of it rankled him. Just a couple of days after Deveau finished his initial testimony, Morehouse had him command the *Die Gratia* and leave Gibraltar for Genoa to deliver their cargo. In his place only Morehouse remained. Yet Morehouse repeatedly claimed he knew nothing and that he had never even been on board the *Celeste*. Now, in mid-January, as Flood had all these affidavits before him, he was incapable of following up on anything. He was now more suspicious than ever and fomenting his plans.

We cannot know, of course, if Deveau and Morehouse were aware that an extra investigation of the vessel could be ordered. It wasn't the norm, and indeed Flood later wrote that he ordered these extra investigations because of the original testimony in open court. A departure of significant witnesses before the case was closed made the crew of the *Dei Gratia* look bad, and this now began to irk Cochrane as well.

At the same time Sir James was examining all these affidavits, on the 31st of January, James Winchester, the owner of the *Mary Celeste*, through his counsel, Cornwall, requested his vessel and cargo be restored to him upon his payment of the salvage expenses. Yet too much had already reached Cochrane's ears. In open court, His Lordship responded:

> There are certain matters which have been brought to my notice respecting this vessel, and I have already very decidedly expressed my

opinion that it is desirable and even very necessary that further investigation should take place before the release of the vessel can be sanctioned, or before she can quit this port. The conduct of the salvors in going away as they have done has, in my opinion, been the most reprehensible and may probably influence the decision as to their claim for remuneration for their services; and it appears very strange why the captain of the Dei Gratia who knows little or nothing to help the investigation, should have remained here, while the first mate and the crew who first boarded the Celeste and brought her here should have been allowed to go away as they have done— the Court will take time to consider the claim for restitution.

The time would extend into March, when Deveau was expected to return. In the interim, the "Flood gates" were opened. Letters went back and forth. The extent to which Flood took Austin's report seriously can be appreciated by this alarming letter he penned to the Board of Trade. Earl Granville received the following:

Gibraltar, 22 Jan^{ry} 1873

Sir,

I have the honour to acquaint you for the information of the Committee of the Privy Council for Trade that early on the morning of the 13th December part of the crew of the British vessel "Dei Gratia" bound from New York to Gibraltar for orders brought into this port a Brigantine which they stated they found on the 5th of that month in Latitude 38° 20 minutes, North longitude 17° 15 minutes at 3 p.m. sea time totally abandoned and derelict and which they supposed from the log to be the American Brigantine "Mary Celeste" bound from New York to Genoa.

They stated that the wind being from the North, and the "Dei Gratia" consequently on the port tack, they met the derelict with her jib and foremast staysail set on the starboard tack.

I caused the derelict to be arrested in the customary manner upon her arrival whereupon the master of the "Dei Gratia," which had arrived on the evening of the 13th of November [sic], made his claim for salvage.

The second mate of the "Dei Gratia" and those of her crew who had boarded the derelict were examined in support of the claim to salvage on the 20th and 21st Ultimo.

But the account which they gave of the soundness and good condition of the derelict was so extraordinary that I found it necessary to apply for a survey which was held in my presence on the 23rd of the same month, the result of which is embodied in the affidavit of Mr. Richard Fortunato [sic], a diver sworn on the 7th inst., the Mr. John Austin, surveyor of shipping, sworn on the 8th inst. and Mr. T.J. Vecchio, sworn on the 9th inst.

From that survey it appears that both bows of the derelict had been recently cut by a sharp instrument, but that she was thoroughly sound, staunch, strong and every way seaworthy and well found, that she was well provisioned and that she had encountered no seriously heavy weather and that no appearance of fire or of the explosion or of alarm of fire or of explosion or any other assignable cause for abandonment was discernible. A sword, however, was found which appeared to me to exhibit traces of blood and to have been wiped before being returned into the scabbard.

My opinion in this respect having been corroborated by others, I proceeded on the 17th inst., to make with assistance of the Marshal of the Vice Admiralty Court, a still more minute examination for marks of violence; and had the honour of being accompanied and greatly assisted by:

Captain Fitzroy R.N., HMS Minotaur
Captain Adeane, R.N., HMS Agincourt
Captain Dowell R.N., HMS Hercules
Captain Vanstitart, R.N., HMS Sultan

and by Col. Laffan, Royal Engineers, all of whom agreed with me in opinion that the injury to the bows had been affected intentionally by a sharp instrument.

On examining the starboard of gallant sail [sic], marks were discovered, apparently of blood, and a mark of a blow, apparently of a sharp axe.

On descending through the forehatch a barrel, ostensibly of alcohol, appeared to have been tampered with.

The vessel's Register, manifest and bills of lading have not been found, neither has any sextant or chronometer been found. On the other hand, almost all the personal effects of the master and I believe that of his wife and child and of the crew have been found in good order and condition.

They are of considerable value. In the Capt's Cabin were a Harmonium in a rosewood case, books and music, and others, mostly of the religious tending; gold lockets and other trinkets and jewelry; and female attire of a superior discrimination were in the lady's boxes. The working chart and ship's log were also found on the arrest of the vessel. Both are complete up to Noon of the 24th of November. I transmit copy of the last day's work, and the deck or slate log is continued, copy of which is enclosed up to 8 a.m. on the following day about how the Eastern fourth of St. Mary's (Azores) bore S.S.W. distant 6 miles— she had therefore run considerably less number of knots since the previous noon than that entered in the Slate, the longitude of St. Mary's being 25° 9 minutes W. Since then eight weeks have elapsed and nothing whatever has been heard of the master or crew or of the unhappy lady and child.

The ship's log which was found on board shows the last day's work of the ship was at noon on the 24th November when the weather was sufficiently fine to enable an observation to be taken. The position was then by observation in Latitude 36° 56 minutes, North Longitude 27° 20 minutes West. Entries on the Slate Log are carried up to 8 a.m. on the 25th which is the last and at which time she had passed from W. to E to the north of the island of St. Mary's, the Eastern point of which bore S.S.W. 6 miles distant. The distance of the longitude of the place where she was found from that of the island of St. Mary's is 10° 11 minutes East and the corrected distance of the latitude of the place where she was found from that last mentioned on the log is 1. 18 North, so that she must actually have held her due course for 10 days after the 25th November, the wheel being loose all that time.

My object is to move the Board of Trade to take such action as they may think fit to discover, if possible, the fate of the master, his wife and child, and the crew of the derelict. My own theory or guess is that the crew got at the alcohol and in the fury of drunkenness murdered the master, whose name was Briggs, his wife and child and the Chief Mate; that they then damaged the bows of the vessel with the view of giving it the appearance of having struck on rocks or suffered from a collision so as to induce the master of any vessel which might take them up if they saw her at some distance to think her not worth attempting to save and that they did sometime between the 25th November and the 5th December escape on board some vessel bound for some North or South American port or the West Indies.[4]

I shall, however, be thankful for any information and am:
(signed)
Frederick Solly Flood

HM'S. Advocate General and Proctor for the Queen in her office of Admiralty, and Attorney General for Gibraltar.

Quite a mouthful.

The Queen's Proctor must have tardily seen that his theory lacked substantial backup. The very next day he sent off an addendum.

Gibraltar 23 January
1873

Sir, I beg leave to supplement my letter of the 22nd Instant by enclosing an extract from so much of the log of the "Dei Gratia" as is necessary to show the position of that vessel on and from the 24th of November to the day when she met the "Mary Celeste" on the 5th of December from which it will appear that the wind during the whole of that time was more or less from the North, that she was during the whole of that time on the port tack, and that consequently it seems incredible that the "Mary Celeste" should have run during the same period a distance of 7° 54 East at least upon the starboard tack, upon which tack she was when found by the "Dei Gratia."

---

[4] Or "western Islands"— i.e. the Azores.

The circumstances seem to me to lead to the conclusion that although no entry either in the log or on the slate of the "Mary Celeste" later than 8 a.m. the 25th of November is to be found, she had in fact not been abandoned till several days afterwards, and probably also that she was advanced much further to the eastward than the spot where she was found.

I have the honour to be
Fred Solly Flood

I'm not sure what Flood means by the barrel of alcohol was "tampered" with. He says it was down the fore-hold. But he might have confused this with the aft hold. This is where Austin found the barrel of Stockholm tar open. It might have been poorly re-secured, and Flood might have thought this was a barrel of alcohol. Raw alcohol, the actual cargo, will make anyone who drinks of it incapable of doing anything. "Alcohol" was also marked on the head of each cask. Flood seems to be referring to an unmarked cask. If Flood thought this was a separate supply barrel and not the regular cargo, it would add a little more reason to his theory, though he certainly should have checked to make sure what was in the barrel.

As I said, Flood was an horrendous theorist, but the blind sow had rooted out the acorn. The location of the *Mary Celeste* was extremely suspicious, all things considered.

With this, Flood actually got into the disturbing data. For those 9 days or so the *Mary Celeste* would have had to drift 50 miles per day, with minimal sails set, and on the wrong tack. That would mean about 2 miles per hour. It is possible for a ship to drift that much, but all on course and in one direction? Against the currents, against the wind, and only at the last to turn around and head westerly?

Flood included the Chief Mate, Albert Richardson, into the ranks of those killed by the crew. He had more than one reason.

One, Richardson was known as a very able and honest Mate. James Winchester had also arrived in Gibraltar on January 15 in order to claim his ship. He made it clear that Richardson was his nephew by marriage. Two, every day he updated their course on that chart over his bed. The chart was marked up to the 24th and no further. Flood basically deduced that the crew took over on the 25th, killed Briggs, his family, and Richardson. This accounted for the lack of filling out the chart or giving any advance in the daily logs. The mutinous crew then sailed the vessel on without making any annotations and then when off Portugal, or when seeing another ship, turned the *Celeste* westward (thus putting her on the starboard tack) and abandoned the vessel.

The letters, to say the least, were disturbing to Earl Granville. He forwarded them to the British Embassy in Washington. On March 11, 1873, Sir Edward Thornton wrote to Hamilton Fish, Secretary of State, stating in part:

> You will perceive that the enquiries which have been instituted into this matter tend to arouse grave suspicions that the master of the vessel in question, together with his wife and child, were murdered by the crew who would seem subsequently to have advanced the vessel and are supposed either to have perished at sea, or to have been picked up by a passing vessel.
>
> It is under these circumstances that I have been instructed to communicate the enclosed documents to you, in order that if the government of the United States should think it expedient, investigations may be instituted with a view of obtaining some clue to the cause of the derelict vessel having been abandoned.

The State Department was not amused by the prospects. An investigation by British officials would be costly, and what was the chance of tracing any of the crew, if they had survived, in the Azores or elsewhere and bring them to book?

Horatio Sprague was obviously made aware of what was now

coming into Washington from London. It all had Flood's name on it. The "fussy little man," as Sprague called him, was making a nuisance of himself. . .and a making a noisy nuisance of himself. He then sent them clippings from the Gibraltar *Chronicle*. At the same time as the Hon. Flood was penning his letter to the Board of Trade, he was guiding the quill of the local press. The first report was on the 21st of January, the day before he first wrote to the Board of Trade in London. The article almost parrots his official letter.

The newspaper reported the basic facts of finding the vessel and the subsequent investigations, highlighting that John Austin could find no reason for why the ship was abandoned. After that the *Chronicle*, courtesy of Flood, delved into the most sanguine evidence. "But, in addition to the above facts, a sword was discovered which, on its being drawn out of its scabbard, exhibited signs of having been smeared with blood and afterward wiped; further, the top-gallant rail had marks on it, apparently of blood, and both bows of the vessel had been cut, to all appearances intentionally, with some sharp instrument. . ." The article set the stage for mutiny: "but the log of the *Dei Gratia* shows that during the time from the 25th November to the day when she met the *Mary Celeste*, the 5th of December, the wind was more or less from the north, and that she was on the *port* tack during the whole of that period. It appears, therefore, almost impossible that the derelict should have compassed within the same time a distance of 7. 54 E, at all events on the *starboard* tack, upon which she was met by the *Dei Gratia*, the obvious inference is that she was not abandoned until some days after the last entry made in the log. . .Naturally various theories are set up to account for this extraordinary series of facts, and the finding of the sword and the blood stains are held to point to some deed of violence. Be that as it may, the fact remains that up to the present date not a word has been heard nor a trace discovered, of the Captain, or the crew, or the lady and her child. The Captain, B. S. Briggs by name, is well-known in Gibraltar, and bore the highest character. It can only be hoped that by giving the utmost publicity to the circumstances some light may be thrown upon this, at present, most mysterious case."[5]

By giving it "utmost publicity" Flood was basically forcing the State Department and the US Attorney General to start an investigation. No one likes being maneuvered. Therefore if either contemplated a British led investigation, Sprague's attitude no doubt easily quashed it. He saw little logic in Flood's theory, especially considering that the crew's personal possessions were also left behind. Wouldn't mutineers take their own stuff? In fact, he had been amazed by the article. When he had forwarded it to Washington he cautioned them that it was written largely with Flood's help.

On the surface, Flood's personal theory had many weaknesses. But he truly did not see them. He was so sure that he hadn't even ordered chemical tests to be made on the suspected blood stains until January 30, a *week* after he electrified the news and agitated the Board of Trade with his theory. The B of T was one thing— private, official theorizing— but he stepped way out on a limb with the *Chronicle* article. He even included in it a generic reference to the bows of the vessel having been intentionally disfigured. This is the most outlandish aspect of his greater theory, but he had the support and weight of 4 Royal Navy captains and 1 engineer, and that was not to be parsed with.

However, debunking theory leads nowhere. Sprague went after the tangible elements of Flood's hypothesis. He now wanted his own firsthand opinion. He asked a US Navy Captain, R.W. Shufeldt, to go have a look. On 7th February 1873, Sprague wrote the Assistant Secretary of State in Washington: "I have much pleasure in forwarding the report of Captain

---

[5] The italics are actually the newspaper's, thus highlighting Flood's personal view.

Shufeldt of our Navy on the subject of the "Mary Celeste's" situation, the perusal of which may prove interesting to your department— Captain Shufeldt arrived at this port in command of the US ship 'Plymouth' on the 5th instant from the Villafranche, and homeward bound via Lisbon and the coast of Africa. The 'Plymouth' left this morning for her destination." The letter follows:

U.S.S. Plymouth, February 6, 1873:

Horatio Sprague Esq.
    U.S. Consul
    My dear Sir

At your request, I visited the American Brig "Mary Celeste" found derelict at sea Dec. 5th 1872 and brought into this port.

After a cursory examination of the Vessel, and a somewhat imperfect knowledge of the circumstances, I am of the opinion that she was abandoned by the master and crew in a moment of panic and for no sufficient reason.

She may have strained in the gale through which she was passing and for the time leaked so much as to alarm the master, and it is possible that at this moment another vessel in sight induced him (having his wife and child on board) to abandon thus hastily— in this event, he may not be heard from for some time to come, as the ship which rescued him may have been bound to a distant port.

I reject the idea of mutiny from the fact that there is no evidence of violence about the decks or in the cabins, besides the force, aft and forward, was so equally divided that a mutiny could hardly have had such a result.

The damage about the bows of the brig appears to me to amount to nothing more than splinters made in the bending of the planks, which were afterwards forced off by the action of the sea— neither hurting the ship or by any possible chance to result of an intention to do so.

The vessel at the present moment appears staunch and seaworthy. Some day I hope and expect to hear from her crew. If surviving, the master will regret his hasty action. But if we should never hear of them again I shall nevertheless think they were lost in the boat in which both master and men abandoned the "Mary Celeste," and shall remember with interest this sad and silent mystery of the sea.

I am very faithfully,
Your friend and obedient,

RW Shufeldt,
Captain,

Sprague rejoiced, perhaps too much, in Shufeldt's impressions. They were, after all, all he had to counter Solly Flood's conjecture alarming Washington via the British Board of Trade. Unfortunately, they are at best very weak. Time would prove no ship had ever picked up the crew of the *Mary Celeste*. Shufeldt's entire theory actually depended on that one point. A ship standing close by injected the only logic in his theory. Yet it hadn't happened. Without that one mitigating factor, there is simply no weight to his conjecture.

Shufeldt was also ignorant of the place where and tack upon which the *Mary Celeste* was found. These remained Flood's big trump to continue his bulldog grip on his theory. This may have been a nuisance to Sprague, but 4 English captains and 1 English engineer upheld that those cuts were made intentionally and recently. Altogether this meant contrivance was at hand!

From this point forward, literary stereotype has characterized the Attorney General as a blundering little troublemaker. The formula has been to attribute his continuing rampage to his belief that there was blood on the sword and on the vessel. But that was really not Flood's fulcrum at all. The fulcrum was that truly ponderous fact of where the *Celeste* was found and found, moreover, on the starboard tack.

As it stood right now, in February, the results of Dr. Patron's blood analysis had not been officially released, but they were no doubt known by Flood. He had set the dear doctor of Gibraltar to this task in late January. He was to check the stained splinters of wood on deck, the axe cut on the top gallant rail, and those nasty smears on the old sword. The results, of course, were negative. Flood knew he couldn't prove blood, and with that he could never prove his theory.

Negative results left Flood with only one target: the crew of the *Dei Gratia*. As far as he could see it, they had messed with evidence. Austin's survey had proven Deveau's testimony false in many places. There had no doubt been much more evidence which they destroyed just to get their greedy mitts on the salvage money. Flood was setting his course to make sure they would not profit by this.

By March, Deveau was finally back from Genoa. He was surprised at how the whole incident had escalated into piracy, mutiny and murder since he had left. The Vice Admiralty Court sat again. Flood was ready to follow up his theory and had his mode of cross-examination ready. On the 3rd he surprisingly put Morehouse on the stand first. Morehouse went over all the basics of finding the *Celeste*, which we already have heard. He couldn't answer about the cuts on the vessel, as he wasn't aware if the *Celeste* had encountered sufficiently rough weather to account for them. The Rep. for the owners of the cargo, Mr. Stokes, asked him to clarify exactly where they found the *Mary Celeste* yet again. Then after Morehouse's answer, Flood's question came out of nowhere. "When did you first go aboard the Mary Celeste?"

Morehouse: I did not go on board the Mary Celeste at all until she came into the port of Gibraltar.

Flood believed differently. He was ready to trap Morehouse. He was going to get details out of Morehouse first. "What report did your mate, Oliver Deveau, make to you about the state of things he found on the 'Mary Celeste,' at his first visit?"

Morehouse: He said nothing particular about the state of the deck, except that things were in a state of confusion— hatches off— ropes about. The flag, or what I thought was a flag from the port yard arm, we found when we got to it, was part of the upper topsail hanging down torn. I think the sail now shown me in Court is part of the fore topsail. I think it has been cut across with a knife— although I have seen sails torn by the wind in every sort of way, across and against the grain.

Morehouse didn't know what Flood was up to, but he had said too much. Also, he didn't know that Deveau had made an entry in the log stating that Morehouse had come aboard on the 6th of December to give him instructions. Morehouse was sufficiently ignorant of Flood's intent to find more discrepancies that he continued his general trend to minimize evidence. Mistakes in his testimony above include "when we got to it." At this point Flood didn't pursue it. He sat back down, prepared to unleash himself on the prodigal Deveau.

Morehouse's desire to continue to minimize the incident was a poor policy. After Cochrane's first censure on January 31, Morehouse should have realized Flood and Cochrane believed he and Deveau had obstructed justice or even tampered with evidence.

The attitude of minimizing the evidence would be more obvious in Mate Deveau. On the next day he was put on the stand. Flood's big evidence— the cuts on the rail and the "blood stains"— were presented to him. He replied:

Deveau: I saw no remains or pieces of a painter or boats rope fastened to the rail, and I noticed no mark of an axe or cut on the rail. I did not see this cut in the rail now shown me to notice it. The cut appears to have been done with a sharp axe; but I do not think it could have been done by my men while we were in possession of the vessel. I did not see any new axes on board the Celeste, but we found an old axe. I did not replace the rails of the ship found on the deck before I returned to the Dei Gratia the first time. I can form no opinion about the cause of the axe cut on the rail.

Solly Flood: Have you any opinion to offer the Court as to the origin of the blood stains on the deck?

Deveau: I noticed no marks or traces of blood on deck. I cannot say whether there were any or not. We never washed or scraped the decks of the Mary Celeste. We had not men enough for that. The sea washed over the decks.

Solly Flood: Salt water contains chloric acid which dissolves the particles of blood.

Deveau: If there are some parts of the deck or rail scraped, I did not notice them and they were not done while we were on board.

[Obviously Deveau did not understand what chloric acid was].

Solly Flood: Did you pick up a sword on board the Mary Celeste?

Deveau: I saw a sword on board the vessel. I found the sword under the captain's berth. I took it from there, and looked at it by drawing it from its sheath. There was nothing remarkable on it, and I don't think there's anything remarkable about it now. It seems rusty. I think I put it back where I found it or somewhere near. I did not see it at the foot of the ladder. Perhaps some of my men may have put it there. I was not on board the Celeste when the Vice Admiralty Court Marshal came on the ship to arrest her, and, therefore, I did not see him find the sword.

Solly Flood: The sword has been cleaned with lemon, which has covered it with citrate of iron, which has destroyed the marks of the supposed blood, which therefore is not blood at all as at first supposed, but another substance put there to disguise the original marks of the blood which were once there.

Whether Flood genuinely believed that absurdity or whether he was merely trying to discombobulate a witness to see the results is up for debate. If serious, Flood's statement was yet another subtle indictment of Deveau and Morehouse. He is implying that since Vecchio first recoiled at the sword and stains that Deveau and Morehouse, before quitting the vessel, cleaned the real blood off and put other stains on there to approximate the same appearance as when Vecchio first saw it. The reason for doing so comes back to the suspicion on Flood and Cochrane's part that Morehouse wanted the *Celeste* to look a simple dereliction at sea. The result would be a swift and pain-less Vice Admiralty Court and then the awarding of salvage rights and monies.

Flood also had Austin's report talking about the large num-ber of sail cuttings. Then Morehouse testified about how the topsail looked intentionally cut. Deveau had conveniently ig-nored this, and this just became another curious omission or contradiction among many.

At this point in the questioning Flood even declared: "All these questions are necessary in the ends of justice, in order to endeavour to solve the mystery of the abandonment of the ship by her Master and Crew. I alone represent the interests of the Master, Briggs, the owner of the equity of redemption of some of the shares of the Mary Celeste."

One can imagine the impatient or petulant looks on the wit-nesses' faces that prompted Flood to qualify his actions. But he still had good cause.

Flood went for another contradiction. He now asked why Deveau's log claimed that Morehouse came aboard when Morehouse had said he never came aboard. The answer seems impromptu.

Deveau: I kept the log on the Mary Celeste after I got on board, that is to say, I wrote it by memory after we got into Gibraltar. I did not write it down at the time, but the captain of the Dei Gratia hav-ing come on board and said he wished I had done so, I said I thought I still could do it from memory, with the help of my chart on which was the ship's course and the latitude and longitude, and from that I entered the log up as it now appears.

The entry made on Friday 6 December, 1872 is not correct. I see there is stated that the captain of the Dei Gratia came on board, that day, of the Mary Celeste. That is not so. The entry 'Captain Morehouse came on board with a letter of instructions' is not correct. In point of fact, Captain Morehouse did not come on board. He had stated that he should come on board, but he sent a letter of instructions in a boat by two men without himself coming. I cannot explain otherwise how I made the error.

Solly Flood: Has Captain Morehouse already seen this entry and previously spoken to you about it?

Deveau: No, he has not seen the entry or spoken to me about it; my attention is now called the first time to the error by you. I cannot say positively whether the letter of instruction was brought to me on that day or the day before. It was on the first or on the second day.

To me I find it more interesting that Morehouse needed to send over a letter of instruction.

In any case, we get an idea of what it was about from the testimony of Thomas Vecchio later that day. He was summoned by H.P. Pisani, who represented the salvors. His testimony unintentionally undermined much of Austin's survey when it came to the condition and place of the personal effects. Austin repeatedly accentuated how nothing was wet enough to indicate heavy storms. Even clothes in the bottom of chests indicated that no more than an inch of water could have gotten into the cabins. Vecchio had something surprising to say. He testified plainly that the clothes and other personal effects had been *taken off* the *Mary Celeste* and had traveled aboard the *Dei Gratia* on the way to Gibraltar. Vecchio was, in fact, handed them by Morehouse when he arrived on board the *Mary Celeste* to arrest her. Vecchio plainly testified: "The particular position, therefore, in which any article was found by me is not to be relied upon as indicating where it was found when the vessel was abandoned."

What was the reason for this? Did Morehouse not trust Deveau and the two men who would sail the ship to Gibraltar? If so, it still makes little sense to transship personal effects, since Deveau or one of the men could easily have emptied the valuables before sending the sea chests over. Remember, Deveau insisted that Morehouse never came aboard until Gibraltar. How would he have known if Deveau or one of the others purloined anything from a chest before bringing it upon deck? As a security precaution, the gesture is worthless. The sea chests and personal things of those on the *Mary Celeste* were in less way where they were than being stacked aboard the *Dei Gratia*. All the chests save one were found opened as well, so that on either ship anything could have been taken when the chests were not being watched. This also meant that a special trip during high seas was made to send a letter and transship heavy sea chests in return. During this time, Morehouse only had two men aboard with him to handle the *Dei Gratia*.[6]

The bulk of Vecchio's testimony describes how the clothes in the bottom of drawers and in the bottom of the crew's sea chests was heavily wet and took days to dry. Yet in contrast to this he noted that the "chart found in the mate's cabin was in use and was high up over his bed and quite dry and uninjured. The harmonium was exactly under the sky light when I found it, and was quite dry and uninjured. It was of rosewood."

It took a week for the *Dei Gratia* to make port and the *Mary Celeste* had been abandoned for 9 days or so before that. The implication was there yet again that the clothes were artificially wetted or got wet during the transfer from ship to ship.

I have repeatedly brought up the suspicions that the *Dei Gratia*'s crew smudged evidence, and do so here again for one reason. It is the motivation for Flood's entire line of questioning after the court was reconvened. Writers have dwelt upon the bloodstain episode and smeared Solly Flood for proposing such unsubstantiated theories. But none seemed to detect that he

---

[6] Morehouse only had 8 total aboard, including himself. With Deveau and 2 men on the *Celeste*, 2 men in the boat, that left him only 2 crew aboard.

was not intending to prove his theory. He was muddying the water to deny the salvors of what he thought they had not been worthy of because of their own deceits and dishonesty in the whole affair. *They* muddied the evidence so badly just to get the salvage money that the actual final sequence of events aboard the ship could never be known. Flood was determined they were not going to profit from this.

The Proctor was also out on that limb that he had foolishly put himself on back on January 21 when he went public with his theory in the *Chronicle*. Patron's blood analysis would confirm no such blood stains on anything. It should be undeniable that Flood already knew the results were negative, for the blood analysis was never introduced in court and yet Flood admitted that the stains on the sword were no longer blood. Flood's conjecture about the sword being doctored also saved his own face or was merely the adamance of a man who didn't want to admit he could be wrong. More than likely, it was just to give enough inference that Deveau had doctored evidence.

There is also another reason why I harp on the motives for Flood's comments to Morehouse and Deveau. In *Strange Mysteries of Time and Space*, Harold Wilkins declared that Flood made a good case for the *Dei Gratia*'s men having killed the *Mary Celeste* crew and pirated the ship for her valuable cargo. Yet there is nothing in the Minutes or Proceedings that he quoted to even remotely suggest this. Rather, it is evident Flood and Cochrane viewed the *Dei Gratia*'s crew as self-seeking and interfering with justice.

Flood's theory, firmly embedded in print on the 22nd and 23rd January, shows he was suspicious of the *Celeste*'s crew and not of the *Dei Gratia*'s. Therefore his innuendos in March must be interpreted as against Morehouse and Deveau for doctoring evidence. He had already discounted Deveau's testimony about the rigging, with good cause, so it seems he would have felt justified in not only regarding Deveau as a bit dim but also in league with Morehouse as to contributing to destroying evidence. Vecchio had not yet testified at this point, but he had no doubt already confided in Flood some of his experiences with the crew when first arresting the ship.

Wilkins even makes a point of highlighting that Deveau thought he had by accident wiped away the last entry in the log when, in fact, he had not. This is indeed a curious bit of gratuitous information on Deveau's part, but it could have nothing to do with complicity in getting rid of the *Celeste*'s crew. The *Celeste* was 8 days ahead of the *Dei Gratia* at all times and could never have been overtaken. But it could be yet another indication that Deveau had tampered with evidence. Deveau's testimony seemed suspicious to Wilkins, albeit for the wrong reasons, who was a bit of Flood reincarnated, but it seems certain that it was also suspicious to Flood and Cochrane as well, although for the right reasons. In short, there could have been a very interesting last entry in the log that clarified everything but might not have been conducive to an easy sprint through court.

On top of this, both Cochrane and Flood felt Deveau had "done away" with a certain "vessel" which made the analysis of the blood stains a necessity. There are no records as to what exactly this "vessel" was, but Deveau had apparently removed something which Cochrane felt was significant to easily explaining the stains on the sword. It could have been some kind of bottle or phial, imaginary or otherwise, that both Flood and he had felt had held the stain that they supposedly used to make the "fake blood stains" on the sword after cleaning off the "real blood."

On the 14th of March the case was finally tried and ended. Cochrane awarded only £1,700 to Morehouse and the crew (quid per barrel). He also rendered another censure for the "conduct of the master of the 'Dei Gratia' in allowing the mate Oliver Deveau to do away with the vessel which had rendered necessary the analysis of the supposed spots or stains of blood

found on the deck of the 'Mary Celeste' and on the sword."
Although the blood analysis was not introduced in Court,
Morehouse was charged for the costs incurred by the Court for
having it done.

The *Mary Celeste* was finally allowed to sail away to Genoa
with another crew and finally deliver her much anticipated cargo.

Unquestionably, Frederick Solly Flood has attained a bad
reputation with writers. He is accused of irresponsible accusations, a foolish theory, and he and Cochrane have been accused
of muddying everything in order to deny full salvage rights and
pocket money for themselves. Most of these assignations can
only thrive far outside of the context of the men's actual words
and the motive for their actions. They also arose late in the legend of the *Mary Celeste*. After decades of fancy— of pirates,
mutinies, and bizarre tales from supposed survivors— legitimate writers began to explore the incident. They wrote fine biographies of the event. But they clearly were out to minimize
anything that could be taken as "sensational." Flood the man,
out of whom sprang the most sanguine and sensational of the
early theories (and news reports), too had to burn on the funeral
pyre. *Dei Gratia*'s men are lamented as victims of an incestuous
colonial British system. Unreliable evidence and contradictory
testimony for heavy weather and panicked flight is not something that minimizers of the strange case of the *Mary Celeste*
wanted.

Some of it had a root in those who played a role in the affair.
James Winchester journeyed to Gibraltar, arriving on January
15, 1873, hoping to speed the process to get his treasured vessel
released. He, however, quickly learned of the problems with
the case and might have even picked up rumors about Flood's
flood-like reputation. He later wrote that he was certain that
Cochrane and Flood were "goein' to arrest mee for hiring the
crue to make way with the officers the Idear was verry rediculas

but from what everybody else in Gibraltar had told me about the Attorney General I did not know but they might do itt as thay seam to doe just as they like. . .So after tarkin' with the consul at Cadiz, I decided to come home."

Harold Wilkins condemned Winchester as "an illiterate old shellback" who might simply have been repeating rumors. But Consul Sprague knew enough to explain things to Winchester. How much he understood was another matter. Flood may have tried to scare Winchester to see what reaction he could excite. He knew he had no criminal jurisdiction over an American ship that encountered an incident at sea. His letter to the Board of Trade was for the purpose of transmitting to America to see if Washington wanted to do anything. Flood was a bull in a china shop, but both he and Sprague knew the limits of his authority.

Amidst the more-neutral biographies, such as Edey Fay's and Bryan's, is Wilkins *Strange Mysteries of Time and Space*. Edey Fay complimented the germinal article ("Light on the Mary Celeste") but disagreed with Wilkins' conclusions about the *Dei Gratia*'s crew having a hand in murdering the *Celeste*'s crew. Although I agree with Edey Fay, Wilkins had turned up some unusual evidence. He had consulted Lloyd's List and apparently found an erred entry for when the *Dei Gratia* sailed. Their lists show she left New York on October 2. Wilkins presented this as evidence *Dei Gratia* could actually have been laying-in-wait for the *Mary Celeste* and then jumped her at sea. Lloyds also shows, as Wilkins' notes, that *Dei Gratia* was spoken to at sea about 550 miles east of New York. But Wilkins lists the date erroneously as December 6. She could never have made Gibraltar by December 13. The correct date was November 19. This is more in keeping with the evidence *Dei Gratia* left on November 15, 1872, and was therefore incapable of overtaking the *Mary Celeste*.

Wilkins even relied on some of the gut feelings of surviving family members. Albert Richardson's sister, Priscilla, was still alive, as was his widow (at the age of 84), in 1931 when Priscilla wrote Wilkins about the incident. Within her letter she declared: "The mystery will never be solved, as the only people who could throw any light on the tragedy were the crew of the *Dei Gratia*, and they have long since disappeared. . . .Did it ever occur to you that they were responsible? My late brother, Captain Lyman Richardson, agreed with me that they were. The *Dei Gratia* lay alongside the *Mary Celeste* in the harbor of New York. They sailed 10 days before the *Mary Celeste*; but they were waiting for her and towed her to Gibraltar, claiming salvage money. Where had the *Dei Gratia* been to all that time? The weather had been fair, according to her own log, and she should have been far ahead. . .The crew of the *Mary Celeste* were foully murdered by some means. They were decoyed to the other vessel, or part of them, and then the extermination of the rest was easy, as they carried no firearms for protection. I am firmly convinced that this is the true solution of the mystery. Captain Briggs and my brother were first-class sailors and would never have left their ship unless compelled by force."

Priscilla Richardson Shelton's letter is interesting, but I have always found it doubtful to rely on relative's appraisals of any situation, especially when they were not eyewitnesses. For decades the Richardsons had heard the rumors and the stories, and doubtless formed their own opinions, much of them not based on facts. Perhaps some were even based on an article by Wilkins introducing the erred Lloyds reports.

However, the Richardson letter brings up that puzzling and oft-repeated story about the two vessels being docked next to each other in New York. If this is true, it is interesting in this context that none of the crewmen of the *Dei Gratia* could remember if the *Celeste* had a lifeboat on board. Where Priscilla got this information is hard to say. Records don't bear it out, but then like the erred Lloyds List that doesn't mean the two ships were not berthed alongside each other for a while. Supposedly, it was Pier 44.

Charles Edey Fay's *The Odyssey of an Abandoned Ship* was the first to introduce the public to the documents held at the National Archives. As with all books backed by an institution the mantel of being a scholarly work was quickly attached to it. But scholarly is not necessarily to be equated with analytical. Fay makes Historian 101 mistakes. He is anachronistic rather than chronological. I use Solly Flood as an example. Fay takes Flood's established stance that there was foul play and assumes this influenced others, such as Austin in their investigations, before we even know for sure when Flood came to his conviction. When Austin studied the peak halyard in December 1872 and noted it was the original and had not been recently spliced, Fay renders a footnote that this "seemed designed to buttress" Flood's theory that there had been foul play aboard. Yet we do not know that Flood even held to that conviction yet when he went aboard the *Mary Celeste*. Certainly he was suspicious of something else having been involved or else he would not have ordered more investigation. In his January 22, 1873, written statement, he said that the testimony of the men compelled him to these more minute inspections of the ship. It seems more than likely that Austin's survey inspired Flood in his theories. They weren't the best theories, true, but we can't be sure that they crystallized before late January. He even sees fit to add a quick epilogue to his letter to the Board of Trade, explaining why the significance of the location and starboard tack inspired him in his belief.

This in itself showed he completely believed Deveau and Morehouse's general account of things. Once again, he was suspicious that they were trying to pull a fast one and minimize the mystery *aboard* so they could forgo too much inquiry and quickly get their prize money. The intact peak halyard indicated Deveau lied. It could have no bearing on whether the *Mary Celeste*'s crew mutinied or not.

Attacks by Rif pirates had been all too frequent in the oceans off Morocco and Gibraltar. In *Mystery Ship*, George S.

Bryan was faithful to bring to the reader's attention a number of instances where these attacks continued into the 1890s. In each case, the pirates boarded smaller vessels like brigantines and made off with all the valuables, smashed compasses, stole ship's papers, and sometimes kidnapped crews. But in each case they left the ship to drift, such as the French and Spanish ships *Prosper Corue* (1896), *Fiducia* and *Rosita Faro* (1897). Gibraltar, only 11 miles from the Moroccan coast, was in the midst of these Barbary pirates. The Vice Admiralty Court was justified in being suspicious of ships found derelict on the high seas. Rifs had not ventured as far as the Azores (a far as it was known), but Flood and Cochrane only had the suspicious word of Deveau and Morehouse as to what the last entry in the log really read.

Captain James Briggs, Benjamin's brother, had his own theory. He thought that the vessel was becalmed near the ragged coast of St. Mary's. Being pulled into the shore and certain sudden death awaited on her jagged rocks, he thought his brother abandoned the vessel in a more maneuverable lifeboat. Their fate, however, was to perish in the frothing seas from which they could not escape. A wind came again and carried the *Celeste* to safety.

Even James Winchester had muddled facts on the case. Either that or he believed later writers who detailed their own theories. When Harold Wilkins wrote his grandson, Winchester Noyes, then-president of the family company, J.H. Winchester Inc., he got the following response. "I have heard my grandfather give his opinion that gases in the hold caused spontaneous explosions which overturned the hatch cover, and the crew, knowing the nature of the vessel's cargo, immediately took to the boat expecting the vessel to burst into flames. . ." An impossibility since only the fore and aft hatches were *intentionally* off and the main hatch was secured.

Along this scenario, however, comes the granddaddy of all

theories that try to explain the dereliction of the ship. It comes from yet another relative of the missing Briggs family. Dr. Oliver W. Cobb was both Benjamin and Sarah Briggs' cousin. He was so detailed in his re-creation of what the final chain-of-events must have been he has impressed all who have read him. Without showing hints of his own personal views, Edey Fay succinctly summarized Cobb's theory:

In this connection, it may be of interest to mention the fact that Oliver W. Cobb, who assisted the mate of the brigantine, *Julia A. Hallock* in checking the sixteen hundred barrels of petroleum unloaded from the vessel at Naples, noticed that some of the metal hoops around the barrels were bright, the paint having been worn off in places as a result of constant chafing in the hold. It was customary to load such barrels with their heads and bottoms facing fore and aft, and with their bungs up. Wooden billets were stuck in, here and there, between the barrels, in order to keep them steady, but that expedient, apparently, did not prevent some of the barrels from rubbing against each other. If then, there was sufficient friction in the hold of the *Julia A Hallock* to wear off the paint on the metal barrel hoops, is it beyond the bound of possibility to suppose that friction in the *Mary Celeste*'s hold containing seventeen hundred barrels of alcohol could have produced a spark and a resulting explosion?

According to the theory of Dr. Cobb as we understand it, Captain Briggs, confronted by a sudden and imminent peril, and caring for the safety of his wife and child, and the members of his crew, gave orders to launch the ship's boat which was lying across the main hatch. As the wind was, presumably, from the west at that time, and the vessel's course was approximately east by south, it is probable that the boat was launched from the leeward side, which, under the circumstances, would have been the port side of the vessel. As an additional precautionary measure, Captain Briggs may have directed one of his men to break out a coil of rope for a tow-line, so that if the threatened danger should pass, they could return to their vessel. The place where such ropes were customarily stowed was the lazarette, a low, headroom space below the deck in the after part of the vessel. According to Dr. Cobb's theory, they had already removed the lazarette hatch (reported as found off by the salvors) when it may have suddenly occurred to one of the company that it would take less time to utilize the main peak halyard, conveniently at hand, than to bother with breaking out a new, and perhaps stiff, coil of rope from the lazarette. This halyard, a stout rope of about three inches in circumference, and approximately three hundred feet long, stood ready for almost instant use. According to the court testimony, the mainsail was furled. The gaff of this sail would, therefore, have been resting on it, presumably with a stopper on the gaff, the sail and the boom, encircling all three. Assuming that on this vessel the halyard was secured at one end of the gaff (although in some vessels it began at a ring-bolt on the mast-head) and that it ran thence upward and downward, through a treble block on the masthead and two single blocks on the gaff, it would finally descend to the deck where it would be secured to a belaying pin on the pin-rack or to the pin-rail at the foot of the mast. According to Dr. Cobb's theory it would have taken but a few moments to release this end of the halyard and then pull it through the gaff and mast-head blocks until its entire length, with one end still secured to the gaff, would have been available for towing purposes. The free end of the halyards could then have been passed between the wooden stanchions supporting the topgallant rail (the vessel having no bulwarks) and then connected with the painter (rope) of the small boat which, by this time, no doubt, would have been alongside, with most of the ship's company already aboard. The tenseness of the situation can easily be imagined as they anxiously awaited the moments when all hands would be in the boat and they could cast off from the *Mary Celeste* and put as much distance possible between themselves and the danger threatening them. At the end of such a long tow-line, they would doubtless have felt comparatively safe while awaiting further developments.

In continuing his faithful recount of Cobb's theory, Edey Fay clarifies that the Servico Meteorlogico dos Açores reported "calm or light winds" for that afternoon. "And it seems probable that the abandonment of the vessel occurred during this period of calm, as a launching of a small boat on a wild sea would have meant little more than the substitution of a new peril for the one immediately impending." However, by that late afternoon the Servico then reports that a "wind of gale force prevailed" in that area. With some reserve, he considers:

It is barely possible that the boat, while being towed through rough waters, with her nose held down by a taut tow-line, was swamped by the heavy seas, resulting in the drowning of all on board. Had this occurred, however, it seems probable that some remnant either of the boat or her painter would have been noticed by the men of the *Dei Gratia* when they discovered the *Mary Celeste*. According to Dr. Cobb's theory, the tow-line parted at that point where it came over the side of the vessel around the corner of the stanchion.

Unfortunately, for all its influence in the decades thereafter, Cobb's theory ignores the facts. The peak halyard simply was not in the condition that Deveau said it was. Although in a letter to Harold Wilkins, Cobb admitted that there was "something shady" in the testimony of the *Dei Gratia*'s men and that they were perhaps "window dressing" because of seeking salvage monies, he doesn't seem to take to full effect that the condition of the ship would have been the main window of their dressing. There is simply no evidence the peak halyard, or parts thereof, was ever used for a towline. And if Deveau was telling the truth about the condition of the rigging (and thus Austin simply incompetent), the condition of the peak halyard was not unique, for Deveau also said that the fore-braces on the port side plus the starboard lower topsail brace were in "the same condition, all broken." All of these could not have been used for towing. "The gear of the foresail was also broken, with the clew-lines and buntings gone."

A better candidate for a towline might be the missing log line. But then, again, the claim that the sounding rod was lying conveniently by the pump causes me to suspect Deveau's account of the actual conditions aboard when they found the vessel. Excessive speculation on what chronology these dubious clues, when put together, might give us is wasted.

So many have tried to explain the case of the *Mary Celeste*, which of course can never have a true explanation, that they overlook the ramifications of what evidence they throw out-of-school. There is no reason to suspect Austin was perjuring himself. Flood was certainly standing over him telling him the conditions Deveau and Wright had described— this is obvious in every contrast Austin makes— but the halyard spoke for itself and could be examined by others called by Morehouse's or Winchester's people, such as H.P. Pisani. There is simply no convenient evidence to support Cobb's theory.

To Deveau the scene suggested another reason altogether. As we know, he thought the abandonment happened because of misreading the pumps. Although I think this unlikely, and very unflattering to Briggs' ability at captaincy, the sounding rod, if it is legitimate evidence and if it miraculously did not shift about the deck, could genuinely suggest the fear was sinking, not fire or explosion. Theorists can't have it both ways. A lack of finding a towline of any kind is congruous with this, for there is no reason why a crew would attach a line to a ship they believed was about to sink like a deadweight.

Even if we suspect Deveau of being excessively simplistic in his theory, his theory was more justified than theories depending on fire. Austin and Deveau agree on this point. There was no evidence of fire, and there would have been had the alcohol fumes began to burn. Remember, the lifeboat appeared to have been lashed over the main hatch. It was impossible for the crew to have opened that hatch while that lifeboat remained in place. Fire, even the quick blue fire of alcohol, would have left some traces on the ceiling of the hatch.

What are we left with?— that the barrels might have been rumbling from agitation from the heavy sea. But the fact the ship was ventilating itself, including the skylight being open, meant the seas had calmed down. What could suddenly happen now? Also, the barrels were full. There simply wasn't enough space to let the alcohol build up steam. When the cargo was finally checked at Genoa, the equivalent of only 9 barrels had leaked (evaporated). This was indeed considered very small compared to 1,700 barrels in the hold.[7] *Moreover*, the vessel had not reached Genoa until late March, some four months after the last entry in the ship's log in late November. How much of this evaporation happened in those months the *Mary Celeste* idled her time in Gibraltar? Logically, far more than could have evaporated in only 2 weeks at sea before the vessel was abandoned. Thus in late November there wasn't much vapor in the hold in order to be able to blow the hatch off. In the final analysis, the 9 barrels was a very small amount. How much trouble and rumbling could only, say, 1 barrel-equivalent evaporation have caused? Probably nothing.

Cobb's theory was in reaction to all the rubbish that had become so popular in the decades since the vessel entered maritime history. As an aspiring writer, Sir Arthur Conan Doyle had

---

[7] It has been said that 9 individual barrels were found empty. This appears not to be the case. The equivalent of 9 barrels was empty. After refilling those partially empty, with others partially empty, it was noted that 9 barrels worth was wanting.

even written a sensational and popular bit entitled "J. Habakkuk Jephson's Statement." This inspired other accounts of other "survivors" to come forth and hog the limelight. These include accounts of a mate named Henry Bilson, the infamous Abel Fosdyk, and many others. In the end, more survived the *Mary Celeste*'s strange mystery at sea than had ever sailed out on her. Conan-Doyle's account ranks as the most significant of them all, for he alone made the mistake of naming her the *Marie Celeste*. She was known by that name for decades afterward until credible writers finally corrected it.

Compared to these, Cobb's theory seems to have both its feet on the deck. But in his good intention to vindicate his relatives' reputations, he seems to have become a bit of a storyteller himself. Cobb is the source of the claim that Briggs and Richardson had sailed together before, and that he was a tiptop Mate to have. This must put to rest even the notion of mutiny. It was during one visit to the Briggs home, Rose Cottage, that Cobb, wrote Edey Fay, "recalls hearing Captain Briggs congratulate Mrs. Briggs upon their good fortune in having Richardson go with them as first mate on the *Mary Celeste*."

This is not suggested at all in Briggs' last letter to his mother before sailing. It is dated November 3, 1872, in New York harbor, and Edey Fay was allowed by the Briggs family to publish a facsimile of it in 1942. In it Briggs does not acknowledge Richardson in any way that would indicate he had ever known him before. He merely writes: "We seem to have a very good Mate and Steward and I hope shall have a pleasant voyage."

Richardson was, as we have seen, James Winchester's nephew by marriage to his wife's niece. It is for this reason, perhaps, that Briggs expressed his hope he was a "very good mate." Certainly if they had sailed together previously for months on end, Briggs would be more definite about Richardson's abilities. It is for this reason we need not suspect Richardson of mutiny.

As to the reliability of the crew, there is less evidence. Sarah

wrote her mother-in-law while the ship was biding its time off
Staten Island on 7 November, 1872, and the letter went ashore
with the pilot. Of the crew she writes: "Benjamin thinks we
have got a pretty peaceable set this time all around if they continue as they have begun. Can't tell how smart they are."

One of Horatio Sprague's duties was to relate a letter that
came in from a German who knew members of the German
crew. He was quite relieved to find out that they were considered very good and reliable men. But one letter really doesn't
amount to much, not even to an acceptable biography. Sprague
may have made much out of this because it countered his nemesis' theory, Solly Flood. From the personal effects Vecchio was
given, it really isn't necessary to delve into the personalities of
these crewmen. Mutineers would not have quit their ship and
left their own things behind. There simply was no mutiny
whether these were roughnecks or not.

The bloodstains about the deck and on the sword were no
doubt rust or something else less sanguine than blood. Solly
Flood played his game and won. If his accusations didn't get
that much of a rise out of Deveau and Morehouse, it was probably because they had indeed window-dressed too much, and
they couldn't afford any indignity, even its appearance.

Sir James Cochrane was right to censure them twice, and to
deny them full compensation and even make them pay for the
bloodstain analysis. If anybody has made the solution to the
Mary Celeste impossible, or at least prevented one consistent
believable theory, it is the crew of the *Dei Gratia*.

Another contributor was undeniably Solly Flood. He had
uncovered enough to accurately undermine the *Dei Gratia*'s
crew, but he persisted in his narrow theory of mutiny despite
the illogic of it. He never relented, and 12 years later he even
decided to transmit a copy of the Proceeding's Minutes to
Sprague, asking for payment. Sprague immediately contacted
British officials with the Board of Trade. They told him to give
the Minutes back (unfortunately) and refuse. "The property

being then restored to the owners, the action became one of Salvage and the Queen's Proctor ought not to have interfered any further in the action, but Mr. Flood persisted in doing so, not on behalf of the American Government, but as the Queen's Proctor and Advocate of the Queen in Her Office of Admiralty. . . .Vice Admiralty Courts have no criminal jurisdiction. Mr. Flood has no right to make any professional charges after the claims of the owners were allowed. . .but no claim was then made by him for his professional charges, in fact no such claim could be made; he should have obtained his fees from the Crown, as the Crown in Admiralty Courts neither receives nor pays costs."

We get a good glimpse at the character of Solly Flood in this belated episode. He was a fussy, little, aggravating man with a bulldog grip. He made enemies amongst his own peers, and even Cochrane showed his impatience with him in open court. But this shouldn't cause us to color our impression of the facts that he championed. However ineptly he might have theorized, he had some disturbing facts at hand: the location of the vessel, the tack she was on, and inconsistent testimony on the part of the salvors. He was more adept in dividing bone and marrow than Wilkins and other writers. He knew *Dei Gratia*'s crew had no hand in causing the dereliction. But he was wrong about mutiny, and being wrong about mutiny merely adds him to the list of other theorists whose ideas have consistently proved untenable when placed next to the actual facts.

There simply is no definable reason why the *Mary Celeste* was abandoned. And that is why the case has remained such a mystery today. I have not explained it here. Nor do I try. This piece of my compendium is also not a biography of the events. One can read Edey Fay or Bryan for that. My account of it is a resurrection of why it has become such a maritime mystery. I have tried to take the reader through a chronology of events so that one can understand why certain statements were made, why theories hatched and when, and why suspicion surrounded the vessel from the beginning and surrounded the fate of all those who sailed her. These have been lost in explanations and popular accounts, but they are the spirit that motivated the arguments to begin with before the mystery of the *Mary Celeste* became nothing more than a literary piece to rehash.

Despite his ill-regard for Solly Flood, Sprague had been a careful follower of events. He, too, had considered and reconsidered so much of the events as they unfolded. He was from a seafaring family. He had been born in Gibraltar and succeeded his father as Consul, a post he retained for 53 years. Recalling it years later in an official dispatch to Worthington C. Ford of the State Department, he wrote:

> This case of the "Mary Celeste," as you justly remark, is startling, since it appears to be one of those mysteries which no human ingenuity can recreate sufficiently to account for the abandonment of this vessel, and the disappearance of her master, family and crew, about whom, nothing has ever transpired. Believe me.

He spoke the truth. And it is only fitting that a man who admirably tried to remain neutral should have the last word.

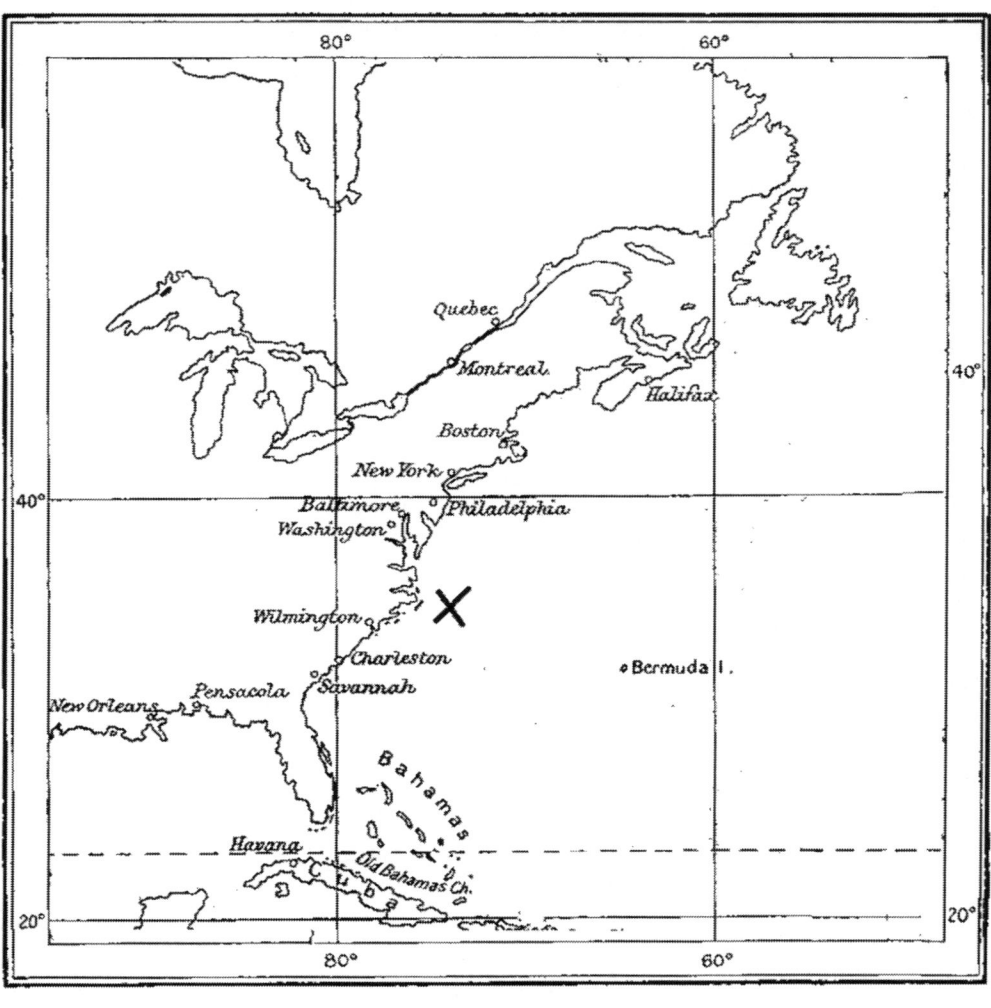

CHAPTER THREE

The
Strange Case
of the
Carroll A. Deering

As strange as the *Mary Celeste*, and one of the most acted upon mysteries of the sea, is the case of the deserted five-masted schooner *Carroll A. Deering*. Returning to Maine from Rio de Janeiro, the *Deering* stopped over at Barbados on January 9, 1921. She was next to be seen off the North Carolina coast by the Cape Lookout Lightship on January 29 at 4:30 p.m. On the morning of January 31, the *Carroll A. Deering* was found hard aground on Outer Diamond Shoals, North Carolina. The ship was ghostly silent; the eleven crew had vanished.

Unlike the *Mary Celeste* comparatively little has been written about the case of the *Carroll A. Deering*, and even less has been speculated about it. Yet it is actually far more of an intriguing and mysterious case than the famous derelict of the Azores. There is even evidence for theories considered outlandish in the case of the *Celeste*, such as mutiny or at least murder having happened. I was apparently the first to put up a detailed article on the World Wide Web. This was based upon all the records I could dig up at the National Archives. Then Patrick Davis, a great grandson of Carroll Atwood Deering (for whom the ship was named) contacted me and gave me the photographs contained herein. I was even informed by another author that it seemed my article was plagiarized and used for the basis of another author's published account. Be that as it may, I didn't bother to pursue it. I was glad to see, however, that Bland Simpson of the University of North Carolina finally published a book on it: *Ghost Ship of Diamond Shoals*. Before this the best rendition was Edward Rowe Snow's in his popular compendium *Mysteries and Adventures Along the Atlantic Coast* (Dodd, Meade, 1948) in the chapter "The Ghost Ship of Diamond Shoals." That title, as you might expect, reflects the attitude of the locals of Cape Hatteras and Ocracoke Island, North Carolina, where sparse remnants of the vessel's bleached bones have attracted curious onlookers until hurricane Ione washed them away in 1955. A few pieces have been salvaged and can be found to decorate roadside places in this very historic part of the United States.

By all seafaring definitions a ghost ship she was. The vessel was manned by no crew in her last hours and yet unswervingly maintained her course of doom to Diamond Shoals. The *Deering* is, in fact, the embodiment of all the legends of ghostly ships. What legend of deserted ships does not have the eerie accounts of interrupted life, such as a meal waiting to be served? How about the ship's mascot found peacefully awaiting rescue?

How about half-marked charts and interrupted journals? This indeed is the *Carroll A. Deering.*

In a sense the *Deering* is also the farewell to the old age of high seas mystery. She was built in Bath, Maine, as late as 1919, by the G.G. Deering Company. She was a huge schooner of 5 masts. Some 225 feet length overall, she evoked the great days when mariners fought to round the Cape and sail on through legendary seas to discover lost islands. Her days were the ebb of the age of discovery, and this tints her photos with more than sepia. It lends that tar and brine and wooden deck smell to adventure at sea. . .and the pre-wireless isolation and "terror of silence" to the mystique of the giant ocean. Frankly, she was obsolete. Few ships of her great size and rigging would be built and used for actual trade purposes anymore. Steam had long surpassed sail for efficiency and reliability.

Those still plying the world's trades in tall ships were like eddies on the side of a river bank. The great torrent of progress had passed them by. Engineers and not quartermasters drove the seas. Officers and not mates governed the ship. Wireless sent regular reports. Radio allowed updated messages to arrive to the ship far out to sea. The terror of silence, that wraith intimately associated with sea travel, was vanquished by Marconi. In its place ships became tied to land by invisible nerves of wireless communication.

With this alone the captain was no longer a lone lord of the sea. He was a representative of the company. Orders could even be sent to change destination or await further instructions. Radio communication made mutiny unlikely and mystery even less so. Wireless was like a magic potion that disenchanted the great sea and defeated its vastness.

The merchant lines were still saturated, however, by sailors of old barkentines, where foc's'cle served and quarterdeck ruled by iron will. Superstitions, old and unrelenting, crept into the steel hulls of coal belching steamers. There the strange lore could be isolated by modern crews and trained officers. But amidst teak decks and slapping sails it still predominated. Those sailors too old to be taught new tricks funneled their quickly obsolescing talents to those tall ships still remaining, those awkward but elegant cousins of the modern steamer. They were at home on sloping decks. They were used to foc's'cle duties and poop deck dominance. New England was still the center of it all. It was full of old seafarers. This proud yolk of the egg that hatched and formed America was steeped in pride. The Yankee merchant had tapped the China trade, fought off Barbary pirates, and enjoyed the American empire, far and flung, when it fell from Madrid's hands into Washington's.

Amongst these old shellbacks would be found sailors from nations where sail still dominated for short distances and common cargo. One of these was Denmark. The schooner was the tendon between the many islands, and hundreds dashed across the North Sea and the Baltic's cold swells to Norway's fjords and Sweden's bustling ports. The old pious New Englander rubbed shoulders with a distant and unintelligible Scandinavian accent or with carob brown lads from the West Indies.

This was the cut of a man's jib in August 1920. They swaggered around New England ports hoping to land a job sailing the Seven Seas, to far ports or to home in Europe or to an exotic island. Reliability was everything. And one thing insured reliability in the owner's mind: a strong willed captain and family reputation.

The G.G. Deering Company acted in accord with long New England tradition and hired a captain of such background: William M. Merritt. The first thing he did was sign his son, S.E. Merritt, as First Mate. This in itself was a fortuitous start. The voyage from Norfolk to Rio de Janeiro would be a long one, and the *Deering* carried no wireless.

The *Deering* idled at Norfolk loading her cargo of coal while Merritt interviewed prospective crewmen. There wasn't much of a dynamic range anymore. But it seemed the interviewees were good enough. They signed their articles before the Master and he set down a description of them.

S.E. Merritt was first, of course. His birthplace was Maine, naturally. At age 29 he was a seasoned and faithful Mate to his father. He was tall at 5.10, a medium complexion from the sun and brine, and his hair was brown. His wages per month were to be $215.00, a hundred of which was to go to his mother.

Next to scribble his name down was Johan Fredrickson of Finland, age: 48; height: 5.6; complexion: ruddy; hair, same; $135.00 per month. He was bos'n and Second Mate. A barely legible hand next signed his name J.A. Benjamin of the French West Indies: Age 51; Height 5.9; description: blond; $150 per month. He was cook. Next: Herbert R. Bates, also of Maine, age 33, height 5.7; complexion: Fair; hair: Light; $150 per month. He was engineer.

All the other crewmen were Danes. N.P. Nielson was the first. He was 24, at 5.5, Fair and Brown. He would receive, as all the Danes would, $100 per month. Niels Olsen: 30, 5.10, Fair, Brown. S. Christian Pedersen: 26, 5.5, Dark, Brown. Peter Sorensen: 19, 5.5, Fair, Brown. Alfred Jorgensen: 24, 5.2, Light, Light. Hans Carl Jensen: 18, 5.9, Light, Light.

The crew had just enough time to get off any letters to their families before they left for the remainder of the year on the long sea voyage. Peter Sorensen wrote his family in Denmark:

Newport News, August 22, 1920.

Dear All

I will just write a few words to let you know that I am all right and that I went ashore from Negros and was signed on an American schooner bound for Rio de Jenairo with bunkers, and I suppose it will take about a month before we return to Newport News; then I shall send home some money and I hope the rate of exchange will be as favorable as now when we come back. I make 100 dollars a month as sailor, which in Danish money will amount to as much as Kr. 680. I know of nothing else to write this time so will close.

Many greetings, son and brother

P. Sorensen

P.S. Write soon

5 M. Sehr

Adr. Carol B. Dering.*[sic]

Rio de Jenairo. Brasil.

Sailing day came in late August. The men scrambled up the ratlines. Merritt stood by Frederickson at the helm as his son walked the deck and shouted the orders to the men in the rigging. The sails unfurled and went taut with the wind. She sailed out, a modern giant amidst the laid-up older brigantines and coastal sailors; an elegant breath of the past amidst the ugly steel mammoths loading their supplies. Her 5 great masts sped her along and she cleaved the blue Chesapeake Bay. Crewmen climbed her rigging, her two mascot cats sprinted about the deck, and her master strode the poop while the faithful helmsman held her to the wind. Except for those coal stained monsters, the scene was no different than the days when the Yankee Clippers departed to their trade routes.

In a bad twist of fate, however, Captain Merritt was taken suddenly ill and the *Deering* had to put in at Lewes, Delaware. The sickness was worse than thought, much worse in fact. Merritt could no longer continue with the voyage and left ship. Naturally, S.E. Merritt also left to dutifully attend to his father, leaving the *Deering* without master and mate.

The G.G. Deering Company rushed to get a new captain. His name was Willis B. Wormell, a very distinctive looking man of age 66. At 6.1 and 198 pounds he was bigger than any of his crew; he was born in Lubec, Maine, on September 16, 1854.

The *Carroll A. Deering* soon after fitting-out.
Photo courtesy of Patrick Davis and the descendants of Carroll A. Deering.

Without the family reliability of the Merritts, Wormell was an excellent choice. He was experienced, totally reliable, a tough captain used to the poop deck before the days of radio. These were the days when it took a captain's unbreakable will to sail a ship 10,000 miles around the world and bring her back to her owners and insurers in one piece.

Without wireless it took an imposing old Ahab like this. He was something out of a Jack London novel. His hair was light ". . .with a prominent streak of gray, slightly wavy." His eyes were blue. He had a light mustache. His forehead was described as "strong and high," his teeth ". . .somewhat yellow from to-bacco; one tooth noticeable for a large gold filling. . .Large frame, well filled out. Round shoulders, one shoulder especially rounded." He also had a ridge on his thumb nail. He was con-sidered a religious New-Englander and a very reliable captain who adhered to the old standards of the sea. For a New-Englander that meant a strong, unflinching work ethic, tough hide, "don't tread on me" attitude, all of which God sanc-tioned. It is perhaps not the most loving God, but one of strict conviction, doctrines and duties.

This showed in Wormell's behavior. He had one peculiarity which was especially noticeable when slightly nervous or intent-ly watching his men ". . .if they were doing something that did not seem to him quite up to standard." He would hold his hands at his side, with the palms facing down at the deck and would repeatedly open and shut his hands. He would some-times do this with his hands ". . .partly behind him. The first shut is rather deliberate, and the successions are quick and closely following one another."

To a crew on the main deck, this might not have been so no-ticeable a trait— from here Wormell was but a towering and glowering Ahab on the poop— but it was a peculiarity all too frequently noted by the helmsman holding the wheel behind him. When Wormell strode the main deck, his eyes judging and critiquing work, it was noticeable to other seamen around, for he stopped and his stern eyes locked upon the miscreant, his rounded shoulders squeezed together, his arms went behind his back, and his fists acted with a mind of their own. This was the man, this was the man indeed for the *Deering*'s long voyage to Rio.

Since the First Mate had also left, this entailed a search for a replacement. Wormell hired-on a Charles B. McLellan. He had little time to check him out. He was handy at Lewes, and too much time had already been spent in delays. Wormell was used to owners pushing time schedules. He had no choice but to quickly get underway.

Finally on September 7, the *Deering* was bound for Rio. Her voyage south is a void so far as we know. Apparently things went well enough. She made good time and she docked at Rio de Janeiro in mid-November,[8] where the cargo was unloaded and the men had a liberty.

Here Wormell met an old friend, Captain George Goodwin, also of Lubec, Maine. Now we get the first hint of problems aboard the ship. Wormell confided in him that his First Mate was worthless and a trouble maker. "Second Mate not much better." Fortunately, Herbert Bates, his engineer, was quite reliable. "He'll stick by me," said Wormell. Goodwin agreed, as he knew of Bates.[9]

As one can imagine, the very statement "he'll stick by me" was loaded. It didn't have to be elaborated upon. Each captain knew what it meant. But there is "worthless" and there is "troublesome." It is not commonplace for a captain to express his anticipation for *mutiny*. A captain's attitude is best summarized by Robert Louis Stevenson in his classic *Treasure Island*.

---

[8] I make this deduction. I could not find any arrival date for her. But since she left Rio on the 3rd of December and made Barbados a little over a month later, one can deduce her speed to Rio from Lewes in September. In full cargo, it would have taken her just over 2 months.

[9] The conversation was had on November 28.

Speaking for the character Captain Smollet, he declares: "No captain, sir, would be justified in going to sea at all if he had ground enough to say that."

This is perhaps not yet the place in the narrative to go into what Wormell might have meant. But for context sake it is best to touch upon it. The sentence, not contended by any historian who has examined the case, reveals that Wormell anticipated some circumstance in which he would need supportive and strong officers by his side. This would suggest a problem with the crew. McLellan's worthlessness in such a situation is underscored by yet another encounter between Wormell and an old sea captain. This was in Barbados on the return voyage. (The *Deering* had left Rio on December 3, bound for Barbados for orders; she was in ballast only.) At Bridgetown by early January 1921, Wormell met Hugh Norton, master of the schooner *Augusta W. Snow*. He clarified that McLellan "has been habitually drunk while ashore." Moreover, "he's utterly unable to handle the crew properly. He treats the men brutally, totally uncalled for."

Neither of these conversations have been challenged by those who have examined the case. But neither has been interpreted either. Both are quite interesting statements, but they are a bit at odds. The latter sounds like it comes from a captain who is too passive, which is not the impression with which Wormell's career leaves one. It does, indeed, sound as if Wormell is worried that McLellan is pushing the men too far but conversely wouldn't be good in a fight if a mutiny broke out.

On the other hand, we get a very different slant on this from McLellan. Norton later had an encounter with him at Da Costa & Company, a familiar supplier of foodstuffs on Barbados. According to Bland Simpson, Norton thought McLellan was partially sober at the time. Of all things, McLellan complained to him that the *crew* of the *Deering* was worthless. "Having trouble with my crew" are the exact words attributed to him. "Considerable trouble," he continued, "on account of they refuse to work. And times I've wanted to punish them, Captain Wormell steps in, interfering, interceding on their behalf— so I've got no authority and can't do anything with them." McLellan then complained he also has to do the navigating because Wormell's eyes are so bad. What is now very interesting is that McLellan tries to bum a job off Norton. However, Norton refused due to his earlier talk with Wormell.

If this encounter is accurately recalled by Norton, this gives us a strange dichotomy. How can McLellan be a brutal thug, and yet be someone Wormell fears will not stand with him in a mutiny? McLellan doesn't sound "worthless" in the sense of being afraid of the crew. Perhaps Wormell feared an uprising when McLellan was drunk? Yet this drunkenness was only (ostensibly) while ashore and not on ship. Perhaps then a mutiny from a crew tired of his brutality? Thus Wormell thought that Bates would alone stand with him.

Yet one must wonder now what good that would do him. If Frederickson was worthless too (or a troublemaker), what good is the engineer standing with the captain? If there is a mutiny amongst the Danish crew, led by Frederickson or another Dane, the ship is lost. Aside from Bates, J.A. Benjamin, the cook, would presumably be the only other loyal man aboard. In this scenario McLellan would be quite parched in his quarters at the time.

The only way to reconcile both accounts is to assume McLellan was lying to Norton. It is more likely that McLellan wanted off ship and naturally had to have a better excuse than that he was disliked by the captain and perhaps disrespected by the crew. Simpson reports that McLellan was later heard, half crocked at the Continental Café, to say "Well, then, I'll get the captain before we get to Norfolk. I will." He was overheard by the First Mate of the *Snow*, Sippi by name, and Norton, and the captain of the *Alice M. Colburn.* Is that it? Was Wormell afraid of McLellan alone?

During an evening stroll along the beach with Captain G.W. Bunker, however, Wormell once again expressed his fear *of the crew*. He told him they were the worst in his whole career.

Mutinies did happen to sailing vessels at the time, but they were more like crimes at sea. The German ship *General Schroeder* came up in the conversation. It had been the summer before that only 1 mutineer out of a crew of 15 enlisted the aid of two stow-aways and took the ship to Russia. That was a far cry from the majority of a crew turning on their captain and taking the vessel, as in the days of the HMS *Bounty*. If Wormell's contempt for McLellan was based on his drinking incapacity, his fear must then have been of Frederickson, the second mate.

Obviously, it's hard to reconcile all this. The memories come after-the-fact amidst the hype of newspaper headlines talking about mutiny and piracy. From the quoted dialogue, it is hard to figure how Wormell could have been worried about McLellan alone. If such a brutal thug murdered the captain, he could hardly hope to command a crew that hated him. The only reason Wormell should fear McLellan is if he got drunk and violently attacked him. That would put McLellan in a pretty pickle when he sobered up. How could he control a crew that hated him? He could never land the vessel and he would have no control in order to make them sail it to another port.

Theorizing along these lines is what makes the next encounter with the *Deering* truly worrisome. The vessel had set sail from Barbados on January 9, almost delayed because Wormell had to get McLellan out of jail for being drunk (interesting if he thought him so dangerous). Sailing north under these circumstances the schooner was next seen off Cape Lookout Lightship, North Carolina. The date: January 29. The Lightship keeper, Captain Thomas Jacobson, was hailed by voice by a crewman on the *Deering*. Jacobson recalled that this man was standing on the quarterdeck. He remembered this so clearly be-

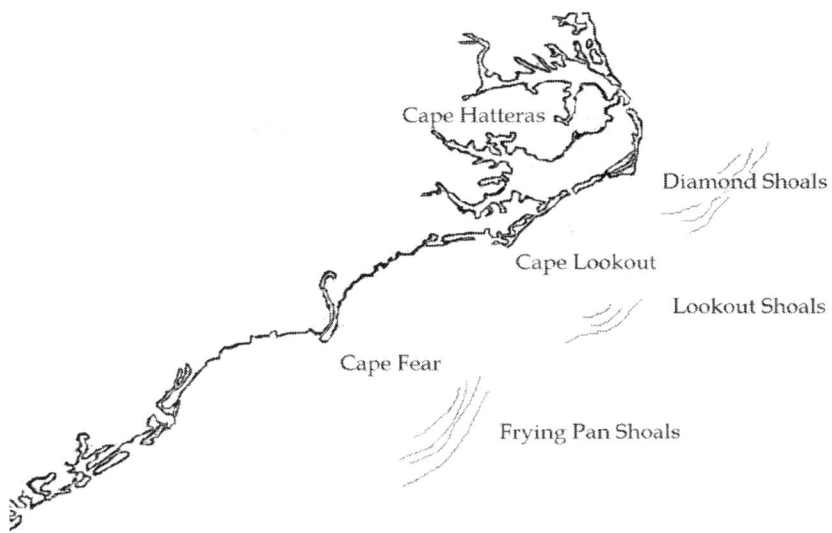

Diamond Shoals in relation to Cape Hatteras and the other shoals and capes off North Carolina.

cause it was so unusual, for *all* the crew were congregated there, a place from which only the officers commanded. Jacobson's description of this particular man later became crucial. He reported that the man shouting at him did not speak, act, nor look like an officer. He was tall, thin, and had reddish hair. Only one crewman fits this description: Frederickson. This crewman shouted to Jacobson that the *Deering* had lost her anchors while riding out the gale south at Cape Fear, please tell the *Deering* company. This said, the schooner continued on its way and glided out of sight along the coast.

Because the Lightship's radio was out, Jacobson attempted to contact a steamer that passed shortly afterward. As it passed, he blew the whistle of the Lightship which required a vessel to respond. The vessel, however, which either had no name or the

The last photo of the *Deering*, taken by Jacobson from the lightship.
Photo courtesy of Patrick Davis.

name covered with a tarp, ignored the horn and continued on
its way.

Shrouded in mystery, at 8:30 a.m. on January 31, the *Carroll
A. Deering* was hard aground on Outer Diamond Shoals near
Cape Hatteras. All sails were set; the lifeboat cables hung at her
stern.

Outer Diamond Shoals is off the coast and completely unapproachable except by boat. Even the best eye strained through
telescopes or binoculars to make out the ship. But all that was
obvious to the lookout stations was that a huge sailing vessel
was firmly aground. Waves slapped her and covered her name
with foam. Like a giant baker's hands they kneaded the vessel
with their crashing brutality and lunging ferocity. They ripped
through her shrouds and jammed her inch by inch deeper into
the sandy bottom.

The Lighthouse Service quickly notified the Coast Guard by
telegram. The next day the Coast Guard Cutter *Seminole* arrived, but due to the pounding surf could not board the vessel
or even approach close enough to get a look at her name on the

stern. She, too, quickly requested information; in reply receiving nothing but a terse "Schooner name unknown whereabouts of crew unknown" from the Diamond Shoals Lightship.

This area of Cape Hatteras had for long been known as the Graveyard of the Atlantic. Its rocky coasts and its churning tides have grasped and beaten hundreds of ships. The coastline was rung by lighthouses and lookout stations, and it wasn't long before such a dramatic sight of a fully rigged schooner raised the interest of the local newspaper. The Norfolk *Dispatch* reported on February 2: "SHIP IS ABANDONED; CREW IS MISSING. All Sails On Schooner Are Set; Coast Guard Still Can't Get Near Enough to Make Out Name."

> Where is the crew of the strange schooner wallowing helplessly in the seas off Diamond Shoals?
>
> Why was the vessel deserted with all sails set?
>
> A coast guard crew that has been frantically trying for two days to reach the strange ship, whose name is still a mystery, are puzzled by the peculiar circumstances under which the vessel was abandoned.
>
> No word of the crew has been heard. All the lifeboats are gone, indicating that all on board got safely away, but whether they made shore at some deserted point to land or were picked up, is so far undetermined.

The questions were valid ones. But although the vessel was officially unknown, the Coast Guard suspected it was the *Carroll A. Deering.* The firm telegraphed the local district to let them know they had been informed by the Lightship that she was in "distress" off Diamond Shoals the day before.

The *Deering* at anchor, 1919. Photo: Patrick R. Davis

The Coast Guard's deduction was correct. On February 4 the Coast Guard cutter *Manning* arrived with the tug *Rescue*. They finally got in close enough to make out her name in moments between the waves splashing and spiking up her stern.

At 10:30 a.m. Captain James Carlson and his men finally were able to board. She was writhing in death, bow and stern twisting in opposite directions. Her deck rose and fell with the waves and rippled back to the stern. The shreds of the topmost sails, all that was left of them, fluttered and whipped the air. Waves licked up the side and splashed down on the deck. They rushed into holds, through windows and down the skylight. She creaked and groaned. Her lower sails were bloated with the wind still driving the ship deeper into the sandbar. Her deck amidships was only 5 feet above the shallow sea (only 8 feet deep here). She had been wedged that deeply into the bottom. (Carlson estimated she was embedded 14 feet into the sand.)

No "ahoy" received a reply.

The search of the ship began. What the wrecking crew and Coast Guard uncovered constitutes the only clues we have, other than that report by Jacobson at the Lightship.

The wreckers had boarded her amidships. The first thing they noticed was that the red and green running lights were burned out. High aloft two red lamps had been hoisted, a signal that the vessel was in distress. But they too were burned out. The midship halyards dangled into the sea and whipped around like wild power cables. Here, amidships, the wreckers were at the lowest part of the vessel's sloping deck. Checking the number 1 hold revealed a disturbing sight. The ship was completely flooded. The upper deck was only about 5 feet above the water. Due to the sloping deck, they went forward where the foc's'cle cabins would still be above the water. They noted that the two anchors were missing and that a kedge anchor was shackled in their place. Descending into one of the fore deckhouses, they found the crew's quarters almost completely empty of personal belongings. Even Bates' engineer's room (on the starboard side) was empty. Below deck they found the galley amidships. Here the sound of the lapping water in the ship was close, very close. On the stove a pot of coffee awaited. Slabs of spareribs were on a large tin platter. A deep stew pot held pea soup. Returning to the upper deck, they went aft. The binnacle was smashed, and the compass was crushed, presumably by the 9 pound sledge hammer found by it. The steering gear was wrecked, and the wheel was broken. The stock of the rudder was thrust up through the deck. Both boats were gone. One had been a 24-foot yawl with a motor; the other was a smaller dory. The ropes from the davits had been cut. They danced about in the churning tides. Descending to the quarterdeck they found the captain's cabin. Except for a few pieces of clothes strewn about, it too was empty of his personal effects. . .with one exception. His precious Bible remained. (Later determined he had had a heavy trunk, grip and kit bag.) To Carlson, it looked as if a spare room had been occupied. In a small room a few pairs of rubber boots lay on the floor. Wormell's bed was unmade. It was wet from the water pounding its way through every board. The table in the chartroom was covered with an unfurled Ocean chart. Yet all the ship's papers, nautical instruments, chronometer and log were missing. Plaintive meows heralded half-starved cats. Three quickly rushed about the feet of the wreckers.

This is the evidence.

It didn't take long for the wrecking crew to determine that the vessel could not be salvaged, and they left the vessel to be pounded into the sea. But before the sea was given its chance, the *Manning* attempted to tow the *Deering* from her place, but due to the rough waters had to cut the towline and destroy the ship by mines. Thus the *Carroll A. Deering* and her clues perished on March 4, 1921.

No great search had been launched immediately after the incident. Because of the orderliness of the abandonment, it had been natural to assume the crew got off safe and would make it to shore. That would put them in touch with most any old timer on Hatteras. But when none ever showed up or were found, it was thought the hard currents, which pull to sea rather than to shore, had drug all the men to their deaths and no bodies or debris were likely to be found. (the Treasury Department had complained that the Coast Guard hadn't searched the beaches afterward and seemed to be giving them no aid whatsoever in trying to unravel what happened.) Thus the windswept beaches of this ancient seafaring shore were silent of clues.

The case of the *Carroll A. Deering* had by this time, one month later, amounted to a mystery of the sea. But it was not a very intricate sea mystery yet. The clues were certainly there. They were like tinder that was waiting to be easily ignited by a spark. But so far it had not happened. Oh, yes, some locals went over the dunes and the grassy knolls of the outer banks with their dogs trying to sniff out trails. The locals had heard about the sledge hammer having destroyed the compass. They had heard about the chart in the chart room being marked in two different hands, indicating Wormell wasn't in command for the last week of the vessel's life. These are seafaring people. They smelled a reason why a crew would make it to land and yet not want to make contact. But by this time the dogs could pick up no clues, and the winds of this windy coast had erased any trails.

Had this been it the *Deering* would have faded into the annals of mundane sea mysteries. The clues would have inspired a few good articles, of course. But time would have worn the details smooth as the sea was even now wearing away what remained of the schooner's wretched skeleton on Diamond Shoals. But something was about to happen that would turn the ghost ship of Diamond Shoals into a world sensation.

Many people, and not just the Treasury Department, had been frustrated by how the Coast Guard seemed to have done very little, and how the lighthouse service also couldn't solve it. The derelict had certainly been news. But now a shocking explanation came on April 11, 1921, when a note was found in a bottle by Christopher Columbus Gray at nearby Buxton Beach. He reported it to the authorities. The note read:

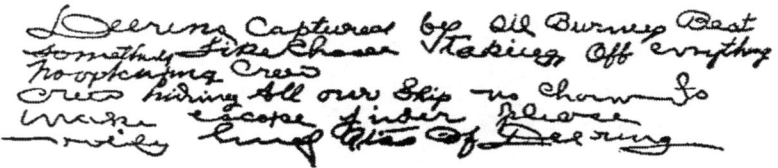

[Deering captured by oil Burning Boat something like chaser. Taking off everything handcuffing crew. Crew hiding All over Ship no chance to make escape. Finder please notify head Qqtrs Deering.]

The spreadsheets were on fire. The authenticity of the note was upheld by Lula Wormell, Captain Wormell's daughter. With true crusty New England zeal she had begun her own investigation. She obtained a copy of the crew's signatures and then also a copy of a letter that Herbert Bates had written to his mother while in Rio, where he had actually written the word "Deering." She was certain they were identical. "But I did not trust to that. I submitted the letters and note found in the bottle to three different handwriting experts, the best I could obtain, and all three agreed that the writing was identical."

She proudly declared the results of her investigation:

> I am quite sure that he wrote it in his engine room while those who had boarded the vessel were on deck. I learned in Washington that the paper upon which it was written was made in Norway and was a sort that is imported to South America in large quantities. It was very finely ruled, with a lavender stripe. . .The bottle, which was of peculiar shape, I found was of a pattern such as is manufactured in Buenos Aires. I'm very sure that Mr. Bates had some of this paper and this bottle in the engine room and wrote the note while undisturbed by those who attacked his vessel.

This was powerful evidence that Lula, with her strong New England bearing, took with her to that "excessively marbled" capital of Washington D.C. Coming with her were Rev. Addison Lorimer and Captain Merritt to encourage a search to be reopened. But neither of them was as formidable as Lula. With the aid of Senator Hale they were able to get the attention of the Secretary of Commerce, Herbert Hoover.

The note in the bottle, archaic and Defoe, wasn't really enough on its own. Herbert Hoover took a special interest in the case for another reason. It was discovered that no less than nine ships of different nationality and varied courses had disappeared around the same time and in the same area. Pirates and worse, Bolsheviks, were suspected when reports came back that unidentified ships were being seen in Russian ports that had had their names blacked out. Thanks to Gray's note, he suspected the *Carroll A. Deering* to have been a Russian victim.

There was much circumstantial evidence to support the "oil burning" boat theory as being a pirate ship. For one, there was that mystery ship that passed the Cape Lookout Lightship. It was absolutely verboten for a ship not to respond to the whistle. Also of especial interest was the s.s. *Hewitt*, with a crew of 42 under captain Hans Jacob Hansen, which was sailing from Sabine, Texas, to Portland, Maine, and should have passed the same area off North Carolina around the time as the *Carroll A. Deering*. Captain Jacobson at the Lightship had never reported seeing her pass. Could she have been the mysterious steamer that refused to acknowledge his whistle? Could it already have been in the hands of hordes of Bolsheviks or pirates? *Hewitt* was last heard from on January 25. More than any other ship, she would remain interwoven with the *Deering* throughout the entire investigation.

There were many more: the steamships *Monte San Micelle* of Italy and *Esperanza de Larrinaga* of Spain were heading out across the Atlantic to Europe; the tanker *Ottawa* sailed from Norfolk for Manchester, England, on February 2, with 3,600 tons of reduced Mexican fuel oil; thirty-three crew disappeared with Captain Williams. Cargo ship *Steinsund*; the Italian cargo ship *Florino*; the Norwegian cargo ship *Svartskog*; the Danish bark *Albyn*; and the steamship *Yute* all vanished in late January or early February. The last heard from any of the vessels was from the *Ottawa* which was in speaking with the *Dorington Court* on February 6, 1921.

The investigation that followed was undertaken by no less than 5 separate departments of the U.S. Government. The man placed in charge was Lawrence Richey, Hoover's faithful assistant. All information that eventually came into official hands concerning the derelict was directed to him.

On the face of it, the investigation looked good for public consumption. Practically speaking, however, there was little to investigate except in the case of the *Deering*. Most of the investigation was, in essence, polite spying. A directive issued to all Consular Officers and their agents at seaports was issued on June 4. In it the consuls were brought up to date on all the particulars of the case, including the provocative note in the bottle and the mysterious steamer which passed Jacobson's lightship and refused to answer any hails.

> Inasmuch as the Navy Department has recently disposed of a number up sub chasers, it is thought that the reference in the message may be to one of those vessels which has been taken over by unprincipled persons who may now be using it as a raider.
>
> The Carroll A. Deering carried a motor lifeboat and a dory, but neither of them has been picked up and no wreckage from them has been found. All the provisions, clothing, and supplies of vessel had been removed.
>
> You are instructed to make discreet inquiries and investigate carefully any clues which may lead to the discovery of the crew of the Carroll A. Deering and an explanation of the disaster. If you succeed in finding out anything which may lead to the discovery of the crew, you will telegraph the Department at once giving full details. Negative information need not be reported.

The object of the communiqué, of course, was pirates. Richey was wise to begin his investigation with the Cape Lookout Lightship report, but he was wrong to concentrate so much on that "mysterious" steamer that passed shortly afterward. Little came back from the consulates for this reason. How does one identify pirates or a sub chaser? Most consuls didn't even know what one looked like.

Meanwhile reports of piracy continued to ignite the press: "VANISHED FLEET MYSTERY EVER, OFFICIALS FEAR," read the New York *Times* for June 23, 1921. The Commissioner of Navigation was quoted as saying: "I have heard many tall yarns of the sea but in this case the facts are there. The *Carroll A. Deering* and the *Hewitt* met some strange fate beyond that of ordinary vessels come to grief." In the article, the English Admiralty wouldn't "flatly" say it was piracy but leaned toward the view.

A "modern 'Captain Kidd' in an oil burning boat" didn't really have the zing as in olden days, so the press highlighted the Red Menace. It was proposed that Red sympathizers had captured the ships and had taken them to Russia. The FBI, in raiding the headquarters of the United Russian Workers in New York, allegedly came across papers detailing orders to capture American ships and take them to Russia. It was noted, in a frenzy of debate, that some of the cargos of the vessels were materials that the Russians could not buy under the western embargo. Herbert Hoover ordered the examining of the cargo lists in order to uncover a pattern.

The entire Red Menace would have been possibly the biggest red herring except for one reason: the *Carroll A. Deering*. No other incident but this one had any evidence. It was the absence of the crew of a sound and stable ship that was unusual . . .and Gray's note was the only link to pirates.

Fortunately, behind-the-scenes Richey was getting suspicious. Weather reports had confirmed that the Atlantic was experiencing the worst hurricane in 22 years last February, and the majority of the vessels that disappeared were heading out into its clutches.

But the idea of a mass pirate attack would fade from the newspapers only after they were given a scapegoat. This would be Christopher Columbus Gray. On August 26, the world was told that the note Gray had found at Buxton Beach was indeed a fake. Without knowing it, Gray confessed to writing the note himself. He told this to none other than an undercover operative. And when the investigators came to Buxton Beach for the coup de grâce, Gray took off like a rabbit to avoid arrest.

Gray's eventual capture was a stroke of luck and ingenuity on Richey's part, and he didn't mind crowing about it either. Earlier that year, after Gray had found the note, he had applied for a job at the Lighthouse Keeper's Station, hoping that his discovery would help get him the job. Through "acquaintances" Richey had a message leaked to Gray that he should come to the Lighthouse Keeper's Station concerning his job application. Gray came, thinking it was only about his application, but was greeted by Federal agents who took him into custody. The full details then came out why Gray had faked the message; he hoped it would get him a job!

When it was all over, Richey made the comment that the entire investigation into the case of the *Deering* was much like a detective story. Richey received the kudos, and publicly the *Deering* case was more or less over. The exposure of the false mystery around the other vessels, and then Gray's exposure rubbed off on the 8 month old incident; and the *Deering* case, if it was still spoken about publicly, was linked in some way with the other vessels lost by storm. The result was that her crew perished in the breakers in their lifeboat.

However, the detective story was not over. There is documentation that conclusively proves that the U.S. Government did not believe the carefully constructed view of the *Deering* and *Hewitt*'s fate to be as the other ships lost in the storm. Nor did Richey believe the notion that the men simply perished in the tide after abandoning ship because of its lost anchors. Long before Gray was exposed, the government was geared to accept mutiny and murder. By late June the State Department had issued another secret directive to Consular agents at seaports. This one contained details of each man's appearance. Richey was looking for *survivors*. These Consular offices were still searching diligently for any seaman as late as 1923, long after the public controversy was put to an end.

The confidential circular of the Department of State issued on June 17th, 1921, File No. 1115 C 22 regarding the crews of the *Deering* and *Hewitt:*

DEPARTMENT OF STATE

Washington, June 17, 1921

CONFIDENTIAL.

DISAPPEARANCE OF THE CREW OF THE CARROLL A. DEERING

To the American Consular Officers at Seaports. Gentlemen:

Referring to the Department's confidential instruction of June 4, 1921, reporting the loss of the American schooner CAROLL A. DEERING under circumstances which are at least suspicious, you are informed that the American steamship HEWITT, carrying a cargo of 8,000 tons of sulphur from Sabine, Texas, to Boston, Massachusetts, and Portland, Maine, disappeared on or about the same date and in about the same locality. There is nothing to connect the two casualties, except the similarity of date and place of occurrence. However, the Department is desirous of obtaining any information possible regarding the present whereabouts of any member of the crew of either vessel in order to determine whether or not there has been foul play.

With this in mind, a description of the master of the CAROLL A. DEERING and a list of the crew of both vessels is appended. The description of the master of the CAROLL A. DEERING was furnished by his relative, and the list and descriptions of the crew of the HEWITT and CAROLL A. DEERING were taken from the Shipping Articles.

You are instructed to place this list among the names of suspected aliens and to check all crew lists of vessels presented to you against it before visaing them. However, if you suspect that any member of either crew is aboard any vessel, the crew list of which is presented for visa, you will refuse to visa it, but will notify the Department by telegraph of the presence aboard the vessel of the suspect in order that steps may be taken to make a complete investigation upon the vessel's arrival in the United States.

I am, Gentlemen,

Your obedient servant,

For the Secretary of State:

WILBUR J. CARR

These descriptions finally gave the consuls something to work with. Months after the disappearance of the crew, the tracing of the same began. There should really be no acrimony extended to the government over why the crew had not been sought before this point. Until the big bolshy scare created by Gray's hoax, there had been little reason to suspect that the crew had not perished in the surf of Diamond Shoals. If they had mutinied, as evidence aboard suggested, then justice had been served. Ironically, the Red Menace scare brought in the bigwigs of Washington, and when the scare was exposed Richey could see that the provocative evidence did *not* indicate the crew necessarily died. There was also the missing *Hewitt* and that mysterious ship that refused to answer Jacobson's hail. On his own, Richey could never have gotten far with a personal dragnet. But in June with the pirate scare still in full swing, he smartly used official channels to set the hounds on still-invisible foxes.

A flurry of communications followed when a sailor was suspected. From the Consul at Rotterdam, on January 31, 1922, the State Department was informed that the Danish steamship *Frederiksborg* sailed for Hampton Roads on January 28 and had on board two Danish seamen, Niels Peter Nielson and Peter Sorensen. They not only shared the same names, but "are identical in every manner to the men with the same names on the schooner CARROLL A. DEERING. . ." The only difference was that Sorensen was listed as 29 not 19.

The FBI was notified and was standing by at Hampton Roads to question the sailors before they could leave the ship. Agent H.S. White contacted the Maritime Exchange in Norfolk to ascertain the position of the *Frederiksborg* but discovered, to his surprise, that the *Frederiksborg* had not left Rotterdam yet, but was still listed as in that port. It appeared that the Consul had misnamed the ship that had departed thinking it was the *Frederiksborg*. The case, since it was outside of American jurisdiction, was considered closed by White. The Niels Nielson and Peter Sorensen, whoever they were, were headed to some other distant port on a different ship, thus being spared interrogation.

During the period of this investigation it was suggested and quickly quashed that the information that two men suspected in the *Deering* case were heading for the U.S. should be released. A communiqué dated February 3, 1922, probably from Richey, states the official reaction clearly: "I think it is extremely important that this information be not given out, at least until after the arrival of the vessels and the examination of the members of the crew who are suspected. I believe that it would be inadvisable to give the information out even after the arrival of the vessels, because it would indicate the method by which the Department is endeavoring to find trace of any members of the crews of the lost vessels who may be alive, and, if there is any reason why the seamen would desire to keep their identity a secret, it could be done by avoiding vessels coming to the United States."

The other vessel alluded to in the communiqué was the s.s.

Tranquebar. An alert Consul at Vera Cruz prepared the FBI with the following dispatch dated December 31, 1921: "Referring to the Department's circular instruction dated June 17th relative to the schooner CAROLL A. DEERING, I have to report that the Danish vessel TRANQUEBAR cleared for Galveston on December 31st. The alien crewlist of this vessel contains the names of H.C. Jensen, No. 14, and Peter Nielsen, No. 24, who answer the descriptions. . ." etc. and so forth.

Agent A.G. Sullivan inspected the crew list of the vessel as soon as she docked at 9 a.m. January 4, 1922, at pier 38. Then the two men were discreetly taken with Sullivan to the office of Hans Guldman, the Danish Consul, in room 425 of the Security Building, Galveston, where, according to Sullivan, they cooperated "very cordially." Sullivan reported: "The subject H.C. Jensen speaks English quite well, but the subject Nielsen does not speak English at all." However, through the cooperation of Mr. Guldman the following stories were brought out. Jensen claimed the only time he had been near Hatteras was on the bark *Elizabeth* in 1919 sailing from Copenhagen to Hampton Roads, Virginia. He had stated that at the time of the incident he was a sailor on a small boat, the *Pioneer* traveling from Copenhagen to Banthelmer. In Nielsen's case, he said he was arrested in Odense, Denmark, on January 1st, 1921, for "intoxication," and after he was released he worked on the docks. Nielsen claimed never to have heard of the *Carroll A. Deering.*

Naturally, the two men's statements had to be taken at face value since there was no immediate way to determine their validity. They were released and sent back to the *Tranquebar.* But Mr. Guldman told the captain to deny them the usual liberties and shore leave until their stories could be verified. Mr. Guldman was very cooperative in the matter, referred to as a real "gentleman" by agent Sullivan and also was a naturalized American citizen. Guldman also told Sullivan he would keep the Department posted on the ship's next port of call. However, between the 14th and 19th of January the *Tranquebar* sailed out of the port for her next destination. The information was never forthcoming from Denmark to confirm their stories and do not exist in any documentation. If any information was ever turned up that did prove the men lied about their positions at the time in question, it came too late and this Jensen and Nielsen could never be linked or not linked with the *Carroll A. Deering* sailors of the same name. The Nielsen and Jensen of the *Tranquebar* faded from the story as hazily as they entered it. Probably more the grateful.

For another sailor it would not be the same. The following telegram was sent July 14th, 1921, to the Secretary of State from the Consul at Constantinople, Turkey:

> B.O. Raney, second assistant engineer United States Shipping Board vessel MOPANG sunk in Black Sea, is proceeding to New York on Greek steamer MEGALI HELLAS.
> We suspect his being identical with B.O. Rainey, third assistant engineer steamship HEWITT. Department's confidential instructions June 8. Have warned Athens and Patras. Details by Mail.
> RAVNDAL

Before he contacted the State Department, Gabriel Ravndal had taken the necessary precautions to insure that Raney would in fact make it to New York and come under American jurisdiction. He sent the following information to the American Consul at Athens before the above dispatch:

> July 11; 8 P.M. The following message should be treated as confidential and urgent. The crew of the S/S MOPANG which was sunk in the Black Sea, is due to transship at Piraeus from the S/S POLICOS to the S/S MEGALI HELLAS. Among this crew is the Second Assistant Engineer Raney whose complicity in the loss of several American vessels is suspected by this Consulate General. Please refer to the June 4th and 17th confidential instructions of the Department. Kramer, the first mate, holds a collective passport for the shipwrecked crew. Without

arousing suspicion please be sure that Raney gets off on the MEGALI HELLAS for New York and cable the Department and Consuls at ports of call. An arrangement should also be made with the Captain of the MEGALI HELLAS to keep the suspected engineer under an informal guard until he can be delivered to the American authorities. A telegraphic acknowledgement is requested.

RAVNDAL

Well, the more specific information Ravndal referred to in his July 14th communiqué was dated July 20th. Besides the above information, Ravndal had discovered that when the 33 members of the *Mopang* arrived at Constantinople on July 6th to be repatriated to the United States, one quickly stood out when he inquired "about the possibilities" of enlisting in the Allied Police Corps at Constantinople. This was Raney. He did not give a reason for this, but did state in regard to his query that he did not wish to return to the United States. Instead, Raney later requested a passport to travel in Europe, but because of his lack of proof of American citizenship, the request was denied and he was told to ship to the U.S. with the other destitute crew for repatriation.

Armed with this information the Consul at Athens and captain of the *Megali Hellas* made sure their interesting passenger was sent safely to America.

A picture of Raney was sent ahead with his thumb print. Raney was of medium height, a cocky and confident young man by his picture, with his cap tilted jauntily to one side, a hand on his hip waiting for it to all be over but enjoying the attention.

Neither Consul Ravndal nor the American Consul at Athens were overreacting to the situation. When Raney finally arrived at New York, he was questioned concerning the entire incident, and if he was, in fact, B.O. Rainey, listed as signing on the *Hewitt* on her last voyage. He was! There was no mistake in this case. This time the FBI finally had the real article. He did, however, have an excuse for being alive. He did not sail out on her, he told them; he had left the *Hewitt* twenty minutes before she sailed. . .so he said anyway.

On August 18, 1921, the State Department finally satisfied Ravndal's curiosity. Wilbur J. Carr responded: "The Depart-

ment appreciates the prompt manner in which you handled this matter and through your efforts the Department of Justice was able to examine Mr. Raney upon his arrival in the United States. However, it has been ascertained that Mr. Raney left the HEWITT about twenty minutes before its clearance from the port of Sabine and was, therefore, unable to furnish any information regarding the loss of the vessel."

The specifics of the examination were never made known and this is the only document, a letter to the Consul, that alludes to the questioning. How it was ascertained, it was never mentioned in the document, and B.O. Raney quickly fades away. It was rather anticlimactic for the Consuls in Constantinople and Athens, considering the subtlety they went through to get Raney to return.

This anticlimactic end is also present in the last documented sighting of a man alleged to be similar in name and appearance to a member of the *Carroll A. Deering*'s crew. This was on September 14, 1922, when a sailor named Peter Sorensen was known to have shipped out on the Danish ship *Kronberg* from Valparaiso, Chile.

The FBI quickly began to check into the movements of the ship and discovered it was at Mejillones, Chile, its first loading point. The ship was then to head for Balboa, Panama Canal, due there October 6th. From there it might go to Jacksonville, Florida, or Savannah, Georgia and then to Philadelphia.

Mr. Doubleda, of the ship's owners, said he would keep the Department informed of the vessel's movements. The FBI agent recommended the offices be contacted at Philadelphia to await the ship. This is the last heard of *Kronberg* and Sorensen, or any part of the case of the *Carroll A. Deering*.[10]

What is rather interesting about the sightings of suspected *Deering* crewmen is that they all represent one of the Danes on board. Never Fredrickson, the ruddy Finlander, Benjamin the veteran cook, and lastly never Bates, the reliable engineer. Only once a possible McLellan was seen— he who has been fingered as the lead mutineer in most critiques. This sighting, furthermore, is one of the most piquing. A Cyril A. McLellan curiously emerged into existence within only a month after the *Carroll A. Deering* dereliction. On March 20, 1921, he was issued an A.B. Seaman certificate #20,694 by the local board of Steamboat Inspectors in Portland, Oregon. The Department of Justice followed this up with an inquiry into the man's address and movements. In response to this, the Collector of Customs discovered that this Cyril McLellan was an untraceable person. He gave his address to the board which issued him his A.B. Seaman certificate as 88 Third Street, Portland— "This is the address of the Sailors' Union," wrote back the Collector of Customs, A. Moore, "and upon inquiry they state that they have no knowledge of this person and it is not found that he shipped out of here on any vessel bound for foreign. The above information from the local Inspector's is all that this office is able to procure."

---

[10] From 1923-on the records of the FBI are still housed at the FBI building, Washington. The relevant documents to complete this last report must still be there. But since I could not prove that Sorensen was dead, they would not nor were required to release anything to me under FOIA.

Neither could the Commissioner of Navigation find anything on a Cyril McLellan ". . .in the records of this office, nor in the records of the Sailors' Union of the Pacific at this port." (San Francisco).

The man was never traced. He emerged briefly in Portland, gave false information, and was never heard from again.

*   *   *

Minus the Bolshevik bogey men and all the hoopla of Gray's fake note in the bottle we now come to the actual evidence of the *Deering* case. Just what does it point to?

The steering gear was smashed. So was the compass. The purpose? Clearly, it would make navigating the Graveyard of the Atlantic impossible. Yes, but beyond this? What would this cause the crew to do? Again, it seems clear they would have to abandon the vessel. Was that therefore the purpose? This seems logical when we consider many other factors which crop up.

Foremost is the information provided by captains with whom Wormell had contact in the ports on the way home, plus the other evidence that suggests Wormell was not in command of the schooner when it passed the Cape Lookout Lightship. Together they spell a crime at sea. Whether this was committed by the majority of the crew as a mutiny or by one rogue officer, the result would be the same. Neither could allow any witnesses to be left to tell the tale. All would have to abandon ship. Members of the mutinous crew would smash the gear and compass to induce the remaining loyal hands (such as Bates) to accompany them in the boats or the individual mutineer/murderer (such as McLellan) would do it to make the crew leave the vessel. The result is a mysteriously deserted ship with only enigmatic clues aboard.

In light of either theory, Jacobson's description of the man who called out to him becomes crucial. This description fits Johan Fredrickson, the ruddy Finlander. If the crew mutinied and killed Wormell *and* McLellan, he would most likely be in charge. But why would he bother to contact the Lightship and have the loss of the ship's anchors reported? Was it all part of the cover to help explain the reason why the ship would be found deserted or, more likely, destroyed in the Graveyard?

If McLellan was responsible for the mutiny, and Wormell was dead and Bates, the reliable engineer, was out of the way, Fredrickson, as the Bos'n, would be the next highest officer. The fact that the Bos'n called out from the poop deck argues strongly for the supposition that the officers were either dead or, in McLellan's case, occupied with covering the other men at gun-point from a secret place so he wouldn't be seen. But why have Frederickson inform the Lightship? Again, it could be to convey the whole nuance that all was otherwise well aboard but that the ship was not properly capable of anchoring.

Alas, in both cases this act implies that the suspect is assuming the ship will be destroyed in the rough waters off Cape Hatteras. If that happened, the last message would truly convince the owners the men had no choice but to abandon a ship they could not bring to a stop. I can't imagine that the mutineer(s) thought the ship would safely beach itself and be boarded. A heavy sledge hammer found conveniently by the smashed gear is hardly going to impress upon any investigator that the crew abandoned the vessel out of fear they could not navigate the waters or bring the vessel to a safe anchorage because of the missing anchors. It implies a not-so-friendly persuasion to leave the ship.

If the crew mutinied, the last meal becomes a problem. It implies they were not aware they were about to abandon ship. However, if McLellan alone was pulling the strings he might not have told the crew what was up until he was ready to spring his plan to desert the vessel.

There should be no doubt that the *Deering* was intentionally aimed at the treacherous shoals of the Graveyard of the Atlantic. A letter came into Richey's office from the master of the s.s. *Lake Elon* informing him of what is possibly the last sighting of the *Deering* before she was found deserted on Diamond Shoals.

In connection with the stranding of the American schooner CAROL A. DEERING on North Carolina coast, January 31st, 1921, I can report that while bound from Sagua La Grande, Cuba, toward Baltimore on January 30th, 1921, about 3:30 p.m. we sighted a five-masted schooner about two points on our starboard bow. The wind was S.W. moderate and she had all sails set and steering about NNW making about seven miles. We passed her about 5:45 p.m. about one-half mile off our port side. We were then about twenty-five miles S.W. true from the Diamond Shoals Light Vessel. From the description of the DEERING, we think that this schooner was her but we could not read her name, there was nothing irregular to be seen on board this vessel but she was steering a peculiar course. She appeared to be steering for Cape Hatteras. We sighted Diamond Shoals Light Vessel about 7 p.m. and passed it at 8:32 p.m. The lookout on the schooner should have sighted Cape Hatteras Light, also the Light Ship at Diamond Shoal a little later than we did but in plenty time to avoid going on shore as the weather was clear and cloudy with good visibility. There was a couple of more ships in the vicinity steering a course parallel with us which should have convinced the Captain of the schooner that he was steering a wrong course.

Hoping this may be of some value we are

Very truly yours

Henry Johnson

Master S.S. LAKE ELON

E.V. Ferrandini, Chief Officer.

Was the *Deering* abandoned by this time? Or was that soon to happen? At 5:45 p.m., January 30th, she was about 25 miles southwest of Diamond Shoals heading straight for ruin. At 7 knots (more likely mph) she would go aground around 9 p.m. At 5:45 p.m. dusk was hard upon them. With darkness approaching, McLellan (or the miscreant) might have smashed the gear and the compass. Amidst the worse navigable seas off the Carolinas, there would have been a relatively hurried abandonment. Little argument would have been given by the loyal crew. These circumstances left little choice.

The meal left behind indicates an evening meal— slabs of spare ribs, pea soup and coffee. The men must have not even bothered with it but went about packing their trunks and kits. Before darkness set they must have abandoned ship. Both boats must have been lowered together, explaining why both ropes were found cut at their ends.

After this it's a toss-up. Did McLellan kill the others in the boats? Did the mutinous crew kill the loyal officers, like Bates or the hated Mate McLellan? Did they all conveniently perish in the rough tides? Or did they all survive and nobody wanted the hassle of trials, courts and years of legal grief. Did all part at the beaches and conveniently their boats left no trace? Or were they picked up by that mysterious vessel that passed Jacobson and refused to answer?

The chart from the captain's cabin is a windfall of information. It is the best evidence we have that Wormell was dead. As it is already known, this conclusively showed that Wormell marked the chart up to the 23rd of January, 8 days before she went aground at Diamond Shoals. After this, another hand took over the marking on the chart. The amount of time— 6 days— it took the *Deering* to traverse from Cape Fear Lightship to Cape Lookout Lightship, which is only about 80 miles, caught Richey's eye as well. It was in this period of time that the captain must have been murdered or died as witnessed by the change in handwriting on the chart. But what caused the delayed amount of time for the vessel to cross that minimal distance of sea? Was the mutineer collecting his thoughts about his plan and ordered the vessel to heave to?

If Wormell was murdered, why take his things too? Surely that would take time. Once again, it could be that the devious progenitor of mystery wanted it to look as if all was well and they simply abandoned the ship due to the anchors and perished in the surf. But yet again this implies that he assumed the vessel would be found intact and boarded. One leaves no clues for Davy Jones' Locker. In this case, why leave the sledge hammer where it was found?

One can second-guess this forever, of course. It's hard to put it all together. Crucial bits of evidence stand out, but they together also create an enigma. For instance, the meal, the sledge hammer and smashed steering gear, the chart, the evidence others used Wormell's cabin, and the ship's three little mascots. The abandonment was unexpected— that a meal was even prepared surely testifies to that— but it wasn't so hurried that the men could not pack all their things and place them in the boats. Why weren't the ship's three kitties taken in this instance?

Perhaps the perpetrator(s) didn't care. Perhaps he(they) had already coerced the crew into the first boat and disposed of them by a gun. When the *Lake Elon* sighted the *Deering* steering for the shoals, this formless murderer, whoever he was, may have been the lone occupant of the *Carroll A. Deering*, carefully kept from the view of the *Lake Elon's* spyglass. The only evidence that he was on board may have been his sinister, distorted shadow casting upon the deck from some place of concealment as he waited to abandon the ship in the motor lifeboat for safety and to assume a new identity, believing, most assuredly, that the *Deering* would meet her fate in the breakers.

But the *Deering* survived to preserve within her cabins and upon her decks a riddle of the sea. Some explanation must be called upon to answer all the chain of events for those days in January, and all the evidence found on the vessel that windswept morning. But this sadly has never been accomplished to the satisfaction of anyone who has ever heard of the strange case of The Ghost Ship of Diamond Shoals.

CHAPTER FOUR

Kalia III
A Crime of Passing

Sailing the Bahamas is the most singularly unique and enchanting experience imaginable. There is no place on the world's oceans like this hypnotic archipelago. Its over 700 islands are but the tips of small hills that mount from two huge submarine plateaus called the Great and Little Bahama Banks. The water around the islands is often only a few feet deep, turquoise over the velvety sand, or a burning Safire at the banks' deepest points, which is only about 50 feet. For hundreds of miles a sailboat can cruise over this aquamarine desert with no land in sight, and yet the bottom is but 10 feet below. Shallow tides magically draw exotic patterns in the sands as if by an invisible finger.

Halos of fleshy beaches surround verdant islands. Many are still deserted. These low lying islands can't be accessed by big vessels. Thus they form an alluring paradox. They are cheek-by-jowl with tourist meccas and yet remain an out-of-reach paradise for the majority of tourists. It is only the small boater who has unlimited access to the true beauty of these outback sentinels. One can still row their dinghy to and step upon an uninhabited lee shore as in the days of the genuine pirates of the Caribbean. The excitement of adventure is all around one. You can wonder if you are not the first or perhaps the second to do so, at least within the last hundred years.

This is not the only contrast in the Bahamas. It is a place of many paradoxes. For example, Nassau is a sprawling vacation destination, with all the amenities. Monuments and old forts recall the days when buccaneers were hung from the yardarm. Yet many small island settlements within only 50 miles don't have power, and some with small airports don't even have night lighting. They are accessible only during the day unless one has a boat. And the Bahamas is not a place where the novice wishes to sail at night. Treacherous crags and shoals abound. Sand Bores can be deadly. These are troughs etched into the bottom sands by the currents. They form constantly shifting mazes and can catch the keel of a boat. At the best of times, one is harmlessly beached until the tides shift the sand yet again. At the worst, one is keeled over and pulled under.

Nature also creates eerie happenings in these tropics. Sudden storms and minicanes strike out of the blue, and unusual mirages thrust an island up into the sky, completely unnerving boaters unaware of the potential for reflections off the shallow banks. Unusual glowing waters also vent up from the shallows

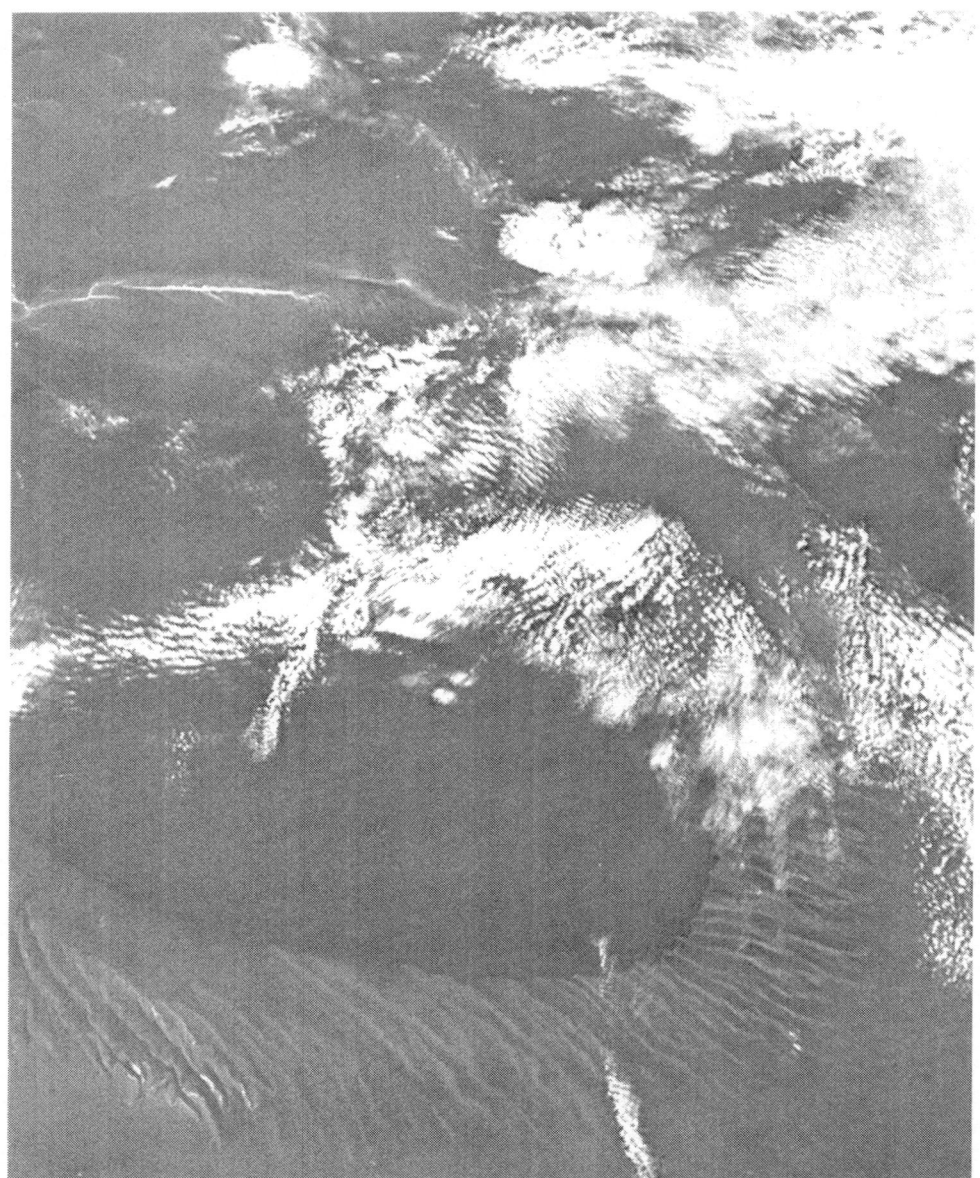

The bulb of the Tongue of the Ocean, as seen from space. Note how the shallow bottom is rippled from the currents, then plunges to abyssal depths. This area of the Tongue is miles across. (NASA)

and glow a green phosphorescence. Shallow though the banks may be, their origin still remains unidentified despite the near-nearness of the bottom for scientific examination. These "glowing waters" ripple and fade away and remain one of the Bahamas' unsolved mysteries. They were the last lights visible from Earth to the astronauts of Apollo 12.

The underwater geography creates odd contrasts too. The Bahama banks are unique shelves. They burst forth from the depths of the Atlantic. Thus shallow water does not gradually fade to deep royal blue. Sailing along the banks the water is a rich translucent turquoise; and the bottom, with its kaleidoscope of turtle grass and marine life, can be carefully enjoyed. But suddenly all can be obliterated from sight by deep impenetrable blue. This area is called the "drop off," where the depths plunge precipitously by thousands of feet. It is an intimidating contrast from sea and air. It thrusts upon the observer that the abyss is never far. This is particularly appreciated along the Exumas and the deep Tongue of the Ocean, an odd gorge cut into the Great Bahama Bank and which terminates in a provocative round bulb.

Paradoxes abound in the Bahamas. They are close to the most civilized industrious nations, but are oddly unapproachable and primitive. Often this primitive allure has proven fatal. Being so close to the industrialized world, they draw adventurers who are completely unaware of the fact that even today 50 miles at sea is really 200 years back in time.

On July 26, 1980, the 38-foot luxury sailboat *Kalia III* was found derelict at one of the deserted cays of the Exumas. The owner was electrician, writer, and adventurer William Kamerer. His wife, Patty Kamerer, had vanished from the yacht, while what possibly was the body of William Kamerer was found in a gruesome condition, curiously in the dinghy and not in the sailboat. When the boat was investigated on July 31, there was no clear explanation uncovered as to why the couple would have been murdered.

The report on this case, couched in the language of officialdom, was entitled: "Report of the investigation of the disappearance of William and Patricia Kamerer on Yacht *Kalia III*— foul play is suspected" and was released on Tuesday, October 28, 1980, after international pressure concerning an alleged cover-up. This report sought to place the details in order.

This tragic and macabre incident occurred near Staniel Cay. There are dozens of outback islands in the Exumas, but very few are inhabited. Staniel Cay is often called a halfway point and "the quintessence of unaffected island retreats" for the simple reason that the small settlement has not been invasive in the several natural attractions. Not least of which is "Thunderball Cave," a grotto for snorkelers and divers alike, named after the 1965 James Bond movie shot in the Bahamas. It is in one of 3 tiny islets located between Staniel Cay and nearby Big Major Cay. The bottom between these two islands is completely see-through, marked only by shadows indicating sea bottom growth.

It was nearby at Pipe Cay that vacationing Illinois State legislator Harry Yourell spotted the white sailing yacht *Kalia III* on Thursday, July 26, 1980, while cruising on board the *Shark II*. This happened when he came in closer to try and identify Staniel Cay amidst the several low lying cays. What he saw at first was eerie, but not necessarily mysterious. The yacht was drifting without any sign of life; and repeated calls to the vessel also went unanswered. So Yourell decided to glide around to the stern of the silent boat to identify its name. As the *Shark II* came around, the name "Kalia III" came into view. Moments later, her dinghy, which was tied to her stern by a rope, coasted out from behind the yacht. In it was the dead body of a man, naked from the waist up, the bottom half "wrapped in something blue." The

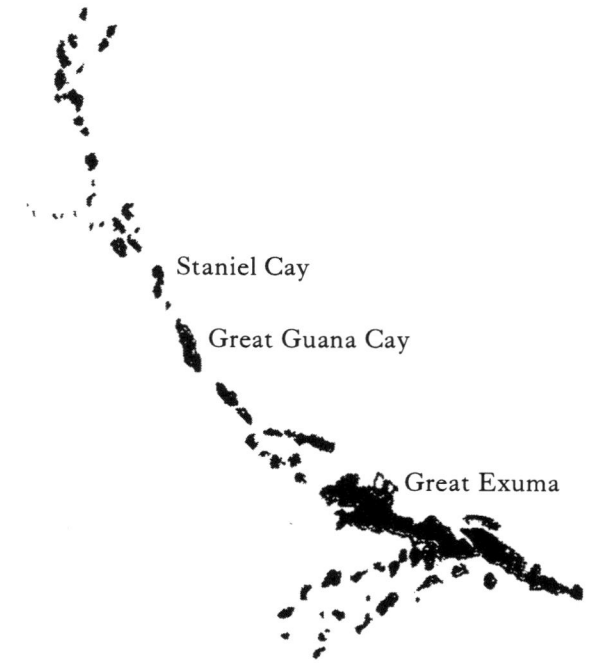

Staniel Cay

Great Guana Cay

Great Exuma

The Exumas chain of islands are in a line southeast from New Providence and Nassau. They lie opposite Andros just across the deep Tongue of the Ocean.

upper part of his body was hanging face down over the side of the dinghy into the water, and covered with blood.

After quickly taking 16 millimeter film of the yacht, Yourell headed straight toward Staniel Cay to report the incident. There Yourell informed Kenneth Rolle, a Staniel Cay islander, about his find. On the double, Rolle called BASRA (Bahamas Air-Sea Rescue) over the citizen band radio and asked them to contact the police. Yet it wouldn't be until 4:30 p.m., July 31, that Nassau was informed of the incident. The message was 5 days in prompting a response.

Meanwhile, in the interim days, Kenneth Rolle had journeyed out to Pipe Cay to locate the yacht himself. He went aboard, dropped the anchor in the sandy bottom, noticed the strong odor generated by the discolored body, and departed. The body was still hanging over the dinghy, faced down, and impossible to identify.

At 5:20 p.m. on July 31, fifty minutes after the police were notified of the body, agents Lundy and Pratt left CID headquarters to pick up a mortician and head for a reserved chartered plane at Nassau airport. But because the plane was not ready, they were delayed for takeoff until 7:15 p.m. The investigators were now at a disadvantage, for Staniel Cay's airfield had no lighting for night takeoff and landing. This meant that due to the approaching dark the pilot would not be able to wait for them at Staniel Cay. Consequently, they would have to stay overnight. In this instance the mortician opted not to go. But he did give Lundy and Pratt his body bag, but he kept his chemicals.

So they were finally off, and at 7:40 p.m. the *Kalia III* was no longer alone and isolated; the roar overhead was the circling plane of Lundy and Pratt. Looking down on the yacht, when the sun was low on the horizon and bathing the islands and rippling water in sparkles of oranges and pink, the white *Kalia III* easily stood out. The yacht appeared to be grounded, its bow in a southeasterly direction. The body was also identifiable laying in the dinghy. "It appeared to be badly swollen to an abnormal size, and discolored." The lower half of the body was "wrapped in something blue," the upper portion was hanging over the side, face down into the water just as Yourell and Rolle had described it.

Satisfied they had found the *Kalia III*, the officers landed at Staniel Cay in order to acquire a boat to go to the isolated cay. There they were greeted by Kenneth Rolle. Mr. Rolle told them the story from the beginning; and also of his unenviable task of journeying to Pipe Cay to anchor the boat. Rolle also told them he was willing to take them to the spot; it would take only 25 minutes.

However, investigation of the incident incurred another delay. With dusk approaching there would not be enough time to get the body before dark and takeoff for Nassau. And due to the fact that Staniel Cay is a stopover for yachters and other visitors it would not be a good idea to tow the boat back to the cay, considering the strong odor, and offend the locals and guests. Judiciously, it was decided that they would head back to Nassau and leave the *Kalia III* in the relatively isolated Pipe Cay area. There was no problem with this, for Rolle observed while he was at the *Kalia III* that the boat was protected on the windward side by Pipe Cay. It would take "a very strong wind to overturn the dinghy." Relieved, Lundy and Pratt left for Nassau; they would be back in the morning with the mortician.

The next day Lundy, Pratt, Rolle, and the mortician proceeded to the sailboat. Upon boarding the sailboat they carefully observed every clue lying about. The report states what they saw:

> They checked the sailboat and saw no one. There were apparent blood stains in the pilot area in the stern of the boat and what appeared to be gun shot marks on the left side of the stern. There were also what appeared to be bullet holes in a red two gallon tin which was tied to a rail on the right side of the boat's stern.
>
> Two spent flare cartridges and four live flares were found at the stern of the boat. The flare gun was not found. A pair of glasses with brown frames was found on the deck of the stern. In the galley there were apparent blood stains.

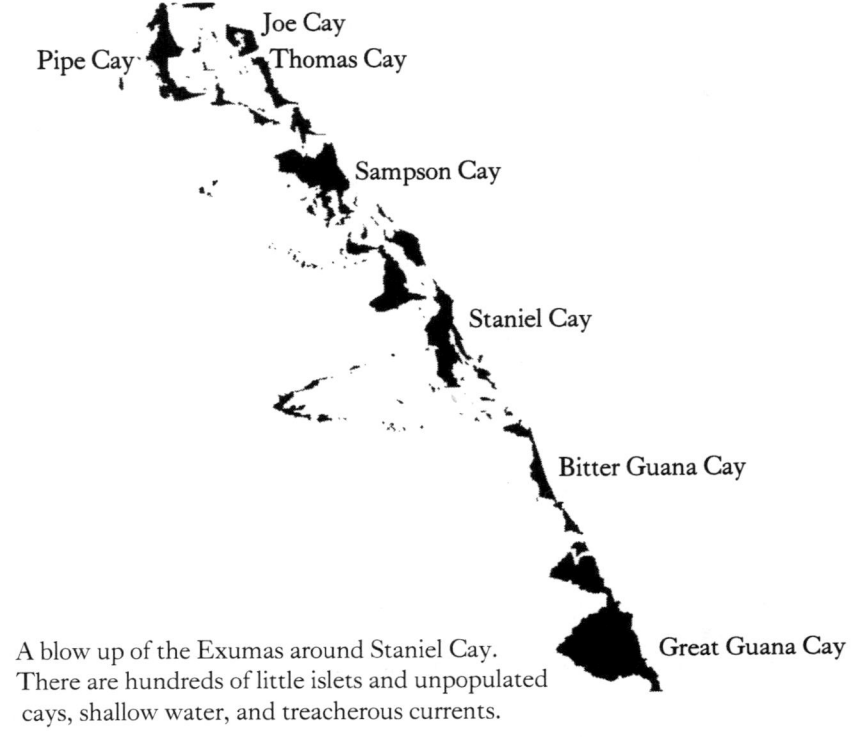

A blow up of the Exumas around Staniel Cay. There are hundreds of little islets and unpopulated cays, shallow water, and treacherous currents.

The dinghy, however, was now suddenly empty. The body had coincidentally disappeared over night along with the blue wrapping. A chilling, but firsthand account follows: "There was a small amount of water in the bottom of the dinghy and on its right side were apparent blood stains. There was a large amount of maggots on the same side."

Upon thoroughly investigating the boat's galley, the US Coast Guard's suspicions proved to be correct: the boat was the Kamerer's. William and Patty's passports were found inside, and the boat's log showed they were sailing the Bahamas "from north to south for several days." The last entry in the log was for July 25, the day before the *Kalia III* was spotted by the *Shark II*. This was written in the hand of Patty Kamerer. The log also confirmed the couple had left Fort Meyers on April 28 and would be sailing around the Bahamas and Caribbean.

The investigation next took to land. Residents were interviewed from various sparsely inhabited nearby cays without shedding any light on the matter. The cay beaches were scoured for the body while the Bahamian defense boat *Exuma* was dispatched to search the waters for any sign of the body or "blue wrapping." Finding nothing, the *Exuma* finally towed the yacht to Nassau.

Inevitably the police were exonerated from any responsibility for losing the body. The case was closed.

The report subsequently said the incident was suspected to be drug related, although it further says: ". . .but there is no hard evidence that it is." The murder of the couple was thought to have been occasioned by the *Kalia III* accidentally stumbling across a smuggling operation in the secluded area they were sailing. The many inlets and isolated cays make it a handy place to conduct this kind of business. From 1977 to 1980, 50 guns, 29 airplanes and 33 boats were confiscated by the Bahamian police in connection with drug incidents. But none of these cases were remotely like the *Kalia III*.

Also, the *Kalia III* hadn't cast anchor, and the sails were not set. They could have been motoring into the area, but there is no report the engine throttle was engaged and the gas tank empty. But the incident clearly had happened at night. What was there for the Kamerers to have seen? Even if there were two boats exchanging drugs, what could two people aboard a yacht make of it? It really doesn't sound like they suddenly surprised any drug transshipping.

Several other questions remain. For instance, what did happen to the body? Was the body dumped by a wave? By a coincidence did a shark finally come after all those days and pull it over the day before it was to be recovered? Who fired the flares? Why was the body in the dinghy and not the boat? What was this blue wrapping? Was the body in the boat William Kamerer? Had he survived the attack? There are logical reasons to fire off flares, but why wounded would he leave a perfectly sound yacht and board the dinghy, only to die? Where did he leave the flare gun? If Patty Kamerer fired the flares, where was she?

I would suggest this scenario. That on the night of July 25, 1980, for reasons unknown William and Patty Kamerer were shot by persons who were also unknown; Patty Kamerer was knocked overboard by the blast of one of the gunshots and William Kamerer was fatally wounded. This explains the "apparent" bullet holes in the boat. Then the vessel carrying the assailants immediately left the scene after randomly firing.

The following hypothetical chain of events can also explain the other evidence. William Kamerer, wounded, quickly shut off the boat's motor. He went into the galley to get the flares, thus explaining the blood inside the boat. The first thing on his mind was not to call for help, but to get his wife who was in the sea somewhere out in the darkness (most likely already dead). He went back up to the deck and fired off the flares in rapid succession, not only as an SOS but to illuminate the surrounding ocean to spot Patty. He was not dressed at the time of the incident, so he wrapped something "blue" around his waist. He took the loaded flare gun to fire more flares and climbed into the dinghy so he could find her and pull her out. In this state he died, the arm with the flare gun hanging over the side where his hand let it fall to the ocean's bottom. This could explain why the body of Mrs. Kamerer was not located, and equally why a body was found in the dinghy. It also accounts for the evidence of spent flares and the various locations of blood on the stern deck and in the galley. And why, in the haste of the moment, William Kamerer sent no SOS, but went into the dinghy seeking only to get his wife, and there to die.

However, the noncommittal nature of the report's language instantly raises some brows and, naturally, some questions on the precise nature of the incident. For by this time the boat had been in police custody for two months. By now if the spots were blood stains, surely this would have been definitely determined. Also, "apparent" bullet holes would have been established as fact, since the bullets could easily be dug out. The "final" report seems anything but. Its language suggests it is nothing more than Lundy or Pratt's preliminary report after returning to Nassau.

The "apparent" murder of William and Patty Kamerer is yet another enigma of the sea. The blue wrapping is unusual, since it is never defined. Surely, Rolle could at least say it was a towel, a sarong, something. If Bill Kamerer was not dressed when the incident happened, he's hardly going to be bashful enough to wrap a blue towel around himself before he goes out into the dark to look for his wife. If drug smugglers murdered them, why not riddle the boat with holes and send it to the bottom and do the job properly? Why leave evidence? From all appearances it was merely a sail-by-killing, one in which there was initially a survivor.

PART II

Steel Mammoths

The USS *Cyclops*. (US Navy photo)

CHAPTER FIVE

A Fate Worse Than Sinking

Steel. Cold hard steel. It inspired the various delusions of 19th century shipbuilding that an unsinkable ship was truly a possibility. With steel there came the engineering skill to weld double hulls and multi water-tight compartments. If by some miracle both hulls were penetrated, only one compartment of a ship would be flooded. This would not be enough to upset buoyancy. The leviathan *Great Eastern*, for example, reinforced this idea. She was the first of the new breed. Once she even rammed a reef and tore open her side. But the water only flooded one compartment and thus did not upset the ship's buoyancy. The *Great Eastern* survived tempest and rocks to become a white elephant. She ended up in the scrapper's yard, the ignoble fate of ships past their prime and use. Until a vessel of such magnitude would sink, such as the *Titanic*, the idea of the unsinkable ship remained.

Powerful ironclads could crash through the waves, belching out smoke from their stacks, no matter what the weather. With the immense sizes steel could provide there could be no fear of storm. Just build the ships big enough, doubled-plated and compartmentalized. Steel inspired so much.

Because of steel engineering many other impressions and stereotypes rode coattail on the "unsinkable ship" theory. Steel prevented fires. Ships could no longer burn to the bar. Steel enabled steam boilers and heavy turbines and ship's screws. Ships could never be without power now. They no longer needed wind. The doldrums of the Sargasso Sea were no longer a worry.

Hydrographic studies, especially in the US, underscored the new confidence. S.D. Sigsbee even noted that out of all the derelicts reported over the 7 years of his study only a few were steamships. The rest were wooden sailing vessels. True, steamships were not as common yet, but seamen instinctively knew not to abandon a sound steel vessel. Steam and steel soon coursed through the Atlantic and through the minds of seamen. Mammoths rode high and dry, now capable of tackling that shrew of a sea. Guarded by these impressions, most seamen knew not to panic and flee a sound steel ship. They fled wood and sail but not steel and steam.

Philosophy and feasibility aren't the same thing, however. In the public arena the former will dominate popular conceptions and not the careful thinking of the latter. With each new ship disaster engineers and architects knew the great mammoths were sinkables. But the idea of the unsinkable ship dominated popular culture. Each new disaster was greeted as a phenomenon and given wide press.

But wireless added the most to our view of a lost ship as an enigma of the sea. As the century turned to the rip-roaring 20th since Christ, sailing the seas was minus something else: the "terror of silence." Warren Tute notes in his *Atlantic Conquest* that by 1899 "Though the Atlantic cable was now over thirty years old, ships had continued to burn or founder in storms with not so much as a whisper reaching land to break the bad news. By the time the twentieth century dawned, although Marconi had proved his invention, the crew of a ship in any kind of trouble still fought a battle for life in utter loneliness when in fact help might be there to hand a few miles beyond the horizon. Wireless telegraphy was to deprive the sea of its ancient terror of silence."

Altogether travel over the sea was indeed changed. Derelicts became fewer. Men kept their heads. Ships made it through storm easier than before and kept the supply and trade routes open and surging with traffic. But something else happened. A paradox. Mystery changed. It did not altogether vanish; it changed. Perhaps it was not so frequent anymore, but when it happened it could not be assumed to be so mundane anymore. In fact, it intensified.

In the days before Marconi's triumph, a ship disappearance was met with many theories. But in the end there could only be a shrug. After all, the sea is vast and a ship relatively small. Who knew what could have happened to it? But as great steel vessels were added to the number of missing ships, those hitherto considered unsinkable, theories grew in complexity. Then when they vanished without a peep over their wireless, the questions grew more ponderous. What is so swift to do this? The genuine sea mystery was born. These are not those humdrum mysteries of bygone days where we simply do not know what happened. These are those mysteries that defy quick explanation.

Wireless meant the ability to send an SOS, thus alerting all others. Wireless meant that there would be regular position reports. Thus if a report was missed, a general position could be determined. Wireless meant others could be notified and they could head to search a certain area. All this would make a ship disappearing a very hard thing indeed. Wreckage of some sorts should at the very least be found.

It was not just the invention and implementation of wireless aboard ships that added to the mystery when one vanished, it was the complex web of wireless and telegraphic communication on land. Every port in most every hemisphere could be connected in a complex network. This put every port in the shipping world in quick contact with each other. There was no way a great ship could be pirated and turn up at another port without the authorities knowing about it. Ports also provided hundreds of nodal points for ships and their crews. Take, for instance, a pirated ship. If it sailed far off its course there was a chance another ship might spot it. Coming to port and discovering that ship had been pirated, wireless placed the witnesses in immediate contact with the owners and various government authorities. Lookouts were immediately posted. At every port of call they awaited the vessel or the crew.

Wireless and telegraph gave us wonderful mental habits of invincibility. It inspired us that progress was surging forward. Thus when mystery did occur it took us and the age of Metropolis by surprise. The hopes and fears, even false assurances and conceits of the age of engineering miracles, made the whole idea of a ship disappearance into something far more than we might make today. We accept that our advances, however grand they have been, still have not overcome nature. But in the early 20th century a new science was intoxicated by the giant leaps and bounds it had made. A missing ship was all the more astounding, and it received far more news coverage and lurid theorizing. It caused all and sundry to pause and consider. In one generation, the old mystique of the sea was at once dashed and then intensified. Was there really something about the sea that we knew nothing about?

The first disappearance to truly shock Metropolis was the USS *Cyclops*. She has become the epitome of the modern sea mystery. She was a huge 520-foot collier (coaling supply vessel), a ship of the US Navy Auxiliary Service, and she was the first Navy ship to vanish without sending an SOS. This more than anything inspired the Navy to believe she had not sunk but that something untoward had happened to her.

There were many other reasons to have reservations about her disappearance. March 1918 rode the closing months of World War I, but the *Cyclops* was traveling in placid waters between Rio de Janeiro and Baltimore, far from the war zone. She was too far away for submarines and mines. If German saboteurs had snuck a time-bomb aboard and blown her up, debris would have been everywhere. In such busy sea lanes some ship should have seen some flotsam. All this made her disappearance very suspicious to the US Navy.

In short, the Navy was ready to agree with the cliffhanger sent to them in a confidential report from the US Consul at Barbados. The *Cyclops* had unexpectedly stopped at this West Indian port on March 3, 1918. In response to the State Department's requests to all consuls along the route of the ship's final voyage to report anything pertinent, they received the results of Consul Brockholst Livingston's quick investigation.

Secretary of State,
Washington, D.C.
April 17. 2 p.m.

Department's 15th. Confidential. Master CYCLOPS stated that he required six hundred tons coal having sufficient on board to reach Bermuda. Engines very poor condition. Not sufficient funds and therefore requested payment by me. Unusually reticent. I have ascertained he took here ton fresh meat, ton flour, thousand pounds vegetables, paying therefor 775 dollars. From different sources gather the following: He had plenty of coal, alleged inferior, took coal to mix, probably he had more than fifteen hundred tons. Master alluded to by others as damned Dutchman, apparently disliked by other officers. Rumored disturbances en route hither, men confined and one executed; also had some prisoners from the fleet in Brazilian waters, one life sentence. United States Consul General Gottshalk passenger, 231 crew exclusive of officers and passengers. Have names crew but not all of the officers and passengers. Many Germanic names appear. Number telegraphic or wireless messages addressed to master or in care of ship were delivered to this port. All telegrams for Barbadoes on file head office St. Thomas. I have to suggest scrutiny there. While not having any definite grounds I fear fate worse than sinking though possibly based on instinctive dislike felt towards master.

LIVINGSTON,

CONSUL

Consul Livingston's communiqué did not please the Navy. The gut reaction was to discount the implication that the ship could have suffered a mutiny or a betrayal to Germany. But it was also hard to explain a captain putting in unexpectedly at a port and claiming he needed more fuel. This, besides the reported disturbances aboard, was truly unsettling.

Mutiny, however, should be easy to uncover. There were 309 men aboard, including the US Consul General of Brazil. If mutiny occurred, then the islands would see a large ingress of unexplained Whites. Consuls were told to report any such occurrence. The alternative was harder to prove. Agents were told to keep a lookout in German ports and report any ship that looked like the *Cyclops*. There were even rumors that the vessel had been seen at anchor in Kiel, Germany.

Since World War I was still raging in Europe in the spring and summer of 1918, the papers and even the Navy could only speculate. But one of the worst accusations dominated the

The *Cyclops*. She was a huge, well-built collier.

spreadsheets: "Cyclops skipper is Hun"; "Cyclops Hun Raider Now"; "Cyclops crewman wrote his family that skipper was pro-German." The Navy would believe no such thing. The commanding officer of the *Cyclops*, George W. Worley, was as English as his name.

Nevertheless, Lieutenant Commander Worley's past had to be investigated, even if only perfunctorily, by the Office of Naval Intelligence and FBI. This investigation quickly yielded the truth of his place of birth. The Navy was surprised. Worley was not born a U.S. citizen. He was born at Sandstadt, Hanover Province, in Germany in the year 1862, under the name Johann Frederick Wichmann. Wherever the ONI operatives would go in their quest to find Worley's past they would inevitably encounter this line when questioning: "Oh, you mean Fred Wichmann." Worley's past it seemed was no secret except to the Navy.

In 1878 young Fred had jumped a German ship at New York and headed to San Francisco. His brothers, Henry and Herman and other family members, already lived there. Young Fred soon joined the family enterprise of Wichman, Lutgen & Co, Distillers Agents. However, during his tenure there was always some form of petty embezzlement going on.

One of his brothers also ran a liquor store. In 1891, now grown, Fred got into this business at the corners of California and Polk streets. When this went belly-up he opened a grocery store at Oak and Broderick streets, while at the same time being heavily involved in his "Captain Wichmann's Roadhouse," a saloon near San Francisco's Cliff House at Ocean Beach. This name is a bit humorous, for it seems he hadn't really been much at sea and had certainly never been a captain.

After this business flopped, Worley went back to the sea as First Mate on a schooner owned by the Austrian Count Rudolf Festitics de Tolna. They got as far as Hawaii on a round-the-world trip when he and his brother-in-law's brother, August Peppercorn, were thrown off. According to Peppercorn, they were ejected because de Tolna discovered that opium was aboard and suspected Worley was secretly smuggling it under his nose.

After this, Worley was later mate on a schooner, taking it to its owners in the Philippines. In this capacity he supposedly shot one of the crewmen and fled. There is another story that he was doing time in an Australian penal colony. Whichever is true, in 1899 he reemerges into the records as George W. Worley on the transport ship *St. Mark*. From here he became an ensign in the US Navy reserve during the Spanish-American War. He worked his way up in the ranks and was made a Lieutenant Commander and given the command of the *Cyclops*.

But a strange trail of brutality and murder followed his career. Amazingly, the first snippets the public heard came 51 years later. In 1969, a former officer aboard the *Cyclops* wrote a wonderful little article for none other than the prestigious journal of the Navy, the *Naval Institute Proceedings*. Conrad A. Nervig had actually been a passenger on the vessel on the way south to Rio. When he was transferred to take up his duties at that port, he thus escaped vanishing with the ship on the return voyage. He was one of the last eyewitnesses aboard ship to be able to speak about circumstances aboard just before the vessel left. As such, *The Cyclops Mystery* has heavily influenced those small vignettes that have been written subsequently on the final voyage of the great ship.

Nervig spoke about his encounters with Captain Worley. "Sometimes I think Captain Worley was born fifty years or even a century too late. He was a perfect example of the tyrannical bucko sailing-ship captains who considered their crews not as human beings but only as a means of getting their vessels to the next port. He was a gruff, eccentric salt, given to carrying a cane but possessing few other qualities."

According to Nervig, a couple of days after the *Cyclops* left Hampton Roads for Rio, the ship's surgeon, Burt J. Asper, confined the young Ensign J.J. Cain to the Dispensary. There he would remain for the rest of the voyage. According to Nervig: "From all accounts this seemed to be a routine matter on ships commanded by Worley. It was the general opinion in the wardroom that this was done to save Mr. Cain from being a victim of the Commanding Officer's unreasoning temper. I do not recall that the doctor made any comment nor that he was in any way questioned regarding the matter; his acts and motives were taken for granted."

In addition to this, Worley soon put his executive officer, Harvey Forbes, under arrest. Worley liked to command a ship his way. His navigation, not always that great, was nevertheless never to be challenged. Forbes had done that once too many times.

Because Cain was in the Dispensary, Nervig, though a passenger, was assigned Cain's duty, the Dog Watch, the lonely tour of duty each night on top of the bridge from 12 a.m. to 4 a.m. It was during this watch that the sleepless seadog would come up and visit. "He seemed a nice man," Nervig penned, but "it was only later that I discovered his peculiarities. He visited me on the bridge during my dog watch carrying a cane, dressed in long underwear, and wearing a derby hat. He would lean on the bridge rail looking at the sea. He has a fund of tales, mostly humorous, but he was quite erratic at times. Without the slightest pause between words, his mood would change to that a very opinionated man— a self-proclaimed genius who thought he had never arrived but should have. It was while in these moods that he'd take out his rage on some unknowing officer. Although he treats me very well— why?— I don't know. It was a part of his makeup."

From Nervig's *The Cyclops Mystery* we come away with the impression of Worley as a mean Jack London type of captain, possibly even a man going insane. Yet there was so much more to Worley that remained undiscovered until I finally uncovered the resting place at the National Archives of over 1,500 papers on the Navy's investigation of the vessel's disappearance. The Navy spared no effort in tracking down every tidbit of his past life. Much in Nervig's article confirms that he told a true story, but it is really only one out of dozens that the Navy garnered. It is also the only one tarnished by 51 years of elapsed time. It is purely from memory. His daily letters to his wife were in the mailbags on the *Cyclops* and lost when the vessel vanished. But the National Archives carries vivid contemporary accounts from former seamen and friends.

Nervig's article is quite intriguing, and its honesty should not be challenged. But there are some things in his memory which should be. He makes no mention of Worley's heavy dependence on alcohol, which is a fact of the man unchallenged even by his closest friends. Nervig also doesn't mention Worley's loath of regular Navy men, which every man and officer who had served with Worley knew.

But most of all Nervig seems completely unaware of something enormously significant: Worley had recently been brought before a Naval Board of Inquiry because 40 of his men had signed a petition after the vessel's last voyage off France. In their petition they had accused him of abuse, drunkenness and dereliction of duty. There was one other thing, but no crewman would put it down on paper. Worley was known to be very Pro-German, and the *Cyclops* was suspected by some of the men to be a nest of 5th Columnists.

The petition mentioned none of this, but hints snuck out at the Hearing. When Worley cross-examined some of the men he revealed how little he had been paying attention. Rather he introduced and tried to make a clean breast of some of the other controversies. For instance, in the case of his cross-examination of Burt Asper, his prime nemesis, he asked about his orders for "lights out" at night. Violation of "lights out" had never been raised, neither in the petition nor in any testimony. Taken by surprise, Asper could only repeat that Worley's proper orders were "lights out." Worley seemed satisfied, though the court no doubt was a little disconcerted by his disengaged cross-examining.

There were reasons, it seemed, for Worley to feel self-conscious. There had, in fact, been a very suspicious set of circumstances discovered on the ship during her last voyage off France. For instance, the boat falls had been found cut. The gun lenses had been put in backwards (thus the ship was virtually defenseless if suddenly attacked) and an unauthorized light had been discovered leading from the deckhouse to the top of the mast. It could have been used for signaling to enemy positions on land and sea.

Captain Worley was also sensitive about another issue not contained in the petition. Right out-of-the-blue he asked in cross-examination how the crew felt about their liberty. This took some by surprise as well. Worley had been accused by dozens of men of impartiality. He gave Auxiliary Service men liberty frequently, but not US Navy men. It was not public knowledge that Worley hated regular Navy men. He had run his ship with auxiliaries, Naval reservists like himself, until war was declared in 1917. War added inductees— ignorant farm boys— and regular Navy men aboard. The *Cyclops* first voyage afterward was to France, the voyage that saw Worley brought before the Mast for his conduct. Both regular Navy men and raw recruits were surprised by how he ran his ship like some old bigoted high seas skipper.

We can safely suspect that dozens did not sign the petition. But both the complaints that were specified and those that remained untouched on paper were well-known to all hands aboard. And those unspecified were by far the most sensitive and dangerous. Perhaps the aggrieving men thought it would be easiest to rid themselves of Worley by concentrating on his indisputable drunkenness rather than trying to weave together hints of treason into solid strands of evidence. Despite being pro-German, Worley might be perfectly innocent. It could be that since the old seadog was frequently under the influence, much was going on under his nose of which he was not aware. With a new captain, perhaps the nest of suspected pro-Germans aboard, which included two officers (Schonof and Konstovich), could be disbanded.

But that was not to be. His private defense before the Board held sway. Worley blamed everything on new recruits. He said they simply didn't know how ships are run. More than this he said he was the victim of a plot. The ringleader was none other than Burt Asper, the ship's surgeon. It was no secret aboard that the petition was circulated by Hospital Apprentice W. Howard. When he wasn't walking it around ship, it was hanging openly in sickbay for any to come by, read and sign. Forty men had done so because of Asper. Worley said this all began for one reason: he had dressed Asper down. Now boldly before the Board he condemned Asper as a sex maniac. He declared he had dressed him down for speaking in loud terms about "women falling for him" and that because of this Asper was in conspiracy with others to remove him as captain. Concerning all the testimony about being observed under the influence of alcohol, and even smelling of it, he said he took a teaspoon of sherry with certain medicines to stave off attacks of beri-beri.

Despite all the damning and consistent testimony, Worley was, amazingly, exonerated by Commander William Whitted, the presiding officer. He wrote to his commander, Admiral N. Abraham, that Worley was a good commander, one of the best, and that the testimony was inspired by malice and by ignorant farm boys newly recruited. Whitted completely glossed over the testimony that Worley chased warrant officers around the deck at gun point, and that he was indisputably inconsistent in discipline and in granting liberty. Whitted and Abraham could both admit that Worley was "intemperate," but they didn't seem to think it would influence his command abilities.

A collier is, after all, not an easy ship to run. It needs more than a sailorman. It needs a man who knows those types of ships and the merchant service of hauling cargoes. Worley was that man. He was a poor navigator, a mean though often humorous sea captain, but he was a good sailorman. He knew ships and he knew the *Cyclops* in particular. The Navy whitewash probably was necessary. He would not have been an easy man to replace.

This attitude may have been the motivating reason to save Worley. But in private the Navy didn't seem to care too much for him, at least to hear Worley talk about it. Of all people, Worley was complaining about how the Navy treated *him*. What his ire seemed to come down to was that he was called before a Board of Inquiry at all. Despite the Navy vindication, the old seadog was rankled by the whole affair. He was even thinking of leaving the Service. He had had only one short voyage since the Board of Inquiry and this was to Halifax, Nova Scotia. Now he was being assigned to Rio. Worley was, obviously, being kept out of the war zone.

George Worley's haughty attitude is actually very disturbing when one realizes it was a recurring attitude. He had actually been called to a trial once before. This was in 1908 and as a result of this trial he truly did leave the Service. While captain of the *Abarenda*, his First Mate had been found beheaded. It was determined that a Scotsman aboard named Dixon had done it. The First Mate, Witchardt, had been so brutal with the men that Dixon was actually exonerated on the grounds of self-defense. But Worley was called to trial, and probably if complicit of anything was guilty of running his ship with such brutal

George W. Worley (*National Archives*)

force. He had hired Witchardt (supposedly his brother-in-law) because he wanted a mate who ran things "deep water style." What Witchardt did to his crew was of little interest to Worley so long as his ship made its ports and functioned properly.

The rumor going about was that Dixon was actually "laying in wait" for Worley and Witchardt got in the way by mistake. From the scuttlebutt, Worley certainly didn't have very clean hands over the Dixon affair. Supposedly, his Second Mate on the *Abarenda*, Peter Gadeburg, also tried to blackmail him over the whole affair. He said he would testify in Worley's behalf if he was promoted to Witchardt's post. Worley refused, and Gadeburg apparently turned State's evidence, and this is what brought Worley to trial for complicity.

In spite of being cleared, Worley nevertheless took it as a personal insult that he was even brought to trial. He was not a man who liked authority. This is certain. He alone ran his ship *his* way.

Whatever the reason, Worley left the Service. One can assume he didn't feel safe in the Navy Auxiliary. When he came back perhaps he realized it was far safer here than in the Merchant Marine, where a captain doesn't have the immunity of a Naval Reservists uniform.

All this was water under the bridge as the *Cyclops* left Hampton Roads for Rio in January 1918. But it was a bridge under which there was still a current. Asper was still ship's surgeon, and many who had signed the petition were still aboard and hated their captain. Nervig's article, from a man completely unaware of this sordid history, takes on new life now. He writes how Worley mistreated Forbes and Cain, both regular Navy men, and this is something we can now understand. He writes how Asper protected Cain just to spite Worley, and this too we can understand. Asper and Worley were deadly nemeses. Nervig writes how glum the officers always were and how little they spoke in the wardroom. We can understand this if they believed that Nervig was the captain's pet. There is certainly much Nervig wasn't told, but in light of the Navy's secret investigation we know he captured enough of the expected nuances to give us a clear picture that Worley's brutal ways had not subsided, even after a scandalous Board of Inquiry.

This is reconfirmed during the vessel's first voyage after the Board of Inquiry. The *Cyclops* had that short trip to Halifax. W.J. Jeffers, a seaman aboard from August 20, 1917, to January 2, 1918, also wrote the Navy to inform. "While we were in the fleet at Port Jefferson, the Captain and Doctor were drunk most of the time. He would not give us liberty that went on aboard at Norfolk, but the men who served in the Auxiliary with him were granted liberty at any time."

The effect of the whitewash Worley received from Abraham and Whitted is keenly testified to here, for Jeffers came aboard only a couple of weeks after the Board of Inquiry and yet testifies to the exact same abuses the petitioners had brought against their drunken Captain during the earlier voyage to France.

However, Jeffers continues with more disturbing information, and the Navy considered him quite reliable.

He [Worley] was always bringing outside men aboard while we were under way to Halifax, Nova Scotia, Canada. The Captain tried to anchor at sea, but he could not get water to anchor in, so he went round and around for a long while, and then got under way again. I was standing gun watch on the quarterdeck next to his room. He gave the order, dark ship. He would not stand on the bridge but in his room and his lights were burning. I walked in and said "Sir, your lights can be seen" but he paid no attention to me, and later I told him again. He told me to get out and shut my mouth, and in a few minutes he flashed his lights three times, and then he told me to go turn in my bunk, but I would not do it. When we docked in Halifax he put me a prisoner at large and then gave me five days bread and water, when we got under way to the fleet he put me in the brig but gave me my meals from the fleet to Norfolk, Virginia.

Should this act be regarded as a crude and impoverished attempt on Worley's part to contact German agents? Or was his notorious sense of humor at work baiting Jeffers so he could have fun and throw him in the brig?

It is a difficult question to answer. But from what the Navy was learning from independent sources, there may have been no humor behind Worley's actions. One source was an old business friend, Frank Staude, in San Francisco. He showed them a disturbing letter. In 1913/14, before the US entry into the war, Worley had finally visited the land of his nativity. He wrote how he became quite impressed with Germany, its industry and efficiency. About this same time, after he came back to America, he continued to brag about his homeland and that it would win the war. Pro-Germans were throughout the US Navy. Before the war there was nothing wrong with it. But from another source, Paul Roberts, the Navy learned that around this time Worley started embarrassing or abusing crewmen on his ship who were anti-German. He used to laugh loudly and rejoice at wireless news of German victories and was very abusive to his men during these moments. He also had the habit of "putting an ignorant Greek" seaman at the wheel and locking all others off the bridge. There he commanded his vessel *his* way.

Everything *his* way.

The old seadog's tail feathers had certainly been ruffled over being called before a B of I, but despite this he did remain in the Navy unlike in 1908. Yet he said this would be his last voyage. He sold his home and car and had his wife and baby girl in a rental until he returned. Not long before sailing his wife feared their daughter, Ginny, was sick with scarlet fever, but Worley would not call a doctor. He was afraid he would be quarantined and not be able to make the voyage. For some reason Worley had to make this voyage. The fever broke and Ginny recovered. Worley knew what fevers were like and was right. It was only a fever, but his refusal to call a doctor revealed how, for whatever reason, he needed to make this next voyage, even to the point he would not get his daughter aid for something as serious like suspected scarlet fever. These chain of events were looked on with great suspicion at the time, and to this day they raise an eyebrow.

Thanks to Nervig we have a brief glance at the voyage south to Rio. But after he is transferred to his new duties aboard the *Glacier* (interestingly, commanded by Peter Gadeburg, Worley's old enemy), everything falls silent until Barbados. (The *Cyclops* had left Rio on February 16. She stopped off briefly at Bahia on the 22nd; Nervig recalls seeing her come in from the north rather than the south, and then she left the next day for Baltimore.) Worley surprised not only Barbados but the Navy Department when the *Cyclops* pulled into Bridgetown on March 3. This was an unscheduled stop. When Worley visited Brockholst Livingston he set into history the last things known of the *Cyclops*. In light of what we have seen, the Navy and indeed we today should be concerned.

On March 4, 1918, after only 18 hours in port, the giant *Cyclops* left. After the vessel failed to make Baltimore on the 13th of March, the Navy and the State Department started the ball rolling. The investigation became immense.

Captain Worley was indeed a complex character. His past was mired by two hearings, rumors of murder, embezzlement, drunkenness and drug-running. Much cannot be proven, but there is much circumstantial evidence to support the claims.

After the disappearance there was one thing and one thing only that vied with the theory that the *Cyclops* was betrayed to the Germans by "Fred Worley." This was the idea that German spies or saboteurs had planted a time-bomb aboard the vessel and succeeded in destroying her at sea. Had it not been for this, the public verdict would have long been in and firmly fixed on the seadog.

As flimsy as such a theory may at first sound, it was not the product of mere idle public whim or press sensationalism. On

May 6 the news hit. The New York *Sun* broke the story with the arrival of the *Vestris* into New York harbor. The article stated in part: "Passengers from Rio called attention to a story that stirred Americans and anti-Germans in the city two weeks after the *Cyclops* had been reported missing. An advertisement appeared in one of the Rio dailies printed in Portuguese, saying that at a certain date a Mass would be said at a leading Catholic church for Alfred L. M. Gottschalk, American Consul-General at Rio, who was a passenger on the Cyclops and who was referred to as a 'distinguished north American Consul.' The advertisement bore the names, as signatures, of one of the principle members of the American consulate at Rio and other friends of Mr. Gottschalk. Investigation the next day revealed that none of the men whose names were affixed to the advertisement knew anything about it, and the pastor of the church declared that no one had arranged for a Mass for Mr. Gottschalk."

There is one major problem, and the press and the Navy picked up on it right away— the notice was declared to have appeared in the Rio newspaper about 3 weeks *before* the *Cyclops* was even posted overdue on April 15. At this time nobody but the upper echelons in the Navy knew the vessel was late.

The New York *Times* elaborated the next day: "Mysterious Advertisement In A South American Newspaper Hints Cyclops Was Sunk." The article called attention to a parallel, reminding readers that the German ambassador in New York placed advertisements in newspapers warning American passengers not to embark on the *Lusitania* before she left on her final voyage from New York and was torpedoed off Ireland. "While the advertisement at Rio was not in the nature of a warning it may have been another recourse by German agents to the advertising columns to transmit a report of their operations. It was the first time that an intimation had been given that the Cyclops had been sunk."

The passengers of the *Vestris* suggested that it was placed in the papers as a way of alerting the large German colony in Brazil that "the German government was still active and to spread and keep alive the German propaganda in Brazil, whose participation in the war so far has been passive." Fear that the country might also enter the war as an ally against Germany could also have stirred up the German agents in Brazil, emboldening them to try this sabotage coup. Proclaiming their inside knowledge of the *Cyclops*' sinking with a fake ad for a requiem mass "for the repose of the soul of Consul Gottschalk who was lost at sea when the Cyclops was sunk" was really the only way spies could have surreptitiously signaled their success to the greater German spy community.

The *Times* confirmed that the requiem mass ad was in the paper two weeks after the *Cyclops* left Barbados. This would place its publication around March 16-18, a few days after the *Cyclops* should have been overdue at Baltimore. This in itself should have suggested that there was a close watch on ships entering and leaving American ports. When the *Cyclops* did not arrive, agents waiting at Baltimore could have sent a message to agents in Brazil. "Success."

This coincidence of timing is rather disturbing, and it argues for the greater theory of sabotage to be taken seriously. But finding the answer as to how the bomb got aboard is a daunting task. When it was determined that no one had boarded the vessel at Barbados— thus there could be no German spies aboard— there was really no other option but that somehow a time-bomb was slipped aboard at Rio. Considering the gap of weeks between the vessel leaving Rio and departing Barbados, it seemed inconceivable that a bomb could have been time-set at Rio to blow up weeks later. Therefore it was assumed the bomb would have to be set off by someone on board the vessel. In that case, unless the culprit secured a way to safely flee the vessel he would blow up with the others. The only other option was a rare chance that spies could have smuggled a time-bomb aboard during the loading at Barbados. But one must also consider into this theory that Barbados was an unscheduled stop. The spies would have had to act on the spur of the moment. Rather fleet of foot, to say the least. . .unless Worley was privy to it and put into Barbados for that very purpose.

By this time ONI was already suspicious of Alfred L.M. Gottschalk. As soon as the *Cyclops* had been publicly declared missing, the Navy had started an investigation of his past. In a coded message sent to Rio on April 16, 1918, the investigation had been ordered with a brief: "Cable your confidential opinion as to the loyalty of Consul Gottschalk."

It was an unpleasant surprise for the Navy to receive in reply on April 18 from their agent Hil in Rio de Janeiro the following: "Before entry into war, he was very pro-German. He endeavored to transmit German Red Cross Funds, of which he was the custodian, to Germany, through the National City Bank of New York. I cannot give any instance of his lack of loyalty to the United States. His chief fault lay in his being a newspaper man and secondarily Consul General. This, together with a disagreeable personality, caused Americans and other foreigners to dislike him intensely."[11]

Another ONI operative (not mentioned by name in the report) made a supplemental report on May 13 after the requiem news articles had been published. The operative speaks from personal knowledge. "Mr. Gottschaulk [sic] whom the Operative knows personally was not very popular with the members of the American Colony in Rio de Janerio. No one knew of his departure until a letter was received from him by members of the American Colony in Rio de Janerio having been mailed in Bahia." The operative reports the results of his interview with another member of the S.S. *Vestris*, Mr. W. Van Dyke, who was a representative of the General Electric Company. Van Dyke

---

[11] This reference to a newspaper man must imply a man who catered to the publicity but in substance did not do his job well. Gottschalk had been a reporter some 20 years before. According to Rio papers he had been a journalist e.g. *A Lanterna* April 15, 1918.

states something quite intriguing, and his source was qualified to know. "He further mentioned that officially Consul General Gottschaulk [sp] was supposed to have boarded the Cyclops at Bahia, yet he had been informed by a United States Naval attaché, C. Jungling stationed in Rio de Janerio, that Gottschaulk [sic] had actually boarded the vessel in Rio de Janerio." (Nervig had mentioned that one of the officers aboard, Carroll Page, had gone ashore at Bahia before coming to see him on the *Glacier*. It is possible he mailed the letter.)

Why the secrecy? Gottschalk's pro-German views were well known in Rio. Furthermore, "Mr. Van Dyke in speaking of the latter remarked that rumors had also been current in Rio de Janerio to the effect that Gottschaulk [sic] was Pro-German. Mr. Van Dyke admits that previous to our entrance into the War, Mr. Gottschaulk was an admirer of German methods and efficiency, but further than that he did not given any credence to such rumors."

Nevertheless, Van Dyke added to the theory of betrayal. He stated that he had been en route to Buenos Aires when the *Cyclops* was at Rio. When he returned the *Cyclops* had already headed north. "Sometime thereafter reports were current in Rio de Janerio that the Cyclops had disappeared." Among the many rumors it was said that the ship had sailed to Germany. Van Dyke never mentions any knowledge of the requiem mass ad. His account stands independent of that, and as such it confirms that rumors of the *Cyclops* disappearing were in circulation in South America long before she was being publicly reported overdue.

What was the motive for Gottschalk's secretive departure? Some had heard the excuse that Gottschalk had said he was returning in order to enter the US Army as an officer to do his part in the war. But if so there is no need for such a clandestine and deceptive departure as he took. This was completely at odds with his personality and penchant for publicity.

Prior to entering the Diplomatic Corp., Gottschalk had been a war correspondent for the New York *Herald*. During the Spanish-American War in 1896 he was attached to General Brook's division conducting the Puerto Rican campaign. The New York *Herald* had a flattering spread on him in their April 15 edition, stating that in 1899 he left the paper for commerce. "Seeing the opportunities in Latin American commerce," he became a sugar planter in Haiti and Santo Domingo "but was discouraged by successive revolutions." Going out of business he became the Collector of Customs at Monte Cristo, Santo Domingo. Then in 1902 at the age of 29 he entered the consular service.

A. L. M. GOTTSCHALK,
U. S. consul general at Rio Janeiro,
Brazil.
(Harris & Ewing photo.)

For all Gottschalk's brief stint as a reporter, the moniker of "newspaper man" still clung to him. Though he hadn't worked on a paper for almost 20 years, he had apparently kept the attitude of a publicist; the implication of his detractors was that this was more often for himself than for his country's service. Taking into account the ONI operative's secret report stating how disliked Gottschalk really was, the *Herald's* view of Gottschalk appears all the more like a tailored publicity release, reflecting an image Gottschalk alone preferred to paint of himself. "Since going to Brazil Mr. Gottschalk had been credited with having had much to do with swaying the feeling of the people against Germany. He was a popular speaker there and possessed great influence."

If Gottschalk is to be regarded as a clever spinmeister and a camp follower of cheap newspaper spotlight, a military enlistment might be a logical step on his part. Politically it would put him in a better light, certainly in his hometown of New York where he was well known. He might indeed have been feathering his nest for a political platform in post war elections. Would this not seem smart?

However cunningly he may have been able to manipulate the press and public opinion, the military establishment had seemed wary of him. He had tried to get enlisted before at the outbreak of the war, but apparently nobody in the military helped him. There is thus little evidence that Gottschalk was returning to the United States to enter the army as the rumors said. He had already tried 10 months before when war was declared and received no response. It is even less likely now while only returning to Washington on a short leave of absence.

There was no question Moreau Gottschalk was very pro-German and *very* disliked. General sentiments from staff in Rio de Janeiro were one thing, but a startling letter was received at the Secretary of State (May 13, 1918), from a member of the US Diplomatic Corp., making specific allegations against Gottschalk and his claim to be enlisting in the Army.

The letter was from Mr. J.E. Conner. It contains a scathing opinion of Gottschalk based on his behavior at other consular posts. The letter went silently through channels. The Secret Service (Captain Burke) delivered it in person to the ONI New York office. From there it was forwarded to Washington. Leland Harrison soon forwarded to Captain McCauley, in charge of Office of Naval Intelligence.

If it is desired to solve the mystery of the Collier "Cyclops," I would suggest that you begin upon the theory of the complicity of the Consul General at Rio de Janeiro, A.L. Gottschalk.

If there was any foul play anywhere in the shipping of the seamen it must have been from the last port of call, Rio de Janeiro, and with the cognizance of the Consular Officer there. Reports to that effect have appeared in the New York papers namely that there was foul play, hence mutiny and the loss of the vessel, though I have as yet seen no intimation as to the complicity of the aforementioned

Gottschalk. Quite to the contrary, indeed, was an announcement of the loss of the vessel, to the effect that the said Gottschalk was returning to offer his services in the war. In other words his press agent was on the job. My theory as to the loss of the Cyclops is that through the connivance of the same Gottschalk, the vessel was handed over to the Germans, who either destroyed her after making themselves secure, or possibly interned her in some out of the way port of the world, and that in any case the same Gottschalk will later turn up as the central figure in a romance of his own construction, claiming to have been under duress all the time.

These things I know about the self same Gottschalk: that he was too much of a coward to fight on any account. Second, that before the war he was an ardent pro-German and I have no doubt that he continued to be so while in Brazil. I have myself heard him speak most disparagingly of our country while praising Germany inordinately, and that too as an official at the time of the U.S.A. The former Consul General at Vienna (Mr. Denby) might have something interesting to contribute as to his conduct in that city, where he spent something like three months, doing nothing apparently, while he was supposed to be around inspecting consulates.

I am ready to take my oath in court that, in my opinion, the same A.L. Gottschalk is (or was, if now dead) a man of no integrity of character, a man given to misrepresentation and lying according as it suited his purpose. I had abundant proofs of his lying in my possession at one time, and with the assistance of the Department of State can prove the case; I am ready to go further into this if you send a representative to see me.

J.E. Conner

The Navy didn't waste time following up on this. In the subsequent interview at ONI's New York office, Conner explained that he had served 7 years in the Diplomatic service. "He was in St. Petersburg when Gottschalk was in Vienna and later St. Petersburg." Conner's attitude hadn't changed from his instigating letter. "He further stated that he believed Gottschalk to be unscrupulous and a man who used every effort to further his own interest, rather than those of the government he represented." Conner also noted that Gottschalk spent all his vacations in Berlin and preferred to associate with Germans. There were also other statements that Gottschalk made that led him to believe he was completely pro-German. "Mr. Conner gave the impression of being absolutely honest and the information as given was not due to any personal spite, although he fervently stated that he thoroughly disliked the man." Conner also gave the name of "Mr. Harris," the former Consul General at Stockholm who could speak of Gottschalk along the same lines.

How much did the Navy believe Conner and if believing how much did they think it was relevant anymore? There is no record whatsoever in all the papers amassed at the National Archives or in the State Department documenting an attempt to contact Denby or Harris. The above report, dated May 31, 1918, was only 14 days before the Navy would officially do something remarkable. They would declare all aboard the *Cyclops* to be dead, "lost at sea."

There is nothing to indicate what made the Navy take this action. But it was probably safe to say that part of the reason was for insurance, both for the families and the Navy. The cargo was valued and insured for $500,000 dollars.

But none of this tells us what happened to the *Cyclops*. And, indeed, the Navy didn't particularly believe the declaration either. As soon as the Armistice was being prepared the Navy had sent Admiral Robison to Germany to determine what happened to the ship and to check if any of the crew was indeed there in a POW camp. Yet no trace was ever found. The Germans knew nothing. The ship hadn't been torpedoed, mined, captured, sunk, sabotaged or interned.

Further investigation of that enigmatic requiem mass doesn't turn up spies and plots either. Despite its rather obvious importance, it could never be traced, that is, there is no solid evidence the ad *ever appeared.*[12] Had the Navy ever found solid evidence for it, they never would have pursued so many different angles and theories. Hil at Rio never mentions it (there is no record anyway). There are numerous clippings from Rio newspapers in the State Department papers dated April 15 or later. All cover Gottschalk's life, his South American career, and praise him warmly. He definitely was popular with the journalists. But in none of them, though my Portuguese hangs on my rusty Latin, can I find a mention of the mysterious requiem mass.

This rumor appears to stem solely from passengers aboard the *Vestris,* and from there it cannot be traced except as Brazilian scuttlebutt. What paper? No name is ever given. Those aboard the liner had merely heard of such an advertisement. It would seem that such a thing would and could be quickly backtracked; just have the embassy send a clipping. . .but there is no official word from Richard O. Momsen, Gottschalk's majordomo, either.

Even more peculiar is Momsen's own long letter to the State Department giving details of how the *Cyclops* was loaded. This letter, dated April 27, makes no mention of the advertisement. If he had not yet known about it surely Washington would have informed him in early May when on the 6th the *Vestris* arrived New York and all the newspapers carried the story. But there is no subsequent dispatch from him detailing an investigation to discover the truth of it. The papers also said that the chief diplomat at the embassy had signed the advertisement for the requiem mass. That would be the ambassador or perhaps even Momsen himself. Surely had he heard of such a claim he would have sent a dispatch refuting it or confirming it. Yet there are none. Until April 15, the embassy staff apparently didn't even know the *Cyclops* was overdue.

---

[12] I never found any record of it, and I don't think the Navy did either.

With the end of the war there came the end of all the "exciting" theories— mutiny, treason, betrayal, capture. Ultimately all this translated down to one thing: the *Cyclops* must have merely foundered in a gale or storm. There was a blow that swept the Carolinas on the 10th of March. Or perhaps she suffered the much suspected shift of her weighty cargo. At any rate, this is what was now proposed in the public forum.

Behind the scenes, however, the Navy didn't buy it. No matter how much it once promoted the storm (during the war), it later refused to accept it. The Navy had known the gale could have nothing to do with it. Given the known speed of the *Cyclops* (less than 300 miles per day), she could only have been around the Tropic of Cancer on the 9th of March and off Florida on the 10th, far south of the storm off the Carolinas.

Notwithstanding this the Navy investigated the publicized rumor that the small freighter s.s. *Amalco* had sighted the vessel battling the heavy seas off the Carolinas. According to the Navy informant, a Mr. Freeman of Boston, "log of ss Amalco shows that on night of March ninth USS Cyclops was about five miles distant. March tenth heavy gale damaged the Amalco."

The Navy immediately tracked down her captain, Charles Hillyer. An agent of ONI interviewed him and confirmed that while 80 miles south of Nantucket Light Ship on the 9th or 10th of March Hillyer encountered what he called the worst gale ever. "The heavy seas which washed over the ship strained the hull and machinery badly, stove in the lifeboats, wrecked the bridge, carried away the topmost light, and all but sent the Amalco to the bottom." Unfortunately, Hillyer also immediately denied that the *Cyclops* "was seen by himself or by the men aboard the *Amalco*. He assured me that no such entry had been made in the log. He stated that each night he read over the day's log, and if correct he signed it. If it contained a mistake he had it corrected before signing."

Thus ended the only alleged clue to link the *Cyclops* with a

The *Cyclops* at anchor. US Navy photo.

storm. With a refreshing deferral to the facts, the Navy declared the *Cyclops* was a true mystery, the "greatest in its annals."

The theory that the *Cyclops'* heavy cargo of manganese somehow shifted and sent the vessel to the briny had little practical merit as well. Richard Momsen's letter explaining how the *Cyclops* was loaded set in place many specifics, from the number of buckets of manganese loaded in each hold to the number of stevedores working on loading the ship; and even more important to the discussion at hand Momsen set down a description of what the *Cyclops'* holds actually looked like and how she was loaded.

Momsen's information was based on his personal interviews with E. G. Fontes, "who handles most of the manganese ore" for Morro de Mina Manganese Company, the contractors for the ore. Fontes reminded Momsen that The Brazilian Coaling Company (Cory Brothers) were in charge of loading the vessel and that they have been loading manganese since 1901, "practically from the beginning of the export business in Brazil." Momsen clarified for his superiors that it appears the "only ship loaded by them that was lost was the 'Cambire' [Ed. *Gambier*], a British sailing vessel which was sunk— some years ago— immediately outside of the harbor of Rio. . ." and, which Momsen clarified quickly, "without any crew having been lost in the disaster."

Gambier was a far cry from the huge *Cyclops*, and not just in hull design and size. Mr. Fontes praised the great vessel as a "self trimmer," meaning a ship equipped with special dunnage (stowing, insulating or other material to adjust and trim her holds and secure cargo). This "special dunnage," as it is called, consisted of a section of horizontal wooden platform "to prevent the ore from coming into contact with the ship's plates." On the port and starboard sides of the holds "there were two diagonal, sloping board platforms to prevent a like pressure on the ship's plates." Momsen added: "This is considered to be ample dunnage." The diagonal wood platforms would also prevent a dangerous shift of cargo if the *Cyclops* should roll at sea, and this would aid in preventing the ship from capsizing. Also, it would tend to separate the manganese from any coal dust remaining at the bottom of the hold, as that would have settled on the plates underneath the wood dunnage.

The only problem that Fontes could see was that there were no between-decks holds, so that the "ore was necessarily all laden in the bottom of the hold." Since all the weight was on the bottom of the vessel, could it have broken in twain? This, too, is a popular theory, but it is effectually nullified by Momsen's report.

When the *Cyclops* sailed, she "drew 33 feet of water aft and 29 feet at her bow." Fontes was certain that the *Cyclops* could easily have "drawn 35 feet of water without being overloaded." Worley personally supervised the loading. The night before sailing, noticing she was heavy in the stern, he ordered more cargo in the bow to "equalize her buoyancy." Fontes stated that the ship carried 10,800 tons of manganese and could have carried at least 2,000 more. This would seem to be correct, as he recalled Worley saying the *Cyclops* could handle 12,000 tons. However, Worley did not want to sign for more than 10,000 tons (no doubt due to its weight and contract specifications). The difference of 800 tons would be determined upon arrival in the United States in the usual manner.

Both the supervisor of loading vessels, Manual Pereira, and Captain William Lowry, the agent for the United States Shipping Board, verified Fontes' statements. Worley, it seems, was well aware of the heavier weight of his cargo, and would not load the *Cyclops*' holds to capacity. We can almost hear the voices of all those who gave evidence against Worley's personality: that he was a drunk, poor navigator, brutal and strict. . . but that he was "a good sailorman." The seadog truly knew ships and cargo . . .and especially he knew the *Cyclops*.

There was also little chance the wood dunnage was crushed. When the loading began the buckets (which contained 900 kilos each of manganese) were lowered all the way to the dunnage and then dumped. When the hold began to fill, they were dumped 25 feet over the rising manganese pile.

Amongst the many theories trying to explain the *Cyclops*' disappearance there are 2 theories of particular importance. Both come from Naval officers who served aboard the vessel at one point. The first was from Lieutenant Commander Mahlon S. Tisdale in an article published by no less than the *Naval Institute Proceedings* for January 1920, in which he made what appeared to be an ironclad case for the *Cyclops* "turning turtle"— in other words, capsizing.

This article *Did the Cyclops Turn Turtle?* has proven to be an influential source for a number of reasons. One is that it influenced Josephus Daniels, the then-Secretary of the Navy, to support this notion; two, when the Bermuda Triangle enigma gained such popularity in the 1970s, Triangle fever inspired an entire genre of books and documentaries which resurrected the old article and used it as one of the logical theories to account for the ship's disappearance (other than that of the Bermuda Triangle mythos, of course). The entire article was even reprinted in the 1977 paperback *Riddle of the Bermuda Triangle*, edited by Martin Ebon, a compendium of theories, articles and interviews on the Bermuda Triangle phenomenon. Ebon accentuated the article's authority by noting it appeared first in 1920 "and therefore has an immediacy and closeness to the subject that cannot be equaled by narratives written at a later date." Therefore Tisdale's article is much still with us, strengthened by the fact that it appeared in the prestigious journal of the US Navy.

Regrettably, what anthologists into the Bermuda Triangle didn't know was that in the April 1920 issue of the same *Naval Institute Proceedings* Tisdale's theory was exploded and laid to rest, in such a way, one must add, that it reflected badly on Tisdale. Commander I.I. Yates was the author. He took exception to something that Tisdale recalled Worley saying. It was actually the cornerstone upon which Tisdale's arguments were built.

Tisdale had recalled that while on his 10 day stay on the vessel he noted the topside tank hatches had been left unsecured. He was shocked when groping forward during heavy weather to find that each one could potentially fill with water as the great vessel shipped seas over her deck. He secured each one as best he could and then reported on the bridge. The seadog wasn't concerned at all. "He laughed at my earnestness and said that they were *always left off* in accordance with instructions from the navy yard (I won't mention the yard, as I never saw the circular during my time in the colliers), as the air was 'better for the bitumastic.'[13] The skipper was worrying not at all about the tanks. We were cavorting around the old ocean like a frisky colt, but, true enough, were taking no green seas over the main deck. As I have said, we were light and high out of the water. The Captain wasn't worrying about his cargo."

Tisdale's theory for her final voyage depended on the topside tanks also being unsecured. He speculated that if the *Cyclops* rolled to one side, sending her heavy cargo shifting, the topside tanks, with their hatches unsecured, would have filled with water and increased her roll until she quickly capsized. This would have plunged the vessel keel over, capsizing her before any could get out.

It seemed plausible until Yates' article refuted it a few months later. Every Navy man knew that the *Cyclops* was berthed at Norfolk. Therefore Yates wrote his article, feeling compelled to defend the Norfolk Navy Yard. No such instruction had ever been issued, he declared, and after exonerating the Yard he included interviews with the captains of the *Neptune* and *Jupiter*, sister colliers to the *Cyclops*. Both Naval officers made it plain that in a light condition, as the *Cyclops* was when Tisdale was aboard for a short stay, the topside tanks were probably filled with water anyway in order to maintain ballast. So it was immaterial whether the hatch covers were secured. Also, it seemed certain that Tisdale didn't understand Worley's notorious sense of humor. "Captain Worley was always making jokes," W.J. Kelton, Captain of the *Neptune*, recalled, "and was author of the celebrated 'Tame Lion' story of 1910-11 which was given such publicity that the Department wrote him to put ashore any lion he had on board. It is probable that Captain Worley answered Lieutenant Commander Tisdale in jest on being taken to task for leaving his covers off."

---

[13] Meaning it was better to let the asphalt coating of the tanks breathe.

Tisdale looked bad, hasty and ill-informed. The idea about the *Cyclops* "turning turtle" was essentially laid to rest.

The other popular theory actually comes from Conrad A. Nervig in his article *The Cyclops Mystery*, published in the same journal in 1969. His theory was that the vessel broke in twain. This was based on his remembrance that he saw the deck undulating, that is, conforming to the swells and the synchronicity of the waves. These were signs of "bad contractions," meaning the ship's back could break easily at any time. Although he brought it to Worley's attention, he recalled only his captain's superior dismissal: "Son, she'll last as long as we do." In the end, Nervig declared this was indeed true.

It is interesting, and a bit disconcerting, that Nervig never approached the Navy with this information before. Out of all the letters in the Navy's files written by former crewmen the absence of any letter from Nervig is what is the most surprising. This is not a small point at all. The Navy investigated every lead, but in all the paperwork amassed there is no interview with Nervig, or any letter on his behalf desiring to give such an interview to the Navy. No other seaman ever reported this "undulating" problem developing, and there were many who wrote in.

It is more likely that Nervig never wrote to the Navy because he hadn't anything significant to say. In later life his memory may have been contaminated by other experiences in his career at sea, and he applied these to his last voyage on the *Cyclops*. I say this for several reasons. Nervig's presence is most significant in the documentation by his absence, and this extends to a gem of a find— the officers' list for the voyage *south*. Nervig's memory was that he was an officer aboard with assigned duties. But this was not the case. The Military Personnel Archives in St. Louis confirmed he had only been a passenger. He had been assigned to the *Glacier* and was in transit. It may be that when Cain was committed by Asper that Nervig was asked to take over duties. This is natural to expect and easy to accept. But nevertheless that is not Nervig's memory. He even claimed that Worley tried to prevent his transfer at Rio, when all the time Nervig was already assigned to the *Glacier.*

In examining Nervig's ship assignments before being transferred for passage on the *Cyclops,* I discovered that he was on other colliers; a much older one was the *Orion.* It is possible therefore that what he recollects of "bad contractions" 51 years after-the-fact applies to other, older ships on which he served.

Speaking about the *Cyclops'* launching in 1910, Captain Kelton of the *Neptune,* who was one of her first officers under Worley, was even quoted in Yates' 1920 article as follows: "The *Cyclops* had just been delivered from Cramps and was unusually well built, in fact Cramps lost money in building her, and no caulking of seams or butts was found necessary after her first cruise to Europe to coal the squadron at Kiel. The *Cyclops* was the most seaworthy of her sister ships, but she rolled to wide angles."

Nervig's memory is clearly confused. Moreover, in those 51 years since his strange voyage with the mad seadog he had become one of Hollywood's top editors, editing such films as *A Tale of Two Cities, Northwest Passage, King Solomon's Mines* and *The Bad and the Beautiful.* He is the first recipient of an Oscar for editing (in 1934) and shared an Oscar for editing *King Solomon's Mines.* A bit of that dramatic world could have influenced his story of the *Cyclops'* last voyage. He died in 1980 at the age of 91 after a long and accomplished life.

We may never be able to solve the riddle of the *Cyclops,* but a clue to her final resting place may give us some fresh insights. Two years after the vessel vanished, a retired sea captain walked into the Navy Recruiting Center at Kansas City on March 18, 1920, while on his way back to Chicago. His name was Captain Donald J. Fraser. He had been pleasure sailing the Bahamas in February. South of Bimini, at the group of crags called the Riding Rocks, he came across telltale wreckage. He told his story and the Navy was electrified. Commander John K. Richards wrote to the Chief of Naval Operations, Admiral Coontz.

"Mr. Fraser, while cruising off the banks of the Bahamas in February, 1920, was caught in a small hurricane and forced to take shelter behind the nearest land. This land happened to be Gun Key. While exploring the Key and vicinity he went to what is known as the first Riding Rock, a small Key of about 15 acres situated about 8 or 9 miles southwest of Gun Key in the following approximate position: Latitude, 25° 34' 30" N., 79° 15' W. While exploring the beach of this first Riding Rock he came across a quarter of a clinker type boat whose dimensions were approximately those of a Naval lifeboat. Printed on the bow of this piece of wreckage where the letters U S, then a blank, then Cyclo. Mr. Fraser also stated that there was signs of other letters or letter following the O. The above leads me to believe that the final translation could have readily been USS Cyclops."

In addition to this, Fraser found a notebook the "size that is normally used by Naval Navigators in keeping their rough notes." Although there was a lot of writing on it, the "action of the sea had made all of it illegible." Fraser, however, thought it might be important, so he hid it under a hundred pound rock 25 yards up the beach. Amongst the lifeboat there was more debris. A large "copper circle had been smashed until it was absolutely flat, but was of about the size of the normal Naval Franklin Life Buoy." There was a lot of wood about and other flotsam, but since Fraser wasn't acquainted with all the equipment a Navy ship carried he couldn't be sure any of it was proof of the *Cyclops*. He also saw to the west a long dark shadow under the sea, about 2000 yards from Gun Key, that might be the outline of a sunken ship. Richards was sure that if Naval Operations wanted to pursue this, Fraser would be "only too pleased to definitely mark a navigational chart of this area in order that the exact situation of the Cyclops described above could be located." All Naval Operations would need to do would be to send a chart to him at his address in Chicago.

Richards concludes: "From my conversation with Mr. Fraser this morning his attitude and his familiarity with nautical terms, phraseology and other things pertaining to the sea would indicate that the statements given above were based on facts and not conjectures."

There seemed no reason for the US Navy not to take this seriously. And indeed they did. Admiral R.E. Coontz himself sent a letter to Fraser in Chicago. On April 1 the Admiral received a tardy reply in which Fraser asked pardon for his delay. He had been out of town and now he elaborated to Coontz. Unfortunately, Fraser wasn't too clear. In trying to place the area of the First Riding Rock from Gun Key he made it sound as if the remains of the whaleboat were on Cat Cay. He said the remains were "in a direct line southeast from Gun Cay lighthouse to the nearest point of North Cat Cay, visible at low tide. This is a matter which is rather hard to explain on paper. I intend to get in touch with the Admiral commanding Great Lakes Naval Training Station tomorrow, and perhaps between the two of us we will be able to figure it out."

Without waiting for Fraser's details, on April 17, 1920, the Navy decided to act. "You are hereby directed to dispatch some suitable and available vessel of those under your command to Gun Key, Great Bahama Bank," read the order from Coontz to the Commandant of the 7th Naval District. "There is a strong possibility that the U.S.S. Cyclops would have passed within a short distance of Gun Key in the course of her voyage," continued the order. "The information is of such a definite nature that it seems most important that efforts be made to determine whether or not there is sufficient wreckage there to determine what vessel was wrecked if not the U.S.S. Cyclops."

Admiral Benton C. Decker, the Commandant, decided to go and investigate. While he was combing Gun Key, a letter came in from U.S. Naval Training Station, Great Lakes, Illinois, to

Naval Operation in Washington. Coontz read something surprising. Lt. Commander E.J. Foy thought Fraser a man of "considerable intelligence" but thought that he was also quite hazy "when questioned about the articles which he claims to have discovered." It is hard to imagine Fraser behaved this way with them. Initially with the Kansas City officer, John Richards, he was rather explicit about the letters on the whaleboat, which in itself would seem to insure that this was wreckage from the *Cyclops*. Something apparently had changed in him by the time he walked in to chat with The Great Lakes Naval Training Station officers. "The impression left here was that there was little probability that Mr. Fraser had discovered anything of value. Still in view of the importance of the subject, it is believed that even a remote possibility might with advantage be investigated. . . .As this matter has been the subject of correspondence between Mr. Fraser and the Chief of Naval Operations, it is reported now simply to inform the Department of the impressions left here by Mr. Fraser."

One wonders how Coontz took the presumption of the officers at the Great Lakes. He had Richards' detailed letter in his hand, plus Fraser's later letter confirming the cays by name, though not entirely in the clearest manner.

What happened to make Fraser so hazy and bestow such a reaction on the officers? True, there was significant inconsistency already between Richards' letter and Fraser's own later letter to Coontz. (Richards' letter did not say that Fraser found anything on North or South Cat Cay; he said it was at the First Riding Rock about 9 miles to the southwest. In Fraser's own letter to Coontz he said it was on the Cat Cays, which are a part of the Biminis.) But his recollection of the "articles" he found was still "so definite," as Coontz had put it, that this discrepancy should not cause one to use it to overshadow the significance of his discovery.

Yet therein was the problem for the Navy now. The Great

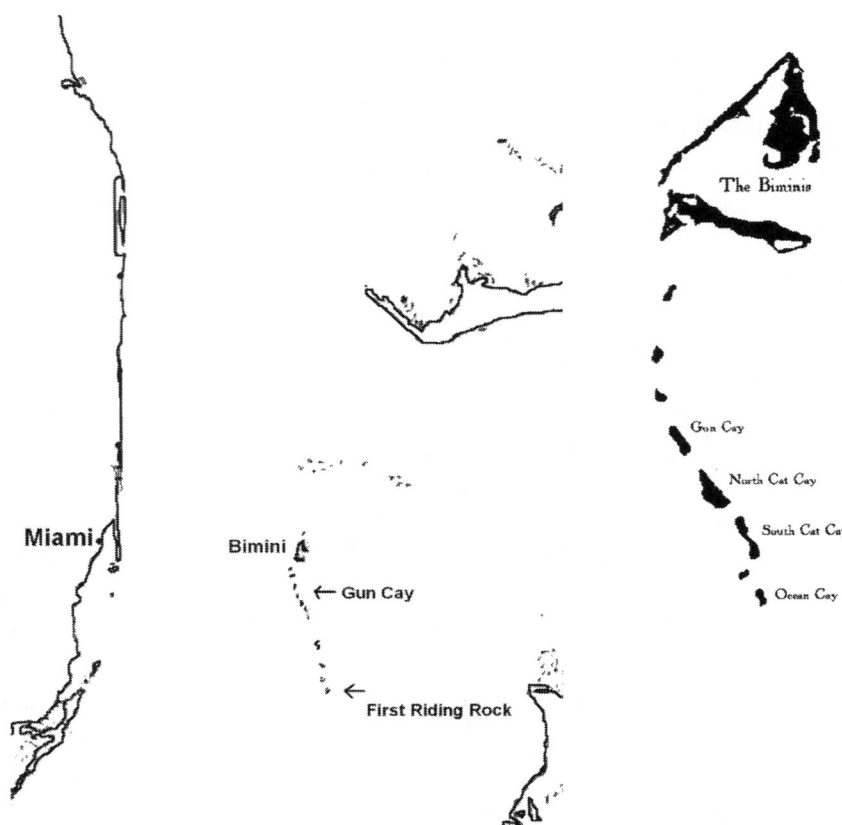

According to Fraser he found the debris at the First Riding Rock, the southernmost islet south of the Bimini Islands. The inset shows where Gun Cay is situated in the Bimini chain.

Lakes officers thought he was now hazy about this. In fact, it seems Fraser was consistently becoming hazier the more contact he had with the Navy.

His apparent contradictions were also added to by a Navy clerk's mistake. When copying Fraser's letter to Coontz to make the infamous Navy triplicates, "west" was changed to "east" for the direction from the cays where Fraser saw the huge shadow under the ocean.

Admiral Decker was now walking up and down the Cat Cay beaches reading copies of both Richards' and Fraser's letters. Comparing them only revealed the inconsistencies. Inasmuch as he had so far not found anything on the cay, he returned to Key West. On April 30, he wrote a long letter to Fraser.

Dear Sir:

There was referred to me a copy of a letter from you to the Chief of Naval Operations dated April 1, 1920, and the letter from Lieut. Comdr. John K. Richards to the same officer, all referring to your experiences in discovering evidences of the wreckage of the U.S.S Cyclops.

I visited Gun Key harbor and walked over the Northern and Southern end of North Cat Key and South Cat Key, for the purpose of discovering the evidence you speak about. I was unable to find any remains of a row boat, tho passing these points about low water. At the Northern end of North Cat Key, I found two or three large stones, possibly two feet in diameter, that showed signs of having been moved, but did not discover any book under them, nor did I see any signs of wreckage of the boat, nor were there any evidences of any wreckage such as you've made in the statement to Lieut. Comdr. Richards. This leads me to make further inquiries from you, with the purpose of securing further information on so important a subject.

(1) During the hurricane, did you anchor in Gun Key harbor?
(2) How did you recognize the harbor?
(3) How did you determine the latitude and longitude given by you in your statement?
(4) How far from your anchorage did you proceed before you sighted this boat, your statement to Lieut. Comdr. Richards, stated that you went to what is known as first Riding Rock, a small Key of about 15 acres, eight or nine miles southwest of Gun Key.

(5) How did you measure the distance; did you proceed in your boat outside or inside; was there any surf?

(6) How did you land and what was the appearance of the small Key from a distance?

(7) What was the characteristics of the beach where you landed: sandy or rocky; smooth or jagged?

It appears that the description given Lieut. Comdr. Richards, and the one contained in your letter, cannot be reconciled; however, if you can, it would be a great favor if you would explain to me the difference.

The last part of your statement of April 1, you speak of a reef or the possible remains of a vessel about 500 yards east from the point North Cat Key. This, of course, is impossible considering the shallow water to the eastward.

I trust you will find it convenient to answer these questions, because it is of great importance that I should clear up this matter, as your statements about the letters on the bow of the whaleboat indicate almost to a certainty that this boat did belong to the *Cyclops*.

Hoping you will be able to answer my questions, in order that I may continue the investigation, I remain

Very sincerely,

Benton C. Decker
Rear Admiral, U.S.N.
Comdt. 7th Naval District.

What must Fraser have made out of Admiral Decker's letter to him? He must now have been more confused by the Navy's mix-up of the direction from the cay to the shadow 2000 yards out *west*. By May 24, he hadn't yet responded to Decker . . .nor would he ever. Nothing is recorded afterward in the Navy's records, but we may safely surmise the Navy gave up the investigation. The upshot was that Decker scoured the wrong islands and had a copy of Fraser's letter with a significant, indeed, critical typo.

It is not surprising that Decker received no reply. Fraser had been cooling for some time. He took a month to reply to Coontz. He was "hazy" when he finally hauled himself in to the Navy at the Great Lakes. He unquestionably must have received Decker's letter, but it is clear he never responded.

Why?

I suspect Fraser's haze and then silence was his defensive reaction to the unexpected interest the Navy showed in his innocent but dutiful report of wreckage. To cut to the chase, should we frankly ask a single pointed question? Namely, was our dear Captain Fraser a rumrunner? In 1919, Prohibition was passed and clandestine rum running into the United States from the Bahamas became a big and profitable business for old mariners. Some even came out of retirement to run the "devil's brew" into the US. A central staging and storage area for the contraband "West Indies Goods" was none other than Gun Key in the Bahamas. A major destination was Chicago. Is it possible that Fraser was an early rumrunner? Seeing it as his duty to report the famous ship's wreckage, did he then become fearful afterward in Chicago that a Navy investigation might spoil the hideout and trade of a growing (and in Chicago, violent) business upon which Fraser depended?

One can second-guess it forever. However, either way one slices it the type of wreckage should have compelled Decker to a thorough search of the surrounding islands. If Fraser was confused, Decker was clearly lax. He should have checked out First Riding Rock where, in Richards' summary, Fraser found everything.

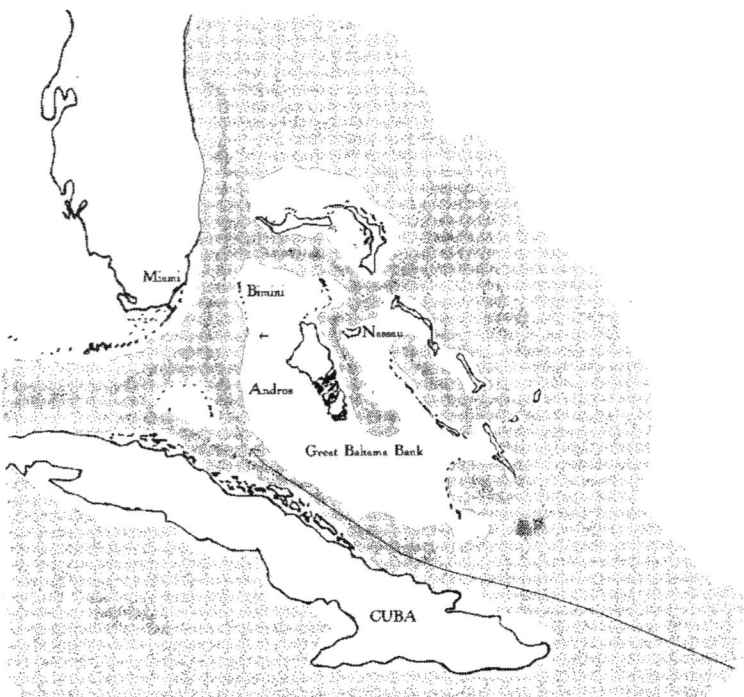

The Cyclops' course through the Old Bahama Channel, the likely place where she was lost.

The Navy investigation of Fraser's tip was anything but an investigation. Yet it is more than safe to assume that Fraser's tip was a sound and good one. Thus we have a clue as to where the *Cyclops* met her fate. It is somewhere in the deep channel off Andros Island, south of the Riding Rocks or possibly further south in the Old Bahama Channel.

Does this location offer any other clues? One thing is incontrovertible. The *Cyclops* was not headed to Germany. She was also far south of any storm. With this understood, we have to accept the *Cyclops* was lost in perfect weather very close to the Bahama islands, Cuba or southern Florida.

This coincidence raises the disturbing questions of mutiny and treason. Where would be the best place to scuttle a ship and still escape? Somewhere right along here would actually be the perfect place. Could mutineers have waited to take the vessel and blow it up here? A small group could get back into the United States relatively easily in the Captain's launch, since it had a motor; or, a sail could be rigged on one of the ship's lifeboats. Passage to the US wouldn't take long. It would require crossing the Florida Straits to the Keys or sailing the Old Bahama Channel to Cuba and from there to any port of call. Mutineers might head home through Florida; traitors might ship from Havana for faraway places and eventually to Germany.

The hardest part of the scenario is to conceive how the complete and assured destruction of the ship could have been carried out so that no other survivors but the mutineers /traitors/saboteurs alone could be guaranteed. Perhaps timed charges set to ignite both coal and manganese? The ship would blow up in a huge and sudden conflagration. The tattered lifeboat could be one of many the vessel carried or it could have been the Captain's own launch. As noted, the latter would have been easiest to launch. A rather poetic sense of justice makes me like to think that if treason occurred the traitors fled the ship in the Captain's boat but were captured in the explosion and the boat destroyed, their lives forfeit by the unseen hand of fate, thus wiping out any survivors to ever tell the tale.

To this day the disappearance of the *Cyclops* admittedly remains the Navy's greatest mystery.

CHAPTER SIX

Tardy Clues:
The *Marine Sulphur Queen*

Any discussion on vanishing ships must always mention the disappearance of the 504-foot T-2 tanker *Marine Sulphur Queen*. Debris was some two weeks tardy in turning up, and its discovery only made this last voyage more mysterious. The *Sulphur Queen* was last heard in routine conversation over her ship-to-shore radio while approaching the south of Florida from Texas, and thereafter disappeared with 39 hands on February 4, 1963. There had been no SOS. For two weeks it was as though the vessel was held in "limbo." Then several articles finally turned up, grouped in the same location. *MSQ*, like so many others in these tropic latitudes, has become an enduring Bermuda Triangle story. But there is much more in the *Queen* which has seldom been brought out. It is fitting that we should take a look at this old case anew and see what it holds for us.

The *Marine Sulphur Queen* was an all-welded vessel of 4,057 net tons and 7,240 gross tons. She was 68.2 feet at the beam, 39.2 in depth, and 504 feet overall. The vessel was originally built in 1944 as a tanker, but was converted in 1960 at the Bethlehem Steel Co. shipyard in Baltimore to carry molten sulphur. This adaptation required considerable remodeling of the vessel's internals, which entailed removing some of the transverse bulkheads in order to install a 306 foot long, 30.6 foot wide, and 33 foot high tank down the center of the ship to carry the molten sulphur. This center tank was then divided into four sulphur-tight compartments. All this was done in adherence to both the American Bureau of Shipping and the U.S. Coast Guard standards.

Because of the extensive work required to redo her insides to accommodate her new cargo, the *Sulphur Queen* underwent other structural renewals. This included replacement of four keel plates 5, 6, 7, and 14; eroded welding in the bottom plates was built up as well as leaking welds in the rudder plates. All of the deck longitudinals in the way of the sulphur tank were renewed as well as all deck longitudinals and web frames in the wing tanks, where it was found necessary. After her insides were finished in 1961, she was certified to haul "Grade E liquids at elevated temperatures," which included sulphur.

The *Marine Sulphur Queen* satisfactorily plied her trade of sulphur for two years in this condition. On January 17, 1963, she was re-certified by the Coast Guard while at Beaumont, Texas, and remained in Class by the American Bureau of Shipping in regard to the condition of her hull and machinery. This inspection was her biennial (two year check), which required the checking and passing of the general alarm system, steering gear, engine telegraph, fire hose, navigation lights, portable fire extinguishers, life preservers, all machinery, all accessible spaces, and also the port boiler; all this was found in satisfactory condition. Where something was found under standards, it was pointed out and repaired: some of the lifeboats were repaired and passed by the inspector; the *Sulphur Queen* also got 11 new life rings. The Beaumont office of the FCC inspected and issued certificates regarding the good conditions of her radio, both on board and in the lifeboats. And after the Bureau of Shipping made the annual examination of the hull, machinery and boilers, the ship was declared seaworthy.

The Master, James Fanning, and key officers, had all served on board the *Sulphur Queen* before, and the crew held all certificates required by the Coast Guard. The harbor pilot that directed her out of the harbor when she departed Sabine Sea Buoy verified the steering gear was in good order.

This is the condition she was in on February 2, 1963, when the pilot was put off, and the complex ship laden with 15,260 long tons of molten sulphur departed Beaumont, Texas, with a crew of 39, en route to that venerable port of Norfolk, Virginia. She cleared the land, slipped over the horizon and was gone.

Subsequent communications with the ship were normal and routine. Fanning gave his ETA at Norfolk as February the 7th. He was also instructed to give a 48 and 24 hour notice before arrival. These never came. The vessel never arrived. Somewhere along her course she silently vanished.

The Coast Guard was finally informed on February 7 that the vessel was overdue. At once they transmitted the information via "hot line" to RCC New York. An hour and twenty minutes later a radio check "All Ships Urgent Broadcast" was initiated 3 times per day until the 16th of February.

The Coast Guard began its search on the 8th, after being informed by RCA radio of the last contact point. The following illustrates the immensity of a Coast Guard search for a vessel.

8 February— Day search— trackline from Beaumont through Florida Straits to Norfolk, a distance of 1,630 miles. Seven aircraft were used in 72 flight hours, searching about 58,000 square miles. This trackline search covered 30 miles on either side of the vessel's estimated track.

8-9 February— Night search— three aircraft flew 23 flight hours and searched 22,000 square miles.

9 February— Day search— since vessel was not found along proposed track, a considerably expanded search plan was used. Nineteen aircraft flew 114 flight hours and searched 95,000 square miles.

9-10 February— Night search— two aircraft flew 12 flight hours and searched 8,300 square miles.

10 February— Day search— nineteen aircraft flew 136 flight hours and searched 76,700 square miles.

11 February— Day search— fourteen aircraft flew 86 flight hours and searched 55,000 square miles.

12 February— Day search—ten aircraft flew 42 flight hours and searched 22,000 square miles.

13 February— Day search— two aircraft flew 16 flight hours and searched 11,000 square miles.

The sum total of the search was 499.6 hours, with an overall 348,400 square miles searched by the Coast Guard, Marine Corps, Navy, and Air Force. Yet nothing was located except the busy shipping traffic proceeding routinely on their course. Each ship was questioned about sightings with the *MSQ* and yet all of them (42 in all) had seen nothing.

Although the lack of finding anything in response to such a huge search seems inexplicable, we must remember that the Coast Guard was not precisely aware of where the vessel had vanished. Thus its entire trackline to Norfolk had been searched, and this contributes much to the impressive number of square miles covered.

Unfortunately, most of this was wasted time and effort. A private message sent from the vessel, and its eventual response, marks a limited area where the vessel must have come to grief. At 1:25 a.m. on February 4, a member of the crew, speculating in wheat futures, transmitted a personal message to his brokerage firm via RCA radio. The response would not come until 11:23 a.m. on the same day. RCA radio tried to contact the vessel and relay the broker's reply, but the two attempts were met without success. It is here, sometime within those ten hours, that the *Marine Sulphur Queen* was overtaken by her fate.

T-2 tanker *Marine Sulphur Queen.*

The places it the *MSQ* in the Gulf of Mexico. Because of the location of the ship's last radio message, and the volatile nature of the Castro regime, the Coast Guard received "tips" that invariably ended with the suggestion to look in a Cuban port. In this case, the FBI investigated such leads, but found no evidence to support them beyond the imagination of crank callers.

An examination of disaster in association with the sea consistently reveals a never-ending stream of paradox. What a huge search failed to find was sighted by accident by a passing boat.

On February 20, a message came from the Deep. The crew of a U.S. Navy Torpedo Retriever at a point 12 miles southwest of Key West noticed 2 objects floating in the water and retrieved them. One turned out to be a fog horn and the other a life jacket. Sifting them from the ocean, they noticed the stenciled name "Marine Sulphur Queen." The search was reactivated.

Forty-eight aircraft sorties totaling 271.4 flight hours covered the area of the Florida Straits and the Dry Tortugas. Seven vessels scoured the sea lanes. In addition, the U.S. Navy hauled out sonar and made an underwater search for the hull from 20th February to March 13. Considering the vessel's size, they estimated an 80% chance of locating it. They employed six ships for 523 hours on scene, and 17 aircraft sorties totaling 57 hours. Yet the hull of the *Marine Sulphur Queen* remained elusive.

However, more debris was found on the surface, all grouped together: 8 life jackets, 5 life rings, 2 name boards (when placed together they read 'arine Sulph'), one shirt, one piece of an oar, 1 storm oil can, 1 gasoline can, 1 cone buoy, and one fog horn.

This debris constituted the only chance to determine what befell the *Sulphur Queen.* As soon as it was retrieved, pictures were taken and it was shuttled to Miami and thence shipped to Washington D.C. for examination by four agencies, the Coast Guard, Bureau of Standards, the Bureau of Fisheries, and the FBI: "The consensus of opinion," read the report "was that possibly two life jackets had been worn by persons and that the shirt tied to a life jacket had also been worn by a person. Numerous tears on the life jackets indicated attack by predatory fish." This was all the definite information that could be gleaned.

The most extraordinary thing about the debris came from a further investigation by the FBI. This examination found no trace of sulphur particles on any of it. Yet one would expect to find at least a hint of it, for if the ship had split in twain the huge tank would have been ripped asunder and exuded yellow pools of foul smelling molten sulphur; it would have sizzled into the ocean, setting up a sulphurous gas cloud that should have settled over everything in the area, including the debris. Had the vessel exploded the sulphur would have showered down and blanketed the area.

The vessel had a history of fire. There was no doubt about that. "Numerous fires had occurred in the sulphur-impregnated insulation in the void spaces." But "these fires were of a local nature seldom covering an area of more than a few square feet, and caused little or no apprehension on the part of the crew. They were extinguished with a steam smothering system and fresh water." The fires, however, were increasing in frequency since October 1962. "Witnesses stated that during a voyage in the latter part of December, 1962, fires burned almost continuously in the insulation of the after end of No. 4 tank. Before the last voyage, the cowl type ventilators from the after pump room had been removed and canvas covers installed to reduce the loss of steam from the fixed fire extinguishing system."

Although it seems quite unlikely that these fires could have caused the vessel to explode, the Coast Guard Commandant considered "another possible cause for the loss of the vessel," one that he felt the Board did not consider thoroughly. This "concerns the possibility of an explosion in the void space surrounding the cargo tanks. Hydrogen sulphide and carbon disulphide gases released by the agitated molten sulphur as well as sulphur vapor could have entered the void spaces in sufficient quantities to have formed an explosive mixture."

No trace of any fire, however, had left the investigators with little concrete to go on. Conclusion 9 of the report is more a pragmatic statement of fact rather than a conclusion:

> In this connection, it is to be noted that although a close inspection of the debris identified as coming from the vessel fails to show

any evidence of charring or of an explosion, this fact by itself does not completely discount the possibility that an explosion did occur.

The weather was the only other tangible clue the Coast Guard had to work with. The seas were heavy in such gale force winds naturally. It was estimated that the highest waves encountered by the *Marine Sulphur Queen* were 16 feet. The wind was a strong gale, 25 to 46 knots. Although a 504-foot ship should be able to breast such waves with relative little discomfort, there was the question of her cargo. How would sulphur behave if severely agitated? The investigators set to their task, but found only dismal results in regards to how it may explain any explosion.

Although an explosion of the gases in one of the cargo tanks cannot be discounted, it would appear that such an explosion, if it occurred, would not be of a sufficient destructive force to account for the complete loss of the vessel without the intervention of other causes, perhaps, resulting from the initial explosion. It seems to be a generally accepted fact that an explosion of these gases is, relatively speaking, and dependent upon the factors of quantity of space, not of a high order.

Another T-2 tanker that suffered an explosion of sulphur from within its tank was used as an interpretive case. However, this did not help explain the *MSQ*'s loss. On the other vessel the tanks were not full and "the factors of quantity of space" therefore allowed for the sulphur to become agitated and for the collected gases to explode. In that case, the explosion only distorted the tank without rupturing it. In the case of the *MSQ* the tanks were full which gave little space for the volatile chemicals carbon disulphide and hydrogen sulphide to form and explode if the sulphur was agitated in the rough seas. Also the sulphur on board was of a very pure variety.

This left the Marine Board with only the skepticism about an unlikely accumulation of these gases in void spaces that may have ignited with the smoldering fires by No. 4 tank.

So the pitching seas were considered. It was speculated that sea water could have come in contact with the molten sulphur by splashing down the vents in rough weather. The result could be a steam explosion in a confined space. This too, however, was disagreed with: "However, the more recent thinking appears to discount the possibility of this reaction with the rationalization of the relatively cool sea water would quickly cool and solidify a layer of the sulphur which in turn would act to insulate the mass of the sulphur and the heat therein from further contact with the water."

Despite the lack of finding any pools of sulphur, did the ship indeed split in half? T-2s almost had a proclivity to do so. By the *MSQ*'s time, some ten T-2s had split in half. However, due to their wartime construction and many watertight bulkheads, they had also demonstrated an ability to remain afloat for quite a while or afloat indefinitely. A number of halves had even been towed back to port to be incorporated into other halves to make entirely "new" ships again.

Yet *MSQ* wasn't like the others. Her vitals had been changed. A number of the watertight bulkheads had been removed or altered in order to make room for the sulphur tank. This was thought to have made the ship less likely to remain afloat if she would break asunder. Yet this work was done in accordance with the American Bureau of Shipping and the Coast Guard standards, and the vessel was seaworthy, so certified just before she left. There were others who felt that the 306-foot center tank would actually prevent the ship from splitting in twain. The absence of sulphur on the articles recovered or the failure to locate any floating pools may support this.

Hoaxers weren't even sure how to account for the vessel's loss. At Laguna Madre, near Corpus Christi, Texas, a whiskey

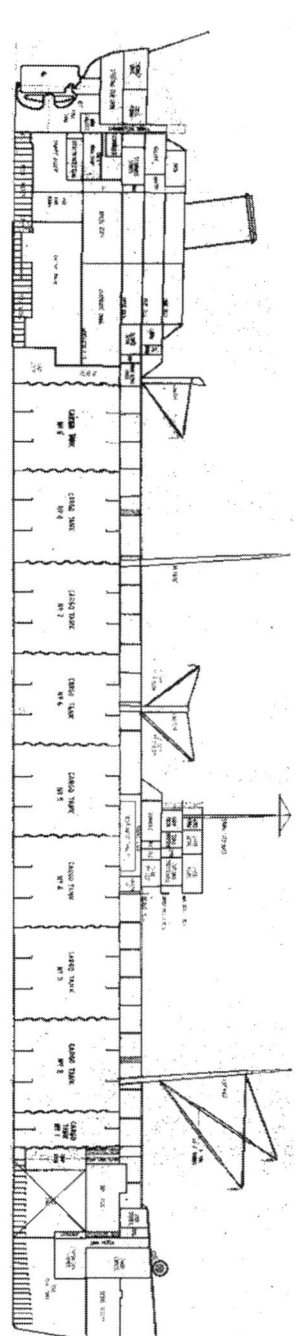

T-2 Tanker cross-section.

bottle washed ashore. On the manila paper inside was written a cryptic message with a ballpoint pen. It referred to an explosion and two men being injured. A crude map was drawn. In traditional tales-of-the-sea fashion an "X" marked the spot next to the word "SHIP." This "X" placed the ship, according the hastily scribbled map, in the western approach to the Florida Straits, the location where the Coast Guard had publically suspected the *Marine Sulphur Queen* of having disappeared.

The theory that grew from this proposed that the life rings were worn by two members of the watch. Although the cause and fate of the vessel remains as mysterious as before, this theory suggests that whatever cataclysm did overwhelm the ship, these two men were the only ones in a position to abandon her with whatever safety means at their disposal. There was no time for an SOS; and the two crew members may have grabbed for the life rings. Only in this way would a note in a bottle, in the way of a last will and testament, be thought of as necessary by the two survivors who realized by the lack of any distress message to the outside that their fates were sealed and, in the amount of time available, left at least this clue as the closing notation of the *Marine Sulphur Queen*.

The note was studied by a Federal examiner. His conclusion was: comparing the signatures of the crew, and in particular a letter by a crewman to his sister, that the letter was indeed written by a member of the *Marine Sulphur Queen*'s compliment.

There was a disagreement. At Washington D.C., at the Geodetic Survey, the Director said it was impossible for the note to have reached the area in which it was found in the interim time since the vessel's loss and the bottle's discovery ". . .unless a strong southeasterly wind had been blowing for several days before and after the dropping."

The amount of time required to write the note and put it in a bottle, tape it and throw it overboard, seem to discount the possibility of it being genuine.

Little really should have been made of this whole note-in-the-bottle affair. The location of the disaster on the note exposes its origins more than the writing experts could. The idea that the ship was near the Florida Keys stems purely from a very inaccurate Coast Guard assessment that was continuously recycled by the news. There is no possible way that the *MSQ* could have been near entering the Florida Straits. The heavy weather through which the tanker passed would require that the ship slow its speed in order to take the troughs safely. The debris, found just 12 miles off Key West, at the mouth of the Florida Straits, had also been *drifting* for 16 days in a rather strong current. It is fatuous to think that if the vessel went down around here the debris still would have been in the vicinity. If only assuming a 1 knot drift as an average based on the variable current drift, the debris would have covered 384 miles in those 16 days it was at sea (384 hours ((from 11:30 a.m. 4 February to 11:30 a.m. 20 February)). Using the debris' location and calculating backward by the drift, this would place the disaster point close to 400 miles northwest of the Keys in the Gulf of Mexico.

Amazingly, the Board even concurred that "the vessel apparently was lost on 4 February 1963 on its approach to, or in the vicinity of, the Straits of Florida." In light of the Board believing (quite rightly) that the ship must have been lost in those 10 hours between 1:25 a.m. and 11:23 a.m. February 4 it is remarkable that they agreed with the investigator as to the location.

It is almost unthinkable that the *Marine Sulphur Queen* was at her full speed. Yet even if at full speed (15 knots) she could hardly have done more than 465 miles at the time of her crewman's stock option call at 1:25 a.m. 4 February. She had only been at sea for 31 hours at this time. If she had reduced speed to 8 knots (standard reduction in heavy weather), she would have been less than 200 miles south of New Orleans. A mixture of full speed and reduced speed (allowing for when the gale

X marks the probable spot where the *MSQ* met that distant horizon.

came on) merely gives us a compromised position between the two above. Yet neither are remotely close to the Straits of Florida, the place where the Coast Guard errantly assumed she must have been. Even if we give her 10 more hours afloat and on course until the brokerage house reply was sent and never rogered (11:23 a.m.) we can only advance her position by 80 to 150 miles or roughly 600 miles out of Texas, and this final distance is dependent on the ship doing full speed in gale force winds. This would indeed place her close to entering the Straits. But with the gale force winds it is highly dubious to even seriously consider that she maintained full speed.

Calculating merely from the drift of the debris, we come to a point about 450 miles from Texas. Coincidently, this is the approximate location where a compromise of full and then reduced speed would have placed her sometime between 1:25 a.m. and 11:23 a.m. 4 February.

The calculations above serve the purpose here to reveal the *MSQ* was nowhere near the Straits of Florida. She was neither making full speed and doubtless she was lost long before 11:30 a.m. She was lost hundreds of miles northwest and the location and tardiness of the debris, a very tangible clue, coupled with the speed of the variable currents, confirms this.

In short, the ship was being looked for in the wrong location. This is doubly true when the Coast Guard reopened its search and looked for the hull with sonar and sidescan.

The Coast Guard mistake is merely one of many that has contributed to the mystery of the *MSQ*. The greatest factor is that the vessel wasn't even searched for until she failed to arrive at port. As soon as she didn't respond to the radio message, and as soon as she didn't make her regular call-ins over radio, the owners should have sounded the alarm to the Coast Guard.

The official report, of course, staying clear of second guesswork, concluded:

> In view of the absence of any survivors and the physical remains of the vessel, the exact cause for the disappearance of the MARINE SULPHUR QUEEN could not be ascertained.

CHAPTER SEVEN

A Requiem For The *Poet*

The disappearance of the *Poet* catapults the ancient terror of silence to new heights— literally. This 520-foot cargo vessel vanished north of Bermuda without sending an SOS but also without, apparently, sending any EPIRB signal. This automatic alarm— Emergency Position Indicating Radio Beacon— floats free from a sinking ship and commences to send out its radio signal. This can be traced by other ships, ground stations, and even by satellites. This tells the rescuers exactly where the vessel went down. It also guides them to the spot and, ideally, this will aid in quick rescue of the survivors. At the very least, if total tragedy has occurred, this will banish mystery, for when quick upon the scene the rescuers should be able to uncover wreckage and this should tell them what happened. Yet this was not to be the case for this huge vessel.

The *Poet* had a long and distinguished career. She was built during World War II and named the *General Omar S. Bundy*. She was a C-4 class cargo vessel, a sturdy pack-laden camel of the sea transporting materiel and troops wherever needed, under fire if necessary. She braved the tumultuous seas of the North Atlantic Convoy system and the heat of the South Seas islands. Her only touch with safety were the radios of that time and the quick launch of her lifeboats should torpedo strike.

All this was past the great vessel now. She had been sold off into private service and plied the seas faithfully for 30 years. She had been rebuilt and outfitted with the latest in lifesaving equipment, automatic alarms and modern radio and telephony. She was renamed from her wartime moniker and given the ultra-peacetime handle of *Poet*. She had no enemies. She feared no mines or torpedoes. Japanese Zeros or German Stuka dive bombers were not going to zoom over her and the chatter of their guns was not going to strafe her to pieces. She was designed to carry food now, not the emissaries of war and destruction.

According to her manifest, the *Poet* was carrying nothing more harmful than a cargo of #2 yellow corn. Loaded with this grain, the 520-foot ship sailed out to sea on October 24, 1980,

The *Poet* in wartime configuration as the *General Omar S. Bundy*.

from Girard Point, Philadelphia, Pennsylvania. At 9 a.m. her master, Leroy Warren, sent an USMER (U.S. Merchant Vessel Locator Filing System) to the Maritime Administration in Washington D.C. stating he was departing Cape Henlopen, Delaware, on a rhumb line[14] course for Gibraltar, then Port Said and Alexandria, Egypt. *Poet's* speed would be 15 knots. She should reach Port Said on 9 November. This message was also relayed to her owners, Hawaii Eugenia Co. of New York:

DEPARTURE CAPE HENLOPEN, 24,0830 BUNKERS RECEIVED 4157 SAILING 6218 ETA PORT SAID 090600.

The last message heard from the *Poet* was at midnight when Robert Gove, the third mate, called his wife on ship-to-shore radio. The conversation was centered around being en route to Egypt, and mentioned nothing else but the basics of the trip.

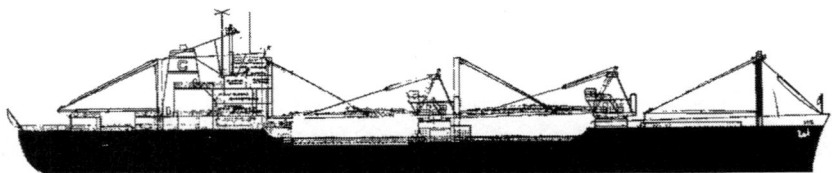

The *Poet* in 1980. She was past her prime, but as cargo ships go she was in good shape. She carried no hazardous cargoes. Only grains.

According to Hawaii Eugenia's company policy, the *Poet* was supposed to send her fuel and position reports every Monday and Thursday; every forty-eight hours she was to transmit her USMER reports. Complying with this, the next contact with the *Poet* should have come on October 26, 1980, but it did not. Somewhere between October 24 and 26, the 11,421 ton *Poet* with a 13,500 ton cargo, and all 34 hands, disappeared.

---

[14] A straight line course crossing all meridians at the same angle on a Mercator chart.

There was no distress from her radio and, more extraordinary, there was no beacon picked up emanating from her EPIRB.

The first indication that there was a problem with the *Poet* came when the Hawaii Eugenia Co. reported her overdue at Gibraltar on November 3. Furthermore, they stated they had received no communiqué from the *Poet* since her departure from Cape Henlopen. In the synopsis of the *Poet*'s loss, the Coast Guard state:

> . . .During the next 5 days, the Coast Guard conducted extensive communication checks with negative results. An air and surface search was commenced on 8 November and the ensuing search, which covered over 296,000 square miles during a ten-day period, proved unsuccessful. . . . .No trace of the vessel, crewmen, or debris was ever found.

A breakdown of the search follows. The first day of the search, the Coast Guard covered 34,850 square miles of ocean in 6 aircraft sorties. The next day they more than doubled it to 85,000 square miles in 9 sorties. Succeeding days totaled 16,000, 32,000, 10,000, and 14,500 in combined sorties of 18. On the 14th of November, 6 sorties covered 41,250 square mile; on November 15, 18,000 square miles were meticulously searched; and 35,000 on the 16th. With the continued negative results, the search wound down to a close on November 17, with only 9,600 square miles covered. A total of 54 sorties were flown from the Azores, Bermuda, and the east coast of the U.S. in the ten day search period covering exactly 297,300 square miles of the Atlantic. After the Coast Guard tallied up the figures, they stated somewhat perfunctorily: "the active search for the *Poet* was suspended."

In the following investigation, the Marine Board of Investigation was treated to several theories concerning what might have happened to the *Poet*. Her grain cargo of #2 yellow corn is not considered dangerous. But an innovative suggestion offered that her cargo sank her. If her corn got wet from leaking bottom plates or piping, the grain may have expanded and the mounting outward pressure on her hull plates could have ruptured the hull, sending the *Poet* to a speedy end by dropping her bottom out in minutes. Along with all the other more fringe theories, this was discounted.

Another theory was at least inferred by Coleman O'Donoghue, a former *Poet* seaman. He claimed that Noel McLaughlin, the ship's baker, told him before the ship left Philadelphia that the *Poet* was "a bucket of rust." O'Donoghue went on to say: "We heard some people on deck say she wasn't seaworthy." However, the Board of Investigation also discounted the notion that the s.s. *Poet* was a rust bucket.

Checking on the last radio contact with the *Poet*, and the next position report due which was not forthcoming, the Coast Guard was able to plot a certain probable radius by course and suspected speed for when she went missing. She must have been a few hundred miles north of Bermuda. The Coast Guard then checked with American vessels that had been in this general area at the same time (24 to 28 October).

There were some ten vessels in the area at the time period of most interest. But none of them reported any contact with the *Poet* or sighted any debris. However, one vessel did encounter an auto distress call. Mr. Edward Mashburn was the radio officer on board the s.s. *Columbia*. On October 27, when some 260 miles south of the *Poet*'s intended course, he picked up a signal. He informed the Coast Guard that he was aft eating when he was notified that at 9:33 p.m. the auto alarm had sounded. He went forward immediately, turned off the alarm, and listened carefully on 500 kHz. Mashburn also listened for other station transmissions; if the 500 kHz is quiet and no one else is transmitting he said he would suspect an emergency was in progress since all stations stop sending and listen in. Mashburn thought that no emergency existed because normal communications continued. He further stated that "false alarms" are not uncommon, especially in bad weather where lightning, static, and many other stations working and calling at the same time contribute to triggering the mechanism. He did, however, just to make sure, maintain a close ear on 500 kHz until 9:48 p.m.

Looking at the USMER reports of the other vessels we may find the reason for the auto alarm sounding. The *American Archer* reported at position 45° 31 N. latitude, 44° 13 W. longitude "Heavy Weather, anticipate reduced speed next 12 hours." *Thomas Lykes* reported a terse "Adverse weather" at position 37° 41 N latitude, 44° 30 W. longitude. *Columbia*, Mashburn's ship, presently was diverting "course because of adverse weather." *Marjorie Lykes* reported similarly "Varied course and speed due to adverse weather." And *Argonaut* reported "Heavy seas." The other ships in the vicinity, *Sam Houston*, CV *Staghound*, *Sealand Pacer*, and *Merrimac* made no remarks on weather. All of these vessels were about 700 miles east of Bermuda, north of the Sargasso Sea.

These reports, in conjunction with the fact that October 27 was already a day past the due position report of s.s. *Poet*, indicates that the weather was the cause of the auto alarm sounding on *Columbia*. It seems that this was a "false alarm" caused by the weather.

But was the weather also the cause for the disappearance of the s.s. *Poet*? The day after she sailed, a "freakish storm," as the New York *Times* put it catching the tide of mystery concerning the *Poet*, swept the area of her intended track with winds up to 70 mph. On October 26, the most probable day that the *Poet* went missing (because of the failure to send her expected position report), another auto alarm had sounded.

Mr. Earl Johnson, who has his FCC Radiotelegraph license and also a Coast Guard issued Radio Officer license, worked part-time and weekends as a marine radio operator at commercial marine radio station WHM, Baltimore, Maryland. He ". . .

heard an auto alarm signal or portions thereof consisting of 4 to 6 four-second dashes at one-second intervals on 500 kHz." Earl Johnson went on to tell the Coast Guard that ". . .The auto alarm signal was clear but weak. The signal did not fade in or out but was steady and then abruptly ended." Mr. Johnson heard this signal on October 26, at 12:00 a.m., but unfortunately he could not determine the direction or distance of the signal. Johnson, however, did note that the radio frequency became silent as other stations listened in. He called the Coast Guard Communications Station at Portsmouth, Virginia, to see if they had heard the signal, but was told that they had not. Like all the other station operators that listened in briefly after the terse dashes speeded across the airwaves, Johnson went back to his routine. It was only a fleeting encounter on a normal clear night and it was quickly over. Not until the 18th of November did he find out that the *Poet* was missing and then he gave the Coast Guard his testimony.

Could the adverse weather, coupled with the rumor that the *Poet* was a "rust bucket," explain why the vessel was singled out amongst the other vessels in the vicinity, and disappeared without trace while the others proceeded?

Part of the job of the Marine Board of Investigation is to determine that. This Board convenes at varying locales depending on the area of the disaster. From this meeting place they sift out evidence gleaned by a number of investigators sent to key places to locate the pertinent records: where the vessel was built, the yards where it was overhauled, certificates of inspections and repairs, etc. Witnesses are called to give firsthand recall of the ship's past. Expert and eyewitness testimony is introduced and heard. Basically, the ship is on trial.

In this particular case the Marine Board of Investigation met at Norfolk, Virginia. And an important part of the investigation was to determine the seaworthiness of the ship. Consideration that the total disappearance of a ship, in a manner assumed to have been so fast as to preclude any distress, and of such destructive capability to prevent, apparently, the EPIRB signal from sending, required a solid explanation.

One of the witnesses to bring his testimony to the Board was the president of Hawaii Eugenia Co., the *Poet*'s owner, Henry J. Bonnabel. He took the stand and testified that the *Poet* was "one of the staunchest and strongest ships in the Merchant Marine." The lawyers representing the families of the lost crewmen disagreed. The rumors of the ship being a rust bucket fed the idea that the *Poet* was unseaworthy.

The real expert testimony would come from the investigators who checked into the vessel's past. This showed that the *Poet*'s hull had been checked out in August of 1980 and was found to be in good condition. That same month the U.S. Government did its annual load line check. Earlier in March the *Poet* had passed her biennial, drydock and tail shaft inspection by the Coast Guard. Her radio telegraphy was also checked by the FCC in August, and found satisfactory. And in October before she sailed the Coast Guard checked and passed her safety and navigation equipment.

The *Poet* had sustained minor damage on her portside hull in Matidi Harbor, Zaire, in 1978. The inspector examined it, but it was not severe enough to warrant immediate attention. He did notice indents on the starboard side of the ship. But they too did not warrant permanent repairs; they were filled with cement and any permanent repairs could wait until the vessel's next regular drydocking.

In a Hazard Category Table drawn up by the Coast Guard, with "A" representing Catastrophic, "B" representing Critical, "C" representing Marginal, and "D" representing Negligible, structural failure as the cause of the vessel sinking in adverse weather was naturally given an "A." In another table showing the *Poet*'s score on probability of such occurrence, it was rated an "L"-"M," or "Possible but not likely" (L), and "Highly Improbable" (M). Those who inspected the vessel evidently disa-

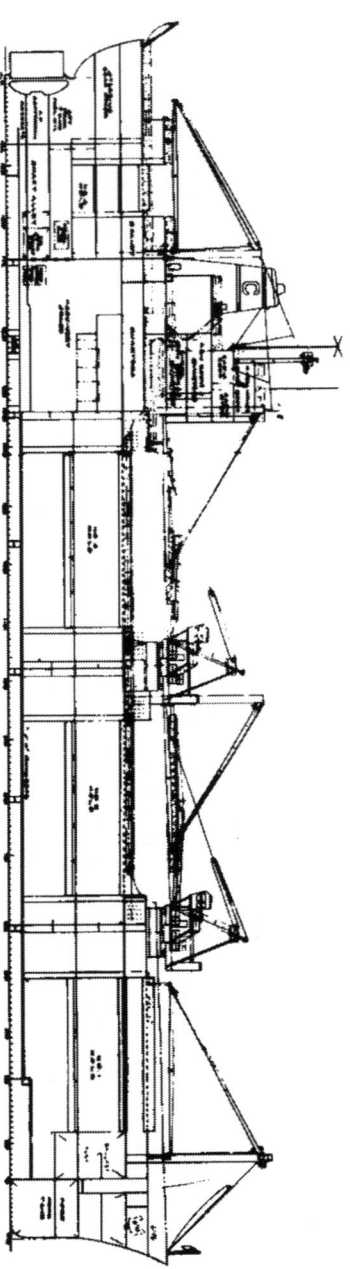

s.s. *Poet* in cross section

greed with baker McLaughlin.

However, the Coast Guard could not completely discount the possibility that structural fault happened since some ships have foundered due to undiscovered structural problems. "In terms of probability of major structural failure, comparison of estimated still water and wave induced loads and resulting stresses to accepted design values and estimated ultimate strength of the hull indicates that the resulting stress levels are relatively low and well below the levels at which one might anticipate major hull structural failure. . .The probability of a major hull structural defect resulting in the vessel breaking in two appears fairly low."

The weather was also checked in detail to see if its pattern indicated any other way in which the vessel could have been lost. When the *Poet* left port a low pressure area moved from a point of 250 miles east of Jacksonville, Florida, to a position off Hudson Bay arriving there on the 27th. It swept right across the *Poet*'s route to Gibraltar. On the 25th the *Poet* should have been encountering the roughest waves and winds of the storm: winds over 50 knots and heavy seas. These should continue for 10 to 12 hours. By the 26th, the storm should be heading west and the *Poet* should have been easing out of the squall with the sustained winds decreasing to 30 to 40 knot range. Late on the 26th and continuing to the 27th, the storm should have moved behind the *Poet*'s track and the ship should be encountering mild sea and weather conditions for the next two days.

One phenomenon was considered. The historical danger the area off the Carolinas has in legend may stem from what is now called the "North Wall Phenomenon" of the Gulf Stream. The area of the North Wall is that part of the Gulf Stream that curves from Cape Hatteras out into the distant Atlantic horizon north of Bermuda carrying the warm tropic waters of the Gulf into the cold Atlantic.

The Coast Guard describes the North Wall Phenomenon as

follows:

> The North Wall Phenomenon is one of rapidly increasing wind and seas in the area of the northern boundary of the Gulf Stream where the sea surface temperatures can change dramatically. In such a region of large surface temperature contrast, a potential for damaging and volatile weather frequently exists. When cold air flows over the narrow zone of warm water, the air rapidly rises. The rising air displaces the heavier, colder air aloft which descends generating strong, gusty winds at the surface.

It was estimated that the *Poet* came under the influence of the North Wall Phenomenon during the 25th while she was northwest or north of Bermuda.

One of the unpredictable elements that might be created in this caldron of waves and winds is a "Rogue Wave." Rogue Wave is self-explanatory. It doesn't travel with the pack, comes from a different direction, is out of proportion and its actions are volatile. At 38° 44 north latitude, 68° 37 West Longitude, which is about 300 miles northwest of Bermuda, on October 26, while still 50 to 60 miles from the North Wall of the Gulf Stream, Mr. Bart Dunbar sighted a rogue wave 40 to 50 feet high that came out of nowhere and capsized his ketch, the *Wandering Angus*. Mr. Dunbar survived. So did the crew of the yacht *Polar Bear* which was on its way to Bermuda from New York, and sank in the heavy seas. The crew was picked up on October 31 by the Polish freighter *Zemia Gdanska*. It is somewhat ironic that the giant cargo ship *Poet* totally vanished without trace.

Baker Mclaughlin may not have known about the conditions of the ship's hull, but he could see and judge for himself the condition of the deck. It is in this light that the *Poet* can be viewed as having a weak spot. The hatch on No.1 hold when last inspected was observed to be knuckled 9 inches up from the ends at the port side center; the skirt and gasket retaining channels were buckled in-board. In other words, it was not watertight. Temporary repairs were done to the satisfaction of the surveyor. But the permanent repairs were deferred until the next dry-docking. The work had been done properly, and at an intermediate survey done in March of 1980 at Beaumont, Texas, no more fractures or released connections in the damaged area were located and once again the permanent repairs were deferred until the next dry-docking (March 1982).

But the watertight hatch on No. 1 hold was an on-going problem, albeit a small one that warranted continued minor repairs to the skirt. Before the *Poet* sailed from Philadelphia, more repairs were done. The Port Engineer recalled a doubler plate was welded to the corner and a part of the skirt bottom edge was "cropped out and a welded insert installed."

Can the rough seas, and the volatility of the North Wall of the Gulf Stream, and the known occurrence of the rogue wave, account for the loss of the *Poet* if the No. 1 hold hatch cover failed, flooding the hold, resulting in the loss of stability? This possibility was given an "A"-"B" in the severity chart, thus indicating the effects of the flooding of No. 1 hold would be "Catastrophic" to "Critical." It would translate to the ship sinking in 5 to 10 minutes; and if the "A" scenario were correct without being able to launch lifeboats or transmit an SOS. In "B" the vessel would have time to transmit a distress and launch the boats. The *Poet* was thus listed as between these two. The above scenario was, however, given an "L" rating in the Probability Table—"Possible, but not likely." No matter what hypothetical event sequence was proposed, whatever did happen was believed to have occurred so quickly as to preclude the transmission of a radio distress.

In any case, the EPIRB should nevertheless have worked, signaling and remaining signaling for days after it hit the water. And it was in working order, no doubt about it. In August the EPIRB was tested and was found satisfactory. If the vessel had capsized, though, it was thought that the EPIRB might have fallen off the bridge, where it was stowed in a float-free container, and crashed on the deck rendering it useless for transmission. As to the failure of the EPIRB, the report states rather matter-of-factly: "No EPIRB signal was received from the *Poet*, meaning the EPIRB didn't deploy, it deployed but failed to transmit, or it transmitted but no one received the signal."

So what did happen to the *Poet*? No one can know for sure. But the Marine Board of Investigation listed possibilities in order of their probability based upon the vessel's history and the known weather conditions:

a) Capsizing due to quartering or following seas.
b) The vessel was lost due to flooding of No. 1 hold from a severe failure of the hatch cover.
c) Structural failure occurred.

b) was given a low probability (L) in the Probability Table only a few pages before these conclusions were expressed. And c) was given "L"-"M— "Highly Improbable." However, a) was given a "J"— "Quite Possible." Therefore the official investigators thought she capsized.

Ironically, in the final assessment, the Commandant of the Coast Guard disagreed.

> The Commandant has concurred with the Marine Board that the approximate cause of the casualty cannot be determined. Although significant credibility can be assigned to any of the possibilities noted by the Board, the Commandant considers it more probable that some loss of hull integrity occurred. If a loss of hull integrity occurred, the ingress of water could have gone undetected by the crew long enough to lead to the sudden loss of the ship by plunging, capsizing or foundering.

The case was closed. But the exact fate continues to remain open.

PART III

Hazardous Duty

CHAPTER EIGHT

Down To The Sea in Ships

The Gloucester Fisherman rightly stands proud upon his pedestal, ship's wheel firm in hand. He gazes faithfully, acceptingly, over that distant horizon that has taken so many. His pragmatic expression is etched in stone, but it reflects the living expression of New England's seafarers. There is no way to avoid the roulette of the sea's whim. Many brave it all their lives. Most come back wounded and spurned, but some never return. The sea takes them. They go down, and the only thing to mark their passing is this stalwart totem reminding the sea it has been and forever shall be challenged in these shores.

New England is a seafarer's land. It was and remains one end of the massive North Atlantic highway. Boston was the gateway to and from Yankee lands. Ships bearing the flags of all the world came to ply their trade here, and from here the young Yankee merchant set out to tap virgin coasts and blaze new highways to old lands. But the Americas had not been fished before. The bounty of the New World was there, but awaiting with it were undiscovered currents, uncharted crags, new weather patterns, and a sea that would introduce itself not with a shake but with a slap.

A rough, coarser people were introducing themselves upon the seas. The first Americans were a unique breed, and much like Virgil we can lament that we are not so great as our forbearers. New Englanders set upon the virgin seas of America like a cowpoke sets upon a bucking bronco to be tamed. Although many were thrown off, they always got back on. It was get back on or perish. Perish at sea and on land, for the seamen kept the lifelines open to America. The sea lanes must be kept open, the breadbasket of the Deep must be accessed.

The first Americans were well-tempered to take on a new land and a new sea. Upon this new land they considered themselves a new people, but they had an old pedigree and a particular type of personality: rugged, determined, unflinching.

Religious persecution cast many of the first Americans here. They weren't running away. They could endure most anything. No one flibbertigibbet sets out to a new, rugged land lightly. But when it came to their freedom to live and express themselves, initial hardship and readjustment was preferable over the endless hawking over their beliefs. This present author's French Huguenot ancestors fled France for Hesse at the revocation of the Edict of Nantes in 1685, and from there one of them, Philippe Brun, answered Catherine the Great's call in

1767 to settle the Volga steppes and become a founder of Nor-
ka, Russia. Some cousins and uncles, I suspect, answered rather
the lure of the New World and came to America. There were
many Reformed who did— Germans from the Palatinate (with
whom Huguenots had married) and from Holland. Here they
were welcomed by their English Puritan brethren and Scots
Covenanters. Calvinists didn't mix much with Lutherans. The
Reformed married with the Reformed, and when Scotland was
crushed in the '45 thousands of Reformed came to likeminded
brethren in America. With them they brought their calamitous
news of the victory of the House of Hanover over the rightful
House of Stuart. The seeds of rebellion were being planted.
Disgruntled Jacobites were determined to have a free land with
no English and Hanoverian overlords. Huguenots (who mixed
much with Scots), being French, didn't mind casting off anything English (Paul Revere was himself of Huguenot origin),
and Reformed Germans came from the Palatinate and didn't
see much use in in these humorless and dour Hanoverians.

My point is that early Americans, especially New
Englanders, were a specific type of personality. They weren't
off-casts. They were a hardnosed, independent religious type
with an enormous work ethic; and I am proud, though my
branch remained in the climes of Europe until the late 19th
century, that many a cousin and uncle, distant and far-flung,
rode the high seas off New England and beat Yankee Doodle's
drum on land.

They harvested crab and lobster, and every form of white
fish. They feasted from the sea and they filled the bellies of a
new world with their produce. It was not an idle game. They
were not great hunters shooting dumb animals. They had to
know a terrain that forever changes. Their weapon was only a
net and their own brains. They needed to learn sailing, the
winds, ropes, ship building and the weather— all this just to
cast their nets.

And, of course, many never came back. It is the same today,

even with all the high tech. They continue to be thrown off that wild steed of the ocean. But New Englanders get back on. Thus rightfully so the Gloucester Fisherman's pedestal memorializes "they that go down to the sea in ships." It is a taken from Psalm 107, verses 23-30:

> They that go down to the sea in ships, that do business in great waters; These see the works of the LORD, and his wonders in the deep. For he commandeth, and raiseth the stormy wind, which lifteth up the waves thereof. They mount up to the heaven, they go down again to the depths: their soul is melted because of trouble. They reel to and fro, and stagger like a drunken man, and are at their wits' end. Then they cry unto the LORD in their trouble, and he bringeth them out of their distresses. He maketh the storm a calm, so that the waves thereof are still. Then are they glad because they be quiet; so he bringeth them unto their desired haven.

Perhaps God instills an allure in the sea, else who would dare its waters? Who would wish to learn all he could of navigation and ships, sea and foam, just to track and anticipate its hidden prey? The seafarer, especially the New England seafarer, is a brilliant lad. But he is a dichotomy. He fled the perils of religious persecution and finally in New England set down roots. But then he went where angels fear to tread in order to make his bread. The new western approaches with all its game did not attract him. He looked back from where he came— the seas— and he risked danger.

For every ante we have made in the realm of technology and shipbuilding, the timeless sea has ante'd up to thwart us. Ships with GPS, built-in floatation, and every other safeguard, still disappear. They wreck and they sink, of course. That shall always be. But to disappear means the sea has won in a careful, quick maneuver. A merciless, hard move that mocks all the science and technology we have.

Thus many still go down to the sea in ships. . .they leave no tale save that the sea is still mighty and will not be conquered. But one thing they do leave behind. The very seas they work, the very occupation they hold, the very traditions they lose their lives for, tell us of their conviction and their characters. Therefore no man perishes mutely. He joins his comrades, all they that go down to the sea in ships, and he joins them right well.

It is these more modern disappearances that give one pause to consider. The ships were well built. Not that the old schooners and fishermen weren't. But with steel we have water-tight bulkheads. We have radio today. Flares. Inflatable life vests and rafts. Perhaps we cannot prevent tragedy, but we should be able to minimize it or at least mark the spot. But still fishermen have vanished, well found, near land and nary a trace found.

In April 1950 the F/V *Four Sisters* vanished near Nantucket Shoal. True, she was 24 years old, but she was stout and all 45 tons kept in order by her master, Gunnar Pedersen. No ship makes New Bedford her home and does not feel the scorn of all the other ancient fishermen if her decks are not kept up, her gear up-to-date and her deck in order. There she left on March 29 for her grounds to fish for scallops. From there she left to Pollack Rip in order to sell her catch (some 700 gallons of scallops). She wasn't even fishing. She wasn't headed far out to sea, nor did Pedersen and the crew have to worry about being caught by a sudden squall with their nets deployed. She was cruising to make the Woods Hole market.

The last seen of her was around 6 a.m. on April 7. She was near buoy 10 east of Nantucket. And that is all. This is the evidence. The Coast Guard Marine Casualty Branch concluded that it must be "presumed that the *Four Sisters* foundered with the loss of all persons on board."

Gusts of wind were the only clue the investigators had to go on. They reached out, like anybody, for anything that can explain what seemed inexplicable. Small craft warnings had gone up on April 3. Then on the 7th, the last day anybody saw the *Sisters*, storm warnings had been hoisted. The wind "velocity in the area of the casualty reached as high as 52 miles per hour with occasional gusts of 65 miles per hour." These are heavy winds, and the seas get rowdy in response. The sea becomes like any creature agitated too much.

But this was a New England, and Bedford no less, scalloper. She was built to ride wave and breast wind. Her high tech for that time was adequate: a fathometer, of course, a direction finder and a radiotelephone. She carried a life ring buoy, 2 fifteen foot dories and life preservers for each crewman. She had one pump, which ran off the engine, and two hand-billy pumps. Ten men were aboard, each a seasoned fisherman.

When the *Sisters* left New Bedford, it was considered too rough for fishing. In these winds ships haul in their nets and jog to shore. But Pedersen and his men pulled it off. They made their grounds and hauled aboard 700 gallons of catch. His last radio communication said nothing of trouble. He was in contact then with the *Dagney*. He asked that they pick up their fishing buoy. It is then that he made it plain they were going to try and make Wood's Hole.

The F/V *Friendship* was also in the same area as the *Four Sisters*, and the Coast Guard could only add with official dryness that she had also left New Bedford and returned safely enough. Official comparisons are one way to be subtle. Exclamation points can never be used in reports, of course. Emotion is excised out. But no sailor is a robot. The Coast Guard are all sailors, and even they have their sublime way in official reports of expressing surprise. As an equal time, they also noted that other boats were in trouble. The *William Landry* was also being searched for and was in trouble. But however relevant it may seem for the Coast Guard report to note that another vessel was in trouble, it was just as relevant for the Coast Guard to have noted that others came through it all right. What it comes down to in the end is obvious: something else must have happened to the *Sisters*— sudden, without warning and without even a chance for flotsam and jetsam. (Monomoy Island and Nantucket were kept under close beach watches. No debris or bodies ever came ashore.) The *Four Sisters* should not have foundered. Moreover, she should not have foundered so close to land and still have left no trace. The Coast Guard search was prompt, as they are always ready for any trouble in these heavily worked waters. (Already on the 9th her owner had declared her overdue.) For 3 days they searched. Over 21,000 square miles were covered. But nothing was found.

What happened? There was some evidence and lots of opinion. It began with another ship's report. The *Friendship* reported that the winds actually reached hurricane force of 75 mph. This is far more than the land stations recorded. *Dagney* said it was far too rough to chance the Pollack Rip Slue.

Yet how would the *Four Sisters* founder? Major hull work from November 1949 to January 1950 completely refitted her. On December 14 she had been hauled out of the water and dry-docked. Her sheathing was removed, then her old caulking, and then she was recaulked. A section of hull planting was replaced, about 5 feet of it. It was replaced properly with the same type of hard 2 inch pine planking. They were secured by nails. Her frame was double 3 by six pieces sawn to shape. Her hatch was wooden, overlaid with a fitted metal cover that lapped down by about 5 inches and was secured by a single hatch bar across the center.

Was that not enough? Did her hatch rip off and the 700 gallons of scallops, drenched with foam and waves crashing in, suddenly weighted her too much and she could no longer ride the waves?

But explaining a possible way for her to have sunk is not the same thing as explaining why there was no debris.

The lack of finding anything inspired the Coast Guard to look deeper into the ship's past. In keeping-up the vessel and refitting it to tip-top shape, had there been a mistake? The Coast Guard considered "that the nail fastening of planking, including butts, was a poor type of construction in the vessel." Did the new patch, in obedience to the gospeline parable, make the condition worse? Did the vessel rip apart and go down like a deadweight, with all hands below decks and no time for Pedersen or his mates to grab for the microphone?

Come that September another vessel would vanish. She was the 104 foot *Theresa A.* She was a US Army built war surplus Casey-type Boat, designated QS 56. After the war many of these boats, and others like them, were sold off, the multiplicity of them no longer of any use to the Army. She had been built in 1944 at Atlantic City, New Jersey, and by 1950 when she was finally refitted for mackerel fishing she was only 6 years old, still a frisky colt. This certificate had come only in May 1950, four months before she would vanish. She had sat out the peacetime post war world at dock until being sold, but her refitting had rechecked and updated all that needed doing. At 104 feet she was a large vessel, and having been an Army Air Rescue ship she had been equipped for soundness and speed.

The *Theresa A.* had set sail from Fairhaven, Massachusetts, on 9 September 1950 to fish on Georges Bank, about 100 miles northeast of that stalwart sentinel, the Nantucket Lightship. In this case we have a clue to her disappearance. At 7:20 p.m. the 12th of September, her captain sent a radio message saying they were in distress and they were manning the lifeboat. Thirty-seven minutes later he sent another. All hands were now abandoning ship.

Despite those 37 minutes of grace, no crewmen survived. Twelve brave lads went into one dory and not one escaped to tell the tale. The winds were heavy, the waves choppy. One fisherman reported the wind got as high as 55 mph. But that alone could not have caused the *Theresa A.* to suddenly founder. It only provides another problem in trying to understand what could have been happening (the captain never stated in the maydays) for that half an hour. High seas can be clarified very quickly over the radio. The vessel was not sinking so quickly there was no time to clarify.

Nor was she alone. On September 11, the *Theresa A.* had been in company of several other ships fishing her grounds off the Georges Bank. Yet no other crew saw remains of her or her dories and crew. This also includes a rescue plane which was quickly at the scene. It had left Salem, Massachusetts, before dark and yet it only spotted the other fishing vessels in the vicinity.

Marine broadcasts to search the area had already diverted other fishing vessels, and now the cutters *Coos Bay*, *Dexter*, and *Eastwind*, were on their way. They battled heavy seas, and were thus delayed, but the aircraft had arrived in time to find something. Yet it only scoured an empty ocean. The searched continued until September 16, and marine broadcasts to be on the lookout continued even after this. But it was all to no avail.

A dry recital of facts only qualifies a few factors which may have contributed to the mystery. For one, there were communications problems, as there frequently is. Thus if the captain of the *Theresa A.* sent a qualifying message as to what the problem was none might have received it. Investigation also turned up that the handling gear in the dory wasn't working on the last trip. Moreover, the method for securing the hatch "was not in accordance with standard practice in that no metal bars were provided." Visible ballast was not secured. No bilge pump was connected to the motor. There was only one other electric powered pump. The hand pump didn't work.

The Coast Guard's informant was reliable. He was Urbanus Stange, the last master of the vessel (up until August). Some of these deficiencies could have been corrected by the time the

THE ARMY "HAS A HEART"

And so we are building 104' Army Aircraft Rescue Boats in record time. Fast, these Casey boats rush hospital facilities far out to sea when brave flyers need assistance. Into them goes all the skilled workmanship that for years has enabled us to say of our auxiliaries:

"CASEY BOATS ARE RARELY OFFERED FOR SALE — THEY SELL THEMSELVES"

When Victory is won, we hope that one of the first new CASEY auxiliaries to have her keel laid may be yours. Meanwhile . . . . . buy U. S. War Bonds and Stamps.

CASEY BOAT BUILDING COMPANY, Inc.
Fairhaven, Massachusetts

An advertisement touting the Casey Boats, the same general hull design that was adapted in the case of the *Theresa A.*

Theresa A. left on her last voyage. The fact there was time for an SOS, two 37 minutes apart in fact, means the vessel wasn't suddenly overwhelmed. Her bulkheads were noted to have been tight while in port, as one would expect of a relatively new army vessel. Thus she was capable of watertight compartmenting. But from the sounds of it, the lack of bilge pumps caused her doom. She slowly filled, perhaps battered from the seas, and there was no way to maintain buoyancy. She slowly began to founder and the men scrambled to their lifeboat.

Did they actually get off? The Coast Guard was skeptical. For instance, during the heavy weather the F/V *Sea Ranger* lost her dory from the waves, and she was riding high. With a ship heavy from foundering, as in the case of the *Theresa A.*, the seas would have been licking and slapping the dory. It is possible that men were both in the dory and boarding her when the seas smacked the foundering deck and lashed the dory wildly from its davit.

Another factor is that she wasn't designed originally for fishing. There's always suspicion in seafarers about messing with a ship's lines and vitals. Indeed, this suspicion has proven justified in other cases. But in this case the vessel was designed as a wartime rescue boat and was seaworthy. Should we nevertheless wonder that in her refit her durability was compromised? Did this set her apart from all her fellow fishermen this day?

All other vessels in her vicinity, the Coast Guard duly noted, made it back to port. One of them, the *Lubenray*, which had been closest to *Theresa*'s position, had decided to stay because the drift was better. The captain reported the seas were high, so much so that he was delayed in getting to the actual scene of the distress relatively nearby, but they rode the sea just fine and so should the *Theresa A.*

Much of the on-scene weather is reported (through the captain of the *Lubenray*), but it really is provided as an incidental. High seas, 55 mile winds, a real nor-easter, but what happened to the *Theresa A.* different from the others?

It seems nothing structurally was wrong with the ship. But the Coast Guard believed "it was possible for water to enter the vessel and that the past general operation and management was not in accordance with the practices of good seamanship." This was the result of the "tendency for some slack practices in the routine operation" of the vessel. Due to the structural soundness, the Coast Guard deduced: "That the crew of the *Theresa A.* did not abandon ship successfully due to the state of the weather."

The Coast Guard offered the remark:

> From the information available in the record of investigation, together with the information obtained from the Department of the Army, with respect to the construction and characteristics of the THERESA A., it would appear that due to her shallow draft and high freeboard, defective steering arrangement, hatch covering and unsecured ballast, the THERESA A. was caught in the trough of the sea from which she could not extricate herself and was overwhelmed by either the shifting of the unsecured ballast or the entrance of water through the defective hatch or both.

However, the Coast Guard stuck its neck out, and rather illogically at that, when it came to their Opinion 17. They admitted that 2 dories had been seen at sea in the general area, but then deduced that they could not have belonged to the vessel "inasmuch as the master reported that they were abandoning ship with one dory." Why could not both dories have been launched? Perhaps one overturned, and the remaining men scrambled for the other. It is hard to say exactly what happened. But the Coast Guard's assumption was fatuous, to say the least. *Theresa A.* was a strong and sturdy vessel, probably taking on water and with no sufficient pumping. She wasn't going down fast. In the first SOS at 7:20 p.m. the master had stated they were taking to the dory. Something might have happened then and they needed to launch the other in the interim. Thirty-seven minutes is a long interim. Something could even have happened after the final message as the captain rushed back to get in the boat.

The Coast Guard assumed that one of the dories had belonged to the *Sea Ranger*, the one which she lost during the storm. It is ironic, to say the least, that these dories should have survived but that nothing of the *Theresa A.* should have survived as a testimony.

If both dories were from the *Theresa A.* she did leave a faint message. Twelve men tried to save themselves, and perhaps none were successful. Her lifeboats survived, but they fled before the men they were supposed to carry to safety. If they were the *Sea Ranger's*, the sea left the final message. One giant clutch grabbed them all and took down the large fishing vessel and her crew and lifeboats and to this day the sea has never opened her fist.

A few months later would see another fishing vessel vanish. The F/V *Penguin* left that venerable New Bedford on February 6, 1951, to go to her fishing grounds about 50 to 60 miles south of Block Island. There she kept company with a number of other vessels, each working its own buoys. Then on the 7th a fresh gale arose. She hove to with the *Holly and James* and *Growier*. It is the unfortunate routine of the sea. One compromises with that primordial temptress. Sometimes it woos her and the gale subsides. Some defy her and continue fishing. Sigurd Matland, master of the *Penguin*, was that man this day. At noon the next day he contacted the captain of the *Growier* and said he was going to ride it out until the gale moderated so he could resume fishing. He was not going to come in until he got a full load of fish. But the other fishers jogged slowly closer to shore to nestle under the wing of the one patron to which the sea must bow— the safe harbor. *Penguin* was no longer in sight, but the other vessels could hear Matland's routine messages. Only after the evening of the 8th was there silence.

Rudolf Matland, his brother, reported the *Penguin* overdue on February 17.

A search found no trace, not an iota. There was the sighting by the *Austin W.* of a lifeboat similar to that carried by the *Penguin*, but this was 30 miles north of her last reported position. Since they saw this on the morning of the 9th it is hard to believe it could have drifted that far that fast. She attempted to recover the boat, but she was unsuccessful in the pitching seas.

"The weather on 7 and 8 February, 1951, was bad with winds up to about 45 knots," the Coast Guard report declared. However, it wasn't that bad, for it quickly added: "The weather was not of sufficient severity to account for the loss of the *Penguin*."

The Coast Guard had good reason to state this. "The *Penguin* had the reputation of being one of the best maintained and able fishing vessels of its size in the New Bedford fishing fleet." She was only 9 years old, still a teenager as fishing vessels go. She was 45 tons, so she wasn't some mammoth that required a financially draining amount of money to keep her tip-top. In the summer of 1950 she was dry-docked and "all necessary hull and engine repairs made; and in December a new propeller and water tank and many other necessities were installed or repaired. She carried 2 dories, one 6-man and one 5-man life rafts, 8 life preservers, and one ring buoy." All were maintained in excellent, pampered condition. She was a good ship, with a good master and crew. Matland's son was his mate, and the others were mostly of his own Scandinavian background. They knew the sea and how wild she can get. The best safety against her is a well-found ship.

Perhaps this deceived Matland not to woo the temptress at all, not even with a gesture of deferring to her modest temper this day. In the weather conditions that prevailed there was no reason really for Matland to have fled. But it might have been wiser. Rather he remained and he vanished.

What did snatch the *Penguin* from amidst her fellow ships? How did the sea grab her without a sound? Six men went into the Deep, and they joined so many others caught at a routine moment.

The disappearance of the *Susan* in December 1953 is even more inexplicable. She was an 83-foot converted Coast Guard vessel, made for battle with villain and with sea. After surviving WWII and being sold into private hands she had been stripped of her armaments, naturally, and several modifications had been done to make her a sleek fishing vessel. Her pilot house forward had been removed and one was built aft. A 40 foot tall mast was raised forward. A 400 gallon fuel tank had been installed, as well as a 300 gallon fuel oil tank, both on the deck fore and aft the pilot house. Internally, the engine room was moved so that the space could be converted into a fish hold.

Conversions such as these instinctively worry seafarers. It is changing a ship's pedigree. It is changing a great lady and dolling her up with makeup to make her a strumpet. . .to clean up the attitude a bit. But the *Susan* seemed a sturdy ship. The Coast Guard, being seafarers, had to temper their natural suspicion. They didn't know if adjustments along these lines could have compromised her buoyancy, since there were no sister ships they could find and examine. However, the *Susan* had had 25 fishing voyages prior to her disappearance and had reported no problems. Thus she seemed to have been a sound vessel.

Her captain, Norman Josefsen, was a cautious man, as well. On this trip he had brought the *Susan* into Wildwood, New Jersey. The weather had been choppy and there was no point in fishing. He decided this was a good time to kill 2 birds with one stone and do some engine repairs. It was nothing major. The next day, December 5, he intended to leave port for his fishing grounds.

This he did, and after that moment the *Susan* and her crew entered that distant horizon. No SOS was ever picked up.

On 19 December Mr. Peter Tollesen notified the Coast Guard the vessel was overdue. An All-Points Bulletin was immediately issued and a search was underway. As in the other cases, nothing was found, no wreckage, no flotsam. . .and the *Susan* had quite an array of life saving gear, too. She had an actual lifeboat, not just a dory; a life raft, and life preservers for all aboard.

The weather had been nothing exceptional. Two storms of little strength between the 5th and 10th of December only caused small craft advisories to be raised. The wave heights were a maximum of 9 feet with winds gusting up to 25 knots.

The Coast Guard couldn't figure it. "The weather conditions during the ensuing five days were stormy but not severe. It would appear that the fishing vessel *Susan* has been lost at sea while engaged in fishing activities and that all seven crew members on board have perished. The cause for the vessel's disappearance cannot be ascertained."

Unusual for reports, the Remarks were posted on the front page.

> A review of the record of investigation of subject casualty indicates that the Board has unsuccessfully explored all possible features of the case which might explain or account for the *Susan*'s disappearance. However, it would have been helpful if the Board had included in its report those pertinent facts which were learned during the investigation, and which described such details as type of lifeboat— where and how carried, essentials of conversion, repairs to the vessel, areas fished in, and the experience of former crew members respecting the vessel's performance.

The remark above is almost a complaint. It was the seafarer in the Coast Guard speaking. It was suspicion demanding something tangible upon which to base its reticence to accept the vessel merely vanished. And, indeed, what the Commandant's office wanted would seem pertinent to trying to understand the loss.

But factually what would itemizing these reveal to the Coast Guard? In the end, the cause for the *Susan*'s disappearance would still be a guess. Granted, had they known more there may have been more for the Coast Guard to guess with, but still none of it would constitute a definite solution to the mystery. Even a scow might disappear, plunged below, because of something completely unrelated to the stability or poor upkeep of the vessel. And the *Susan* was far from that.

Perhaps the investigators were right to leave out too much conjecture in this case. They had made the point in the report that they didn't know how the *Susan* might have been affected by its conversion. What else could they do? In the end suspicions are just that. The *Susan* vanished and shouldn't have. She sank, presumably, and yet shouldn't, and shouldn't have done so without a trace or so quickly as to preclude even an SOS.

Yet she did. A search of 200,000 square miles found nothing. As of the writing of the report, the notice to all vessels to be on the alert was still in effect. But no one had made off with the vessel. There had been no mutiny or piracy. Nothing ever came of the alert. The *Susan* was never seen again, nor any of her crew.

The *Gudrun* was a tragic loss that still haunted the fishing fleets at the *Susan*'s investigation. In January 1951 this 245 ton fishing trawler set out from Gloucester, Massachusetts, to fish the Grand Banks off Newfoundland. She was a big trawler, another former US military ship sold into private hands. She carried a crew of 15 men, each with his task of keeping the mammoth fisher afloat and functioning well. She had a fish hold capacity of 270,000 pounds, and her rugged captain, Axel Johannson, a sea savvy Scandinavian, intended to fill it to capacity with flounder and rosefish.

The voyage to the Grand Banks went smoothly enough and

so did fishing in its winter bleak waters. By January 12, the *Gudrun*'s hold contained 200,000 pounds of flounder and 40,000 pounds of rosefish. At this time she was keeping company with a Nova Scotian, the trawler *Blue Foam*. The buddy system is always good, especially in these waters. On a winter day it is a black and white world, something seen only in an old pencil etching. But pickings were getting sparse here now. So Johannson decided to leave the grounds to the *Blue Foam* and head 60 miles westward in order to pick up 30,000 pounds more of rosefish to fill his hold. He signaled the *Blue Foam* his intentions and set sail.

That was the last anybody saw of the weighty trawler. Over 100 feet of ship and 250 tons of steel vanished without trace. Fifteen men gone. And we know she went down. There is no confusion as in the case of the *Susan*. Johannson had sent a message that they were going down. It crackled over the radio receivers at the Coast Guard shore bases at 8:23 a.m. January 14. He stated they were sinking, and nothing else. RCC New York immediately picked it up. However, they were unable to get any messages back through to the ship. They thought the *Gudrun* must have gone under like a rock. Yet unknown to them other stations continued to pick up calls from Johannson for the next 25 minutes. He was picked up on no less than four frequencies, including two Canadian. He was so desperate he tried to reach any and all he could think of. Finally at 8:51 a.m. it fell silent. During this time no station on land, including closer Canadian stations, could get a message back through to the vessel.

The easiest explanation is that Johannson didn't take the time to wait for any messages. He flipped between the frequencies, quickly sending his distress. His men must have been preparing the lifeboat, and Johannson would wait until the last minute before he rushed to step aboard and push off.

Nothing seems amiss prior to the mayday. The *Gudrun* had

A mammoth like *Gudrun*.

sent regular messages. The *Blue Foam* had intercepted one wherein Johannson had told another vessel that he had gleaned 20,000 more pounds of rosefish from the Deep. This was 6 p.m. January 13.

Rescue was coordinated from several points, New York and Halifax being key in the search. Canadian and US aircraft overflew the area but saw nothing. The seas were gray and pitching, as they often are off the Grand Banks. A mild storm was stirring things up, but visibility was over ten miles. It was windswept, but the clouds were vapid and hung like pouting faces on the horizon.

The other fishermen were fine. They diverted course as best they could to look, but found nothing. US destroyers joined in (USS *Powers* and *Larsen*) and merchant vessels en route to the US or St. Lawrence Seaway scoured the area (s.s. *Mauretania*, *American Planter*, *American Scout*), yet other than the rocking waves nothing remained to explain the loss. For 5 days the Coast Guard searched. But the only clue was a lifeboat found by the *Blue Surf* some 60 miles northeast of the distress call.

According to the report it was found the day before, but this must be a typo. It was perfectly sound, only partially filled with water, floating right side up, food locker intact, and the lower boat fall still in the boat. Had the boat been ripped from the ship? It was stored on top of the pilot house aft with the other one, so that it seemed hard to believe it was ripped from the ship except when it went under. But why did the little lifeboat survive unscathed, but the large trawler slip below without clue? If the lifeboat had been launched, why had no man re-mained aboard?

The Coast Guard had to make some guesses. *Gudrun* was heavy at the time of her sinking. She was only 10,000 pounds short of her full capacity. But why should this matter? This is how the trawler earned her bread. She was equipped to handle 270,000 pounds. This was not an "ideal" amount. This was *her amount* to retrieve, and Axel Johansson did not set sail to sea for the sights. Fishing was the work and the hold was meant to hold yea so much. This was the work and *Gudrun* was the noble workhorse.

At 114 feet length and 23 feet abeam, she should be able to handle the rough seas, especially with her Navy built steel hull. She had a new General Motors 1200 horsepower engine, less than two years old. She was extensively refitted in 1949 at a cost in excess of $70,000 dollars.

But the Coast Guard accepted a rumor. "That the exterior doors which gave access to the athwartships passageway in the deckhouse were not watertight." And "That the exterior doors, which gave access to the space under the whaleback forward and thence, via an open companionway, to the crew's space below the main deck, were habitually left open at sea and that this practice permitted ingress of sea water from the main deck forward to the crew's space in heavy weather."

The investigators do not state where this rumor came from, but it wasn't very flattering to Johansson or his crew. In such heavy weather, habits change, of course. Who was to say that the doors were not closed? True, if not watertight there will be leakage. But had not the ship more than one pump? *Gudrun* had breasted some violent seas in the last 2 years off New England and Nova Scotia, why only now would water come pouring in? The Coast Guard assumed because the ship was heavy with her catch. But she had been heavy before. After all, that was her job.

Despite being full, *Gudrun* did not go down like a rock. Some 25 minutes between the first and last distress indicated there was enough buoyancy to abandon ship and hang on the radio. Desperate calls on 4 frequencies, Canadian and American, meant they knew they were lost. But it was not a quick death. They had time to launch boats, even while practically full in their fish hold. Why did none make it?

The Coast Guard deduced that she foundered, and even specifically declared that the foundering "was initiated by heavy seas flooding the crew's space forward through an open forecastle door and that the leakage through and around the deck house doors after might have been a contributing factor." Under more assumed conditions, the Coast Guard declared that the men could not launch a lifeboat successfully in the conditions which must have prevailed. Yet the lifeboat survived, and all life preservers, men and life rafts vanished in the Deep Six.

The loss of the *Paolina* is at an odd contrast to the others. The Coast Guard found two sides of her dory, another unmarked piece, a fishing buoy, and a section of a hatch cover. Then the next day another cutter discovered her 7 foot life raft and a life ring. The *Paolina*, it seems, left quite a trail. But the Guard found no survivor of her 7 men. In a somewhat tasteless way, the report is rather urging its readers to believe that there could have been no survivors, thus is must be understood why the Coast Guard halted the search and diverted to help what would become a very famous sea incident, the *Fort Mercer* and *Pendleton* casualties.

Storms had struck late in the search. The temperature was freezing. The Coast Guard was no doubt right that there were no survivors. But it is never easy to be squeezed into the position to openly say that when loved ones await news. Moreover, so much debris was found— and all the floatables upon which man might cling— so that an excuse must quickly be given but it must always enrage those who hear it. It's an unenviable position the Coast Guard has been put in too many times. It never looks good, and perhaps no excuses should be made. There was little chance by this time that the crew had survived. The books should merely have been closed without a statement indicating prioritizing. It came off very cold and calculated, and no one was happy with it.

The voyage of the *Paolina* began on February 6, 1952, out of New Bedford. Captain Frits Hokanson was on his way to Nantucket Lightship. On February 12, Hokanson was heard twice. At 1 p.m. he bespoke the *Agnes & Myrna*. He reported his position as 32 miles south southwest of the lightship. He had already caught 30,000 pounds of mixed fish. At 7 p.m. he spoke with the *Growler*, reporting himself in the same position. At midnight he was heading back to New Bedford, he said, in order to make the market on February 14. After this nobody ever heard from the *Paolina* until the Coast Guard found those silent reminders from the Deep.

A whole gale had whipped up, but Hokanson said nothing of that. The other vessels continued their fishing, riding waves and slashing the sleet. At over 60 tons and 73 feet long, the *Paolina* was more than capable of handling the weather. She had also had extensive dry docking just months before and her hull brought up to par. According to her owner, she had been "working a lot in the forecastle." Inspection not so surprisingly discovered fasteners were rusted and in some places gone. Eleven planks to starboard and thirteen to port were removed and refastened. "In addition to the foregoing, fasteners for the keel, various frames, and forefoots were renewed. The vessel was recaulked and bottom painted."

But she still went down. It's hard to say how. She left enough debris, so that she wasn't pulled down liked the others without warning. Everything that could float and save lives (and perhaps initially did) was found. Yet there had been no time for an SOS. Seven men went to the briny, and everything that could have saved them survived, the dory in pieces, the others untouched.

The *Doris Gertrude* was another scalloper. She was 73 feet and 60 tons. She was built in 1936 at Cape May, New Jersey, of thick wood frame and planking. She was in 1955 just shy of her 20th birthday. But she had been well-maintained in New Bedford, from where she left on January 11, 1955, to drag for scallops off the Georges Banks. It was the crowded time of year in those parts. She was in frequent communication with other vessels. At 11 a.m. on the 12th she had promised to check-in again with the *Marmax*. She had said that it would be at 11 p.m., after the nightly weather report. This would tell her captain what he was going to do.

The weather was icy and cold, the seas cavorting, but it was not unusual for that time of year. If the report was for worsening weather, she might jog.

At 5:50 p.m. *Marmax* tried to call *Doris* again, but she didn't reach her. At this time the *Doris Gertrude* was south of the Georges Banks while *Marmax* was north. Then 11 p.m. came and went and there was no contact from the *Doris Gertrude* as promised.

However, the vessel was fine. She was in company of the *Linus A. Eldridge*. Both started fishing together at midnight and continued until 3 a.m. January 13. The weather was indeed getting too choppy at this time, so the scalloper pulled in her nets and started drifting until she was out-of-sight of the *Eldridge*.

She was never seen again. Nor was a sound ever heard from her to indicate a problem.

Had there been a problem with her radio? *Marmax* did not pick her up at the expected time the night before, and when she had tried to hail her earlier at 5 p.m. she never got a response. Was *Doris*'s radio only being picked up close range?

Time is a factor here. She was not reported overdue until the 26th after so many others of her kin that had set sail for the Banks had long returned. This was 13 days *after* the vessel was last seen. There was little hope that anything would be found, and it is not surprising that the extensive Coast Guard search found no trace.

Nothing can really explain her loss. The Coast Guard dismissed the weather, as it was nothing untoward "for that location and season of the year." They even speculated that the boat could have been hit by a freighter, but they considered that remote. They considered fire, but that was only a perfunctory consideration. Could she have drifted onto a shoal spot "of which there are many on Georges Banks"? Possible, but one would think that the vessel would have left enough debris for other fishing vessels to have spotted some. A scalloper is a different type of fisher, though, and one of the Coast Guard guesses should be kept in mind. If she had started fishing again, "dragging in rough weather with one drag out," she could have been "pulled down to a considerable list by her own gear and swamped."

Such has happened before. But the official dry summation of events reminds us of the only known facts: "There was no indication of the vessel being in any difficulty. . .and no trace of the vessel or bodies has been found. . ."

There are many "ifs" in the case of the disappearance of the *Doris Gertrude*, but there are no facts to help explain her loss and those of her 11 men aboard.

These stories here, of course, are not merely written as mysteries of the sea to titillate our senses and start us into wistful fancies. The job of a traveler and writer is to bring many parts of the world, and an understanding of them, to all those who inquire. These events help place the New England fishermen and their jobs in context, for these tragedies and many others are well known to them. They have lost loved ones and friends to disaster. There are few who haven't been touched in these waters by the mystery and horror they can hold. They have searched for others and found nothing or have narrowly escaped death themselves. Yet daily they return to the sea. They know their chances. After years of fishing and marking another friend on the missing or dead list, the New England fisherman knows he rides not just a sea but a roulette dealing gamestress who loves her gambols. He still goes out in order to put fish on dinner tables around the country. He doesn't do this out of graciousness. It is his business. Nevertheless, it is not just cold hard cash earning that motivates him. What type of business has such danger to it that money alone can drive one? Few kinds of business have a life expectancy rating. The Gloucester fisherman is a philosophic breed. He must become one. He goes down to the sea in ships and he does business on great waters. The score is being marked against him with each voyage. At one point, his number will be up. His place will be taken by another. The cycle will continue. All are certain it will never be them who is called by Davey Jones. But many, many have been wrong.

This has continued on, and we can take up the narrative of cases in the 1970s. The disappearance of the scalloper *Navigator* is one example where the sea gave back only one clue: a body missing its hands and feet.

The vessel was listed missing between December 1 and 10, 1977, but no remains had been sighted in a rather intense Coast Guard search which entailed some 368 flight hours and 303 hours for the cutters, *Sherman, Active* and *Cape Horn*. (The total area of ocean searched was 104,000 square miles in which absolutely nothing was located even though the percentage for finding a ship was 99% and for a raft 97%.)

Yet one month after, on January 5, 1978, the Italian fisher *Corrado Secundo* while trawling 110 miles off shore hauled in a body in its nets. It was missing its hands and feet. The body was wearing a dungaree jacket and yellow foul weather gear. "Hot Dog" was written on the back of the jacket. A gruesome sight, the body had to be identified by a renewal form in the jacket pocket. This identified him as Richard W. Neild, a *Navigator* crewman.

Although the case of the *Navigator* is officially listed as undecided, it was noted that a squall had hit during her voyage. Other vessels in her vicinity (5 fishers) weathered it just fine, and it should be made clear that Neild was not wearing a PFD or an exposure suit. He either had no need for the suit or no time for the PFD.

The plot, however, had twists. There was an unconfirmed report that the *Navigator* was in contact with a woman named "Hilda" of Freeport, Massachusetts, on 7 December by way of Citizen Band Radio. If this was true it would put the *Navigator* afloat after the worst part of the squall. Unfortunately, no woman came forth to identify herself as this Hilda and confirm the rumor. But the Coast Guard did receive their quota of goofy phone calls. RCC Boston received a call on December 11 from a woman stating she was the wife of a *Navigator* crewman. She declared that her husband intended to sink the ship and then hung-up. Unusual for official inquiry, this made it into the formal report.

Anyway, in whatever way the *Navigator* perished, it must have been swiftly and strangely done and covered by the sea in order for any and every trace to go undiscovered. A strange feat indeed given her dimensions and construction: she was 72.9 feet long, had a beam of 20.4 feet, and was 71 net tons. She could carry 14.14 tons of fuel, 2.98 tons of fresh water and .48 tons of lube oil. Her wood hull was separated by two transverse watertight bulkheads between the forecastle and the fish hold; the other dividing the fish hold and the engine room. She also carried a 12 man dory and a 9 man inflatable Dunlop raft. Both were stowed on the pilot house. In addition there were reported to be 15 Type 1 Personal Flotation Devices, and also an undetermined number of exposure suits were believed on board.

Prior to sailing, the *Navigator* had been a ship well-maintained. She had gone through dry-dock and checked out; she was reefed out and the zincs were replaced; seams were recemented; the hull was scraped and repainted; and the radio equipment was inspected and in good condition. In fact, a somewhat biased attorney's statement was attached to the official report stating that the ship was in ". . .superb condition when left port." Nevertheless the Coast Guard countered the attorney's statements attached, declaring the repairs ". . .are not considered appropriate corrective safety measures for this type of casualty."

Yet officially the cause of the casualty was undetermined. What is sufficient for that?

Among those disappearances that have haunted New England waters there is one type which is far more remarkable than fishing vessels. The tugboat is the bulldog of the sea. Ugly, squat, mean and often indolent while at work. It pushes and shoves, jolts and drags. It is meant to be tough. It is bulldog and sheepdog. It herds and commands. Few wreck and even fewer simply vanish.

The *King Co-Bra* was 66.6 feet long, 16 feet wide, 52 gross tons. She had two diesel engines producing 1,000 horsepower. She was a sea going grunt. Yet she not only vanished but did so with split-second suddenness. The sudden and complete destruction of the vessel is underlined by the fact that the tug vanished late one night while rounding a headland.

The *King Co-Bra* left Grass Island Pier, Greenwich, Connecticut on January 2, 1979, en route to Camden, New Jersey, with a crew of 4 seamen. Her captain, Michael Cowen, reported to the owner via ship-to-shore radio off Atlantic City at 10:00 p.m. giving his ETA at Camden as between 12:00 p.m. and 2:00 p.m. January 3rd. Cowen's intent was to use the buoys off the coast of New Jersey as navigation aids. To do this he would attempt to stay 2 miles off shore. That was the last message heard from the tug.

The vessel was reported overdue at 10:35 p.m. on January 3 about 7 hours after it should have arrived. A "multi-unit air/sea search through 8 January found nothing positive." An oil slick was reported between buoys 8a and 8b off Cape Henlopen, Delaware, and investigated by the Coast Guard cutter *Cape Starr*, but the slick was not located. On January 14, over a week after the search was called off, a passerby at Lewes Beach, Delaware, discovered a life preserver with "King Co-Bra" stenciled thereon. Nothing else was added to the debris. This solitary item was it.

An investigation of the vessel's condition at the time of sailing found her to be seaworthy. The all-steel hull was strong and

A sea-going tug

in good condition. Her 3 VHP FM radios were operable when she left; the inflatable life raft was maintained and stored properly; the radar, depth sounder, and electrical and manual steering were all in order— thus shallow water and reefs couldn't take her by surprise.

An interesting speculation was advanced by the U.S. Coast Guard. When Cowen called the owner and gave his ETA— although he mentioned nothing unusual in the weather or the vessel's performance— he did mention one other thing; he reported he had been running on half speed (in rough seas ships reduce speed) but now was at full (10 kts). A squall had hit that night along the eastern coast and the highest winds were for the evening of January 2nd. Since Cowen signaled he was at full speed, with the implication that he was through the rough weather, the sea had apparently sufficiently calmed by 10 o'clock and business returned to usual. Was it premature? The Coast Guard thought that the accident might have happened ". . .just prior to or after rounding Cape May and entering Delaware Bay." This opinion was based on the experience of one of the *Co-Bra*'s previous operators who said that Delaware Bay would be hazardous in a flood tide and northwest winds. The Coast Guard agreed, since in entering the bay there would no longer have been any wind protection from the Jersey coast, making the seas there unexpectedly rough for the tug. Did the captain, at full speed, run the *King Co-Bra* into unexpected high winds and waves, and then founder?

In the disappearance of a fishing vessel, *Amazing Grace*, 80 miles off Cape Henlopen, Delaware, in 1984, the Coast Guard speculated that a tell-tale clue to its loss rose from the Deep after the prolonged Coast Guard search had failed to find any trace of the vessel. There seemed no other answer since it was unlikely the Coast Guard had missed such an item in their search. This was the fishing vessel's Givens life raft found floating in an area that, calculating by drift measurements, had been searched thoroughly on the previous days. Although they are much fewer than disappearances, re-appearances in the sea possess a curious quality, and all seem to play along the same theme. Parts of the vessel capable of carrying survivors, such as the lifeboats, are found deserted in areas after extensive searches sighted nothing.

It was, in its way, a gauntlet that the sea threw back, challenging or, perhaps better put, teasing us to come again. The Coast Guard picked it up and resumed an intensive search in the area with an excellent prognosis for finding any articles, but located only two other derelict 14-foot out-boards unrelated to the *Amazing Grace*.

The search for this 86-foot fishing vessel, a twelve million dollar undertaking involving 106 aircraft sorties, 564 aircraft hours flight time, and enveloping 192,146 square miles in 16 days, proceeded after a typical description of the missing vessel was broadcast to the Coast Guard by a concerned fishing vessel:

HIS HULL IS MAROON, TRIMMED WITH WHITE RIG-GING. THE HULL OF THE BOAT IS MAROON, RUSTY MA-ROON TRIMMED WHITE. SHE IS ABOUT EIGHTY FOOT LONG. ABOUT TWENTY FIVE FEET WIDE. WITH A BLUE-ISH SUPERSTRUCTURE.

Early the morning of November 14, 1984, the *Amazing Grace* had been only 10 nautical miles distant to the southwest from a sister fisherman, the *Atlantic Pride*. Both vessels were about 80 miles east of Cape Henlopen. Both vessels were also captained by brothers, Cecil Robles on the *Atlantic Pride*, and Paul Robles on the *Amazing Grace*. At this time, Paul Robles' mate, James Bowers (cousin of the two captains), had been in contact with the *Atlantic Pride* in order to arrange a transfer of supplies. It was a routine enough request. In response Cecil Robles then ordered his ship to make for his brother's vessel.

The seas had been choppy, but it really wasn't bad. Waves were about 8-10 feet; winds blowing from the northwest at 35 knots. However, the *Amazing Grace* must have caught an awkward wave with its hold open. An half hour later, Paul Robles reported to his brother that at the present time the crew were busy opening the freeing ports because they had taken a wave over the bow and some water had gotten into the fish hold. It was unfortunate, but a condition he expressed no concern about. Nevertheless, the rendezvous would have to be postponed at this time, for they were jogging toward shore.

The *Atlantic Pride* resumed fishing and was about 7 to 8 miles distant at the time of the last conversation.

Nothing particularly remarkable happened the rest of the day. The *Atlantic Pride* went about hauling in her catch. But later at 12 o'clock Cecil Robles took his mate's watch and attempted to call the *Amazing Grace*. Yet there was no response. He continued until midnight. Yet he received no answer. Radio problems can abound at sea, and the *Amazing Grace* may have already been close in to shore, blocked by a landfall or veiled by distance. Although concerned, Cecil Robles went to bed.

The next morning at 6 a.m., November 15, he awakened and discovered there still had been no message from the *Amazing Grace*. Even more concerned now, Robles attempted to call the U.S. Coast Guard to inquire if they had contact with the vessel, but received no reply here too. However, he was able to make contact with another fishing vessel, the *Carolina Princess*, fishing in the vicinity, and requested they relay a message.

At 10:37 a.m. the Coast Guard received the following call:

> Group Cape May, Group Cape May, this is the (Garbled) *Carolina Princess*, Group Cape May can you hear me? Over. What we are calling you about (Garbled) is if you have seen or heard of the *Amazing Grace*. The Trawler *Amazing Grace*. Yesterday morning at seven thirty was the last time anyone had contact with him. He had water in his ice box, water in the engine room (Garbled) but he was not going to worry about it, to see if he could pump it out. But no one has had real contact with him since. We haven't been able to get no radio contact out of the man whatsoever. We need to see if you can locate him or to look around to see if he is in Cape May. We don't know what to do about it. . . He cut out when he found out what happened and he said he'd get back. We called the Atlantic and everyone has called him, but we have not been able to get him. . .over.[15]

The Coast Guard initiated an immediate communications search to raise the vessel. Vessels most near the suspected area of the trawler were also requested to begin a search. These

---

[15] The captain of the *Carolina Princess* later corrected his mistake in official testimony and said that he meant the fish hold not the engine room.

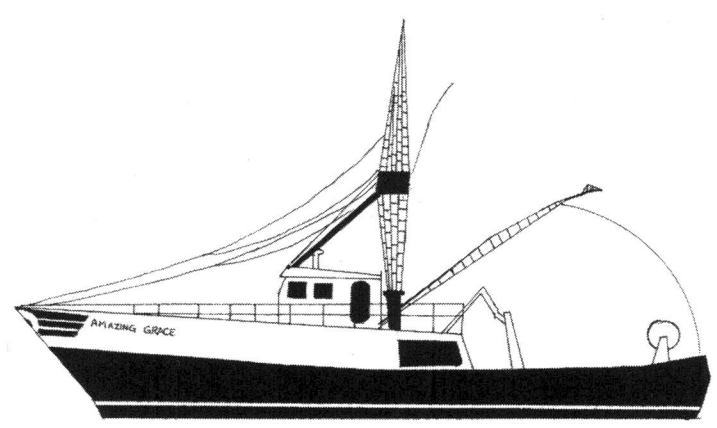

The *Amazing Grace*

ships, the *Captain Malc, Atlantic Pride* and *Carolina Princess,* began searching on the 15th and by that night were joined by other fishing vessels, the *Carolina Lady, Carolina Girl, Carolina Tarheel,* and *Carolina Dream.* Besides this effort, there was also an "All-Points Bulletin" broadcast to all vessels off New Jersey, Delaware and Maryland to be on the lookout for the trawler.

The official action began that afternoon. A Coast Guard jet from Cape Cod and a helicopter from Cape May started a quadrant by quadrant search in the area about 80 miles off Cape Henlopen, easily spotting the fishing fleet below. Also the cutters *Cape Bataan* and *Cape Starr* (the latter later recalled) were also dispatched with another helicopter to supplement the growing search efforts. This impressive amount of manpower and machines was coordinated by the two hundred-ten-foot cutter *Chilula.* Her command bridge calculated the computations at 66% chance of sighting the *Amazing Grace* in the conditions that prevailed. On November 19 the computations were shifted to the probability of finding a life raft when it was obvious the *Amazing Grace* was not afloat. A good 90% chance was forecast.

Now that by-chance discovery yielded that fateful clue. On November 21 the Danish ship *Clifford Maersk* pulled aboard the *Amazing Grace*'s Givens life raft, contacted the Coast Guard and read the numbers over the radio. The Coast Guard immediately traced it to the *Amazing Grace*. This unexpected find prompted the Coast Guard to begin another search in that area. The weather was considered "ideal."

Nevertheless, the results were disappointing. On November 30, the search was discontinued and the subsequent investigation concluded: "The National Transportation Safety Board is unable to determine the probable cause of the loss of the *Amazing Grace*." That wasn't enough. The Board also seemed to have ruled out every possible scenario: "The *Amazing Grace* did not sink due to an explosion, fire, structural failure, or scuttling." The conclusions do, however, go on to state a theory. "The *Amazing Grace* may have capsized and sunk due to continuing pull on one of its clam dredge's wire cables after the clam dredge was snagged on the ocean bottom."

Like a scalloper, the *Amazing Grace* dredged the bottom, and thus the suspicion by the Board was not unwarranted. It had been considered in the case of the *Doris Gertrude*, for nothing else seemed to be able to explain a clean disappearance. But as in that case, it was a guess here too. There was no evidence to support it and, quite frankly, there was evidence to contradict it. The last message of Paul Robles contains that evidence. He stated he was not fishing but jogging to shore.

What did happen? Like in the case of the many others, only the sea knows.

Reservations were expressed about the cause for the loss of the fishing vessel *Heidi Marie* of Stonington, Connecticut, when months after her disappearance another fishing vessel, the *Sophie G.*, owned by the same enterprise, was exposed as being scuttled to receive the insurance money. However, investigations conclusively proved that the *Heidi Marie* was, in fact, legitimately lost at sea with five crew on Tuesday, November 21, 1989.

The Coast Guard began to search for the *Heidi Marie* after she failed to contact her owner, James P. Garbo. In the meantime they had also been tracking an auto-alarm beacon determined as coming from the fishing vessel. It was emanating from about 150 miles southeast of New York over the underwater Hudson Canyon. While searching the area on Sunday the 26th, already 5 days after the ship had presumably been lost, the Coast Guard saw the first of the several brief lights on the ocean that possibly may have been flares.

The first one was seen from a cutter, then another from a jet. The color of these lights ranged from three white, one red, and one orange. On Monday the 27th two more lights were seen; and on Tuesday, a week after the loss, the last light was seen and soon extinguished. During this hide-and-seek of fading lights, the Coast Guard rescuers were led on a merry chase attempting to track them down. However, the sources of the lights could never be specifically determined.

The frustration of coming upon an empty sea when they thought they had arrived at the source of the lights was expressed by the coordinator of the search operations, Admiral Rybacki:

We'll never know if we were seeing signals for help, the lights were so far away and lasted just a few seconds. . .Each time we had a sighting, it gave us new hope as we sent ships and aircraft to investigate. Despite a thorough search, we were disappointed each time to find no one in the area.

One Guardsman expressed his consternation over the fleeting flares (or lights) in a more explanatory way: "It might be a mile away, or it might be 30 miles away. There are no geographical references at all on the ocean. On land there are mountains and hills, but on the ocean, all you've got is the horizon."

During this rather depressing week-long search for the light sources, the Coast Guard was also intermittently picking up scattered debris. On the previous Friday (the 24th) the *Heidi Marie*'s fishing markers were found. So too was a radar reflector, wood beams, and lobster pots; and one of *Heidi Marie*'s EPIRBs was found. All the material indicated that the vessel had been obliterated.

A novel proposition for finding the missing lobster boat was provided by Givens, the makers of the most commonly used life rafts. The president of the company made a statement that the crew could be alive if they had gotten into the raft as the rafts have a built-in rain catcher, storage for foods and can, moreover, withstand 35 foot seas and 190 mph winds. Givens suggested that a spy plane with cameras could fly over the area and photograph it; the photographs could then be studied and the raft spotted.

The Coast Guard, however, concentrated their search efforts a little closer to the ocean. This effort, except for the minimal debris found, produced sad results and the search was discontinued on December 1, 1989, with the definite cause of the lobster fisher's fate unknown.

These and many other have vanished over the years. The number has grown fewer, fortunately, with modern advances in radio and emergency automatic alarms, stronger hull constructions and better training of crews and reading of the weather. The seafarer is still in a stubborn lot. But time has convinced him he needs a bigger edge against that temptress. Computer technology and education has helped immensely. But time has taught the seafarer the greatest respect for the New England seas, and this has taught him caution. To this we owe a higher survival rate today. Yet once in a while a ship, stronger and greater than those before, vanishes and leaves no clue. Its loss is a reminder that the sea still watches covetously over her territory and takes what tithes she sees fit.

But they still go down to the ship in ships. They still do business on great waters. . . .And this accords the sailorman a greater respect than the sea.

PART IV

High Seas Hijinks

CHAPTER NINE

The Pirates of Malacca

The Jakes Ladder Theater Company discovered a rather un-flattering origin of their hired parrot Percy. While rehearsing for a children's television show at the Blandford Forum in the west of England, Percy was set proudly upon the shoulder of the actor playing Long John Silver. Everything went well and *Pirates of Treasure Island* looked like it would run smoothly that night on the telly playhouse. However, Percy suddenly let out with a string of filth contrary to the director's orders.   In

stead of saying pieces of eight, Percy said "piss off mate." Then
he told a couple to bloody well "bugger off." This not only got
Percy sacked, but it made some people curious as to Percy's origins. He was a 17 month old parrot, supposedly of a fine pet
store cultivation and Amazon breeding, who had apparently
quite an unsavory connection with dockside lingo.

There are a number of reasons why Percy excited some attention. Piracy at sea had hit an all-time high in 1999. Thus
when a parrot turned to acting gigs revealed he had less than a
store pedigree his past doings had to be looked into.

Technically, any interdict of a ship on its course, any rob-
bery of a vessel or persons aboard, is classed legally as a piratical
act by the International Marine Bureau in London, which de-
fines piracy specifically as "the act of boarding any vessel with
the intent to commit theft or other crime and with the capability to use force in the furtherance of the act." However, the
1990s saw the reemergence of the old style of piracy. Ships were
boarded, then the entire crew was made to walk the plank,
thrown off the ship or, in one case, bound and gagged and
drowned in the ocean. The pirates then took the ship and its
cargo to another port. Sometimes members of the crew were
spared to help run the vessel or, on occasion, one of the officers
or engineers already on board had been an insider for the pirates.

Ships laden with cargo were not always the object of the pirates. Sometimes empty vessels were taken and then used to
pick up cargos and ply trade for a while. Secluded islands and
free thinking Southeast Asian ports made it easy to sequester
even large freighters, and when the pirates were through with
them they could be sunk or merely abandoned.

It can happen all over the world, but geopolitics hasn't
caused much to change. "Piracy flourishes where it always has:
in the Caribbean where Henry Morgan and Blackbeard once
ruled the waves, off north Africa where corsairs once plundered
the Barbary Coast, in the far east where the pirate junks of the

famed chieftain Ching Yih were the scourge of the South China Sea. . .” declared *The Cargo Letter*, the news bulletin of the Law Offices of Countryman & McDaniel. The politics of these regions makes it easier for pirates to evade capture and make it to a friendly port. But only one reason has made Southeast Asia the hottest pirate zone in the world. It is a geographic one. There is one passage through which most of world shipping passes on their voyages through Indochina: the dreaded Strait of Malacca. This relatively narrow passage off Malaya is unavoidable. It is the gateway between east and west and has been since Marco Polo sailed through here to China. At its narrowest part it is comprised of smaller channels. One is the Singapore Strait. Another is the Philip Strait.

Along these forested shores numerous pirate nests exist. Sequestered lagoons hold speedboats. Limited by the reduced speed of vessels lined-up to go through the narrowest part of the Strait, the lumbering freighters are sitting ducks. Pirate speedboats zoom out and bring their buccaneer hordes. They stay in the narrow void behind the ship's smokestack where the radar sweep cannot detect them. They swarm aboard, wielding their machetes and swords. Unarmed and taken by surprise, the freighter crews were at the mercy of sword swirling villains. . . in tennis shoes.

For example, on January 16, 1999, pirates did just this to the huge super tanker *Chaumont*. They knew enough to stay in the “radar shadow” created by her large funnel. Before the crew was aware, pirate minions had crawled aboard. The deck watch was overwhelmed. Crewmen ran to their quarters and locked themselves in. Officers were beaten and the master's safe was looted. For 30 minutes the huge vessel sailed on in treacherous waters without anybody at the helm, yet mercifully never running aground and spilling its thousands of gallons of crude oil.

The Strait of Malacca is a natural narrow waterway, but it is little known in the western world because it is not the result of

The Strait of Malacca. Long and narrow, it is the main gateway east and west.

engineering. There are no stories celebrating the daring ingenuity as there is in the digging of the Panama Canal or the Suez. But the Strait of Malacca is just as important. Over 500 billion dollars in commerce comes and goes through here. Some 200 ships per day. It is truly the gateway of Indochina. Every flag flutters from thousands of ships each year.

But it cannot be watched and guarded like the manmade canals. The shores of the strait are wild jungles and mangrove swamps. Festering in them, the pirates watch their targets through binoculars. They strike quickly. But they do not strike randomly. They select their ships and, as in the case of the *Chaumont*, clearly understand its blind spots and layout.

These pirates, like all pirates of old, are able-bodied seamen. They have eyes and ears in every port, and they know when ships are leaving and how valuable their cargos are. They are crudely confident, as the attack on the *Chaumont* shows. She was one of many ships taking their turn through this narrow area of the Malacca Strait. There isn't much the other ships' crews could have done. They can simply watch the speedboats zoom up. In some cases they see bursts of smoke as gun battle ensues and then through their binoculars the shocked crews of lingering freighters watch the hordes scurry up to the deck of the chosen victim.

The *Chaumont*, as one of the largest tankers in the world, was not a likely choice to steal. The pirates were petty this day. They merely robbed the valuables and beat the crew. But by 1999 this was becoming rare. Pirates were so bold now that they were taking the entire ships and transferring or selling their cargo in other ports.

These are the genuine pirates of modern day Malacca. They are high-tech seagoing mafia with buyers waiting for the cargos and with tipsters telling them what ships will be vulnerable. They have many disguises and use many means. But one thing they never change: boldness is their MO. They strike from Malacca or they venture out from here to the Bay of Thailand. Coming or going ships must face the Strait of Malacca and take their chance of being next or being surveyed and targeted with deadly intent, and then being the next victim in the Bay.

It got to the point where ship captains and crews were "scared strait." By June 1999 it was clear that the unbridled piracy in this area was dangerous to world commerce. Some 10 ships had been attacked and boarded in the nearby Singapore Straits in the first 3 months of 1999 alone. This was up from 2 the year before. The Singapore Navy and Coast Guard, in tandem with the Indonesian Navy, coordinated patrols. But there seemed little chance of stopping them this way. "Pirates today are well aware of the loopholes that have been created for them and they are not slow to exploit them, escaping from one country's waters to another, knowing that they will not be pursued or prosecuted. . ." declared the IMO.

Waters teemed with sharks as astounded fishermen closed in on a small lifeboat wallowing under the weight of 21 men. They were the entire crew of the *Marine Master*. Pirates had seized their large freighter on March 21, 1999, and set them adrift. In this case, the pirates had the courtesy to bring the tiny raft along in order to pitch the crew off into the sea. These were some of the more civilized pirates. All fortunately survived in the dangerous Burmese waters.

As the case of the *Marine Master* demonstrates, the pirates of Malacca were that confident in the laws protecting them that they could be generous and allow witnesses to survive. But there were occasions in which none of the crew survived. The fate of many was summed up like the M/V *9 Sea Star 4*. She was a smaller vessel, only 461 gross tons. She left Hong Kong with 8 crewmen on October 14, 1999, for Thailand, and was never seen again. Notices asked for anyone who spotted the vessel to please relay it to the International Marine Bureau's piracy reporting center. But "the length of time since the ship was last sighted makes it unlikely that it will be seen again unless reports of its arrival or loss have 'slipped through the net' and this is merely a case of misreporting."

These reservations rang true for all incidents as ticker tape message after ticker tape message came over the machines at shipping bureaus, legal offices and insurers, declaring a new mystery. A typical one:

M/V *Chosun Hope*, with 9,000 tons of jute from Bangladesh for Brazil; *Okavanga*, with 5000 tons of urea from Indonesia for Vietnam vanished.

Pirates have proven themselves adept at disposing of ships no longer wanted. The M/V *Alondra Rainbow* had provoked a huge search after being kidnapped on October 22, 1999. Ten pirates with pistols and swords had scampered aboard the vessel near Thailand. They transferred the crew to the smaller vessel they had arrived in, towed them in this, and then a week later set them adrift in a 20 man life raft, with minimal food and water. They drifted for 10 days before they were rescued by fishermen. But the *Alondra Rainbow* thereafter vanished.

The large vessel was finally recognized on November 16 by the Indian Coast Guard about 200 miles off Goa. When hailed, the captain returned that the vessel was the Belize flagged *Mega Rama*, bound from Manila. The Coast Guard checked the registry, and stood by. This proved no such vessel existed. The vessel was hailed again and told to stop and prepare to be boarded. Nevertheless, the no-named ship continued, forcing the Coast Guard to fire warning shots across her bow. She still refused. Finally, the Coast Guard opened up directly on the vessel. Only then did the vessel stop and the pirate crew rush for cover. They set fire to the vessel in an attempt to destroy its paperwork, and the engineer opened the intake valves in an attempt to scuttle her. However, the Coast Guard was aboard by this time and was able to save the vessel. The long ordeal of the *Alondra Rainbow* finally came to an end.

The Cargo Letter of the law offices of Countryman & McDaniel for November 1999 recapped how piracy was becoming rampant. For 1999 the case numbers were up some 202 reported attacks from 1998. "But, officials say, most high seas crimes never get reported. According to the International Marine Bureau, a ship can be hijacked to order for US $300,000 in the Philippines and delivered in 3 days."

A good example is the 1995 case of the *Anna Sierra*. Carrying 5 million dollars in sugar, she left Bangkok under Cypriot ownership on September 12, and was headed for Manila. As such she didn't have to beware the Strait of Malacca. However, while still in the Bay of Thailand, 30 masked men sped alongside in speedboats and scrambled up to her decks. They put all 23 alarmed crew adrift in rafts and steered the ship over the horizon. Thus the *Anna Sierra* vanished.

Clearly the pirates had put a close watch on ships while in harbor and selected them prior to their departure. They know their cargos and plan to take both ship and cargo to a safe and profitable modern Tortuga. In this case, however they were not aware that the crew made it to fishermen quickly. Piracy alerts were posted.

Several days passed and the ship was recognized in the Chinese port Beihai. The pirates had made a ghastly spelling mistake in the new name they had chosen— "Artic Sea" rather than "Arctic Sea." Also, the original name was still visible beneath the shallow new veneer of paint.

Chinese officials staked-out the freighter and finally went aboard. The crew was placed under guard. "Then began a 9 month war of words and paper to ascertain ownership," presented the Cargo Letter. "After endless wrangling, the authorities gave up. The pirates were sent home to Indonesia. The ship was abandoned by its owner and, to this day, sits rusting in a Chinese port. The losers: the companies that insured its ship and cargo."

This was one of the first examples where a major band of the Malaccan pirates was captured and yet still released. The reasons, of course, were many fold. Piracy in 1995 was only beginning to rear its head on such a bold scale. The level of organization to which it could go was not even fathomed at that time . . .though for years there were isolated events that showed how

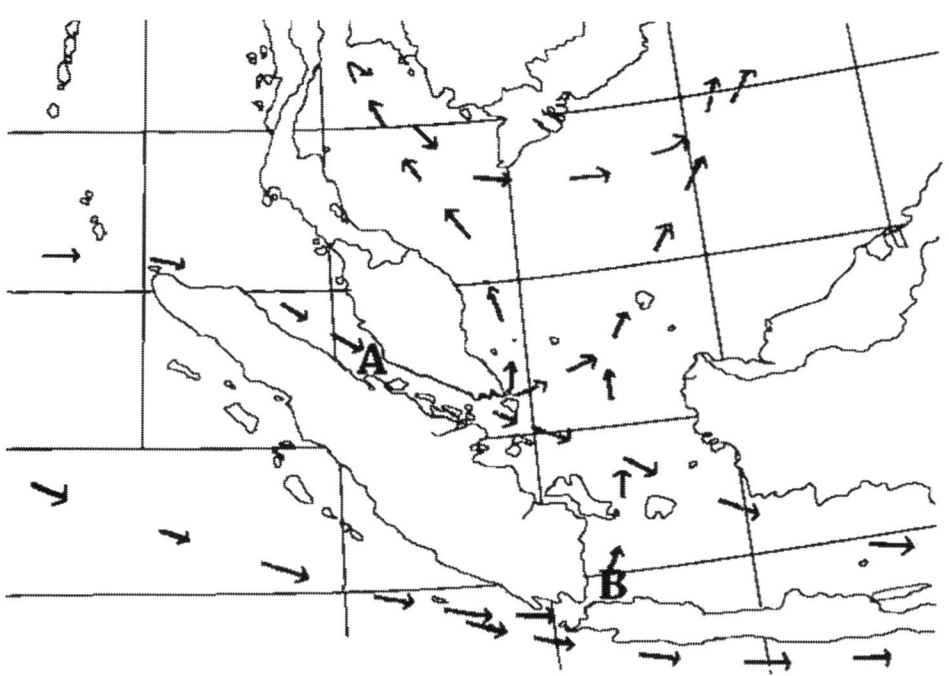

A is the Strait of Malacca. B is the Sunda Strait. Arrows mark the major shipping lanes to China and Australia.

bold and rehearsed the pirates were getting in their attacks.

Previously in June, the *Hye Mieko*, flying the Singapore flag, was hijacked off Cambodia. A small vessel had come alongside. For all intents and purposes it was painted to appear to be a Chinese customs launch. Yet it was a pirate ship. The freighter was forced to sail 1,600 miles to Shanwei, China. This entire time the event was being broadcast around the world. Yet no ship came to its rescue. The only person who did was the owner. He followed it in a small plane. Upon arrival in Shanwei the *Hye Mieko* was impounded. When the owner arrived at the airport he was detained and charged with smuggling cigarettes.

"He was detained," wrote the Cargo Letter, "to cover the crime."

Why is it such a surprise that the high tech pirates of Malacca became bolder and more organized after 1995? They simply did not worry about ships pursuing them and China was becoming a new Tortuga. Because of this, piracy hit epidemic proportions and there was no need for them to curtail their violence. A safe haven awaited them. "In the first 9 months of 1997 pirates killed 45 seafarers, which was a 73% rise over the previous year. The Kuala Lampur Regional Piracy Center, the branch of the IMB, reported: 'While the numbers of piratical attacks have reduced from the same period last year, it should be noted that there has been an increase in the severity of the attacks.'"

When the books were closed on 1997, there were a recorded 247 pirate assaults that year. Fifty-one deaths resulted; thirty people injured. In 1998 the attacks were only 198, yet more deaths occurred. Some 67 crewmen were murdered. Noel Choong, of the IMB, confirmed the trend was holding. "The pirates are getting increasingly violent. Years ago, they would steal the cargo, loot the ship's safe, and rob the crewmen. These days the pirates are increasingly brazen. They steal the entire ship and kill the crew.

By far the most tragic case happened in January 1999. The *Cheung Son* was sailing the South China Sea when she was boarded. Each and every crewmen, 23 men in number, were bound, gagged, and weighted and then flung over the sides to drown. A few days later 6 of the bodies were brought up in fishermen's nets, still bound and gagged. This was the first evidence authorities had that the bulk carrier had been kidnapped.

Chinese officials arrested 7 persons suspected of having been in some way involved in planning or carrying out the event. But the ship remained missing.

It was more than prescient that in November 1998 the IMB made yet another impassioned call for stronger laws. Although it asked for all regional governments to help crush the piracy, the plea was really aimed at China. At this time yet another freighter was missing and feared secluded in a Chinese port.

The *Tenyu* was a smaller freighter that had disappeared in September after having left Indonesia with a cargo of aluminum ingots worth 4.3 million dollars. The IMB suspicions turned out right. Five months after it vanished it was discovered under a new flag and with a new name in Zhangjiagang, a port near Shanghai. It was named *Sanwei-1* and flew the Honduran flag. It now had 16 Indonesian crewmen instead of its South Korean captain and chief engineer and 12 Chinese crewmen, all of whom were still missing and feared murdered.

There is no question that this ship's disappearance was a carefully premeditated act. Shortly after *Tenyu* had vanished, the ingots had been purchased and sold to a Chinese company (in October). Nevertheless, Ms. Guo Xin, the PRC delegate to the IMO, defended China's move to repatriate the men. The visas and passports they carried proved they came aboard ship later than the hijacking and that they could not have anything to do with it. This spin might have looked good to an uninformed audience, but according to Countryman & McDaniel: ". . .the IMB claimed that it was certain that the chief mate on the *Tenyu* when it arrived in China was the same man who had been 2nd mate on an earlier hijacked ship, the M/V *Anna Sierra*. The crew operating that ship was also released by the Chinese authorities."

At the same time as this controversy was brewing there was hope that the *Siam Xanai*, which was also found in Chinese waters, after having been hijacked in Malaysia, would be returned to its rightful owners. Only one of the Thai crewmen had been forcibly kept aboard to help run the ship. The other 16 were thrown from the vessel. Ten of those who sailed the vessel into China were supposedly arrested by the authorities after they put an embargo on the tanker. But China still kept the tanker.

The same can be said for other vessels. In October 1998 China showed no cooperation after the pirated Malaysian ship *Petro Ranger* was found at Hainan. Instead of extraditing the 12 suspected seamen as hoped, they released them. The ship had been hijacked, coincidently also by 12 pirates, while en route for Ho Chi Minh City. The captain and crew had been tortured. Some of the 9,574 tons of gas oil and kerosene had been sold by the pirates and the rest was seized but the Chinese government before they finally let the ship sail.

But the brutal piracy of the *Cheung Son* in 1999 had brought things to a head. Suspected pirates in that case, along with detainees suspected in other cases (totaling 38 men), were finally brought to trial in Shanwei. The pirates were all Chinese except for one Indonesian. They had pirated everything from ingots to gasoline. They had been a large gang posing as anti-smuggling police, and by this method they had hijacked 3 vessels in 1998. The trial began December 10 and lasted for 6 days of testimony. Some of this included how some of them killed the 23 members of the vessel. They had bludgeoned the men before throwing them over. The pirates were sentenced to death.

At the same time as these pirates were being brought to trial, the search had finally ended for a freighter turned international pirate ship. The *Kobe Queen I* had vanished en route to the Dominican Republic in August with a cargo of 15,000 metric tons of steel worth 5 million dollars. She had sailed in July from Istanbul and stopped at Dakar (another hotspot of piracy). After Dakar, the captain, Yuri Levkosky, was supposedly contacted by the owners in Odessa, Babush Marine, and detoured. Yet neither would give details to the authorities on the new location. The ship bunkered at Cape Verde, put in at Lagos, then stood off the coast of Nigeria. In Lagos it was discovered the vessel had taken aboard 6 weeks of fuel and supplies. Then it effectively vanished. When the vessel failed to arrive and it was discovered that it had been told to alter course and the captain had refused to ever elaborate, the *Kobe Queen I* was declared a criminal ship and sought by all world governments.

The extent to which the international pirate networks were intertwined can be found in how the global sea chase finally found the ship off Pondicherry, India. On 24 December 1999, the Madras Lloyd's of London agents, Wilson & Co. Ltd., spotted the vessel anchored off the coast. She was now sporting the improvised name *Gloria Kopp*.

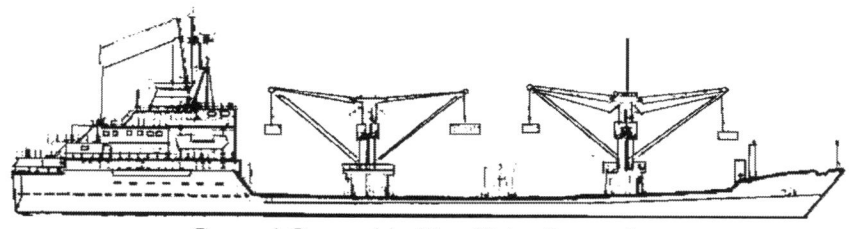

General Cargo ship like *Kobe Queen I*

The pirates were ever-vigilant, however. The ship's watch was keen enough to spot the Coast Guard cutter *Vikram* when still about 6 and one half miles distance and closing. *Kobe Queen* was still within the territorial waters. They quickly weighed anchored and departed. They had the advantage of oncoming foul weather. The sea was already getting choppy, but the huge *Kobe Queen* simply cut through the waves while the *Vikram* bobbed about.

At some 13.5 miles off shore in international waters the pirates felt safe. But the *Vikram* still bore down, fighting the seas and preparing for gunfire. In the distance behind her two Naval vessels had joined the pursuit.

It was clear from the bridge of the pirate ship that with support coming *Vikram* was not going to give up. At this point the pirates rang out with gunfire. The *Vikram* responded. The bursts of smoke continued to belch out from both ships. Amaz-

ingly, the *Vikram* was able to come alongside and the guards-
men boarded the vessel.

A deck battle finally got the Ukrainian crew to surrender.
Yet captain Levkoskey was not amongst them. It is somewhat
confusing as what actually had happened aboard. Supposedly
the chief mate was sent under guard to get the captain in his
cabin. When he opened the door there was Levkoskey hanging
from a nylon rope. Another report said death was by a single
shot. What actually did happen? Was Levkoskey merely a prisoner of the pirate crew and did they hang him at the end in order to place the blame on him or was he truly the scoundrel that
led them?

Piracy ebbed in the early 21st century due to China finally
obliging and trying some of the suspected pirates. Incidents
were down markedly by 2006. But something disturbing was
happening. Trend would be too strong a word, but on occasion
it seemed the pirates were accompanied by militant Islamists.
This had rather alarming ramifications, one which I was sensitive to since December 2001.

On September 11, 2001, I was made painfully aware, as we
all were, of terrorists and their boldness and brutality. . .and the
lengths they would go to carry out their plans. But for me there
was a sense of guilt. Due to my world reputation on the subject
of the Bermuda Triangle, I was often a point of contact by Moslems. The Bermuda Triangle is quite a serious topic to them,
and many Moslems believe it is mentioned with great significance in the Quran. Being regarded as the world authority on
the topic, I grew accustomed to Moslems asking me questions
or just passing along to me why the area and Bermuda has great
meaning. Therefore when in the summer of 2000 and 2001
emailers claiming to be students from Kabul requested my help
in getting them MD-80s to charter for a tour of the Triangle, I
thought little more of it than to dismiss them as an extremist religious sect within Islam. I didn't bother to respond to the
number of requests.

Then on September 11, 2001, we all know what happened. I couldn't help but wonder if those who had organized the tragic attack had been behind the emails to me as one way of trying to get jumbo jets without going to the trouble of hijacking.

By this time the emails had long been deleted from my system and I thought there was little reason in contacting the authorities. However, by December 2001 emails started again. My unusual name and Moslems' deep belief in revelation by dreams was responsible. One Pakistani merchant mariner, a Moslem "who believes in nothing but peace and love," he was quick to clarify, said he had a dream. In this dream he was to encounter two men who would be instrumental in leading him to the last Imam. A number of Moslems believed the last Imam would be revealed on a throne rising from the sapphire sea. This had to be the island of Bermuda. He agreed with this, too. He became convinced by a string of coincidences that could not ultimately be coincidence.

In his dream he would first meet a man whose name would mean "shank of beef." The second man's name would mean "god of beginnings." While after I had regrettably gained weight some may have associated me with a shank of beef, the Pakistani merchant marine officer had already met him. He was a Saudi. My name, my ever-strange name, is not so strange to any Italian. Gian is simply the Italian form of Latin Janus— the god of beginnings. I had qualified my name's meaning on my website's Q&A page, and it was this that electrified my young merchant mariner pen pal. Put together this was proof that Bermuda was the throne, and I was the key to the future of his quest for the revelation of the last Imam to all mankind.

I decided to answer this email.

Basically, I was in my "I Spy" mode. I wanted to know who the ye old "shank of beef" was. Finally, to convince me, my Pakistani merchant mariner copied me and the Saudi, whom I shall call Masam. This is what I wanted, for I quickly began to detect that the Pakistani, whom I shall call Misam, was only a patsy. It turned out to my satisfaction that I was right. Masam was pushy. I was to help get them into the United States or Bermuda. They lamented that they couldn't get into either at this time because of the terrorist attack and the borders were closed to anybody with passports from their countries. They were peaceful and loving. They were merely the victims of current events, but their sacred quest must go on. I was in his dreams too. It all came down to me, Bermuda, and the US of A.

During this exchange I caught Masam and Misam in some lie. I forget what it was now. It wasn't a big one, but they were hardly religious fanatics desperately trying to get into Bermuda or the United States to pay reverence to their last Imam. Something sounded more like "Alu Akbar!" I told them the obvious: that the Bahamas was their only compromise. But they weren't into that.

In fact, it was hard to make out what they wanted aside from wanting in America. The conversation ceased when I wouldn't help them. Were they terrorists? This I will never know. But their front was false. There is no doubt Masam lied. I still think Misam was nothing but a patsy. In retrospect, I still consider it. If they were, I probably was just one minor point of contact in a greater network trying to forge solid contacts to get into America quietly via maritime means. . .and the back door.

But if Masam was a terrorist, it told me they were now snooping around the Merchant Marine and Florida/Bahamas. Through Cuba large amounts of drugs secretly come into the USA. The thousands of islets and keys around southern Florida make it a handy place for smugglers, as the Coast Guard is all-too-often aware. These are violent and clandestine coasts, and it is impossible for the Coast Guard to patrol them minutely. Innocent tourists have been executed gangland style for stumbling casually across drug drop-off points.

Yet far more dangerous things could be smuggled in. Dirty spent nuclear fuel could easily be manipulated through Cuba or the Bahamas and barrel by barrel brought into the US through southern Florida's jungle coasts and sequestered lagoons. The Triangle has proven the perfect place to kidnap yachts and ultimately the best cover. Few if any missing yachts, which are so common, are investigated. The Coast Guard may assume piracy, the public forum the infamous Bermuda Triangle, but these yachts can in fact, and often are, still around and trafficking illegal cargo. The method for seizing boats and shipping dirty spent fuel wouldn't be any different than the method for kidnapping a vessel to use it as a drug runner. Once enough dirty fuel was stockpiled in America, a dirty bomb could be built in a rental house, abandoned warehouse, wherever, in any American town, and set off as a reprisal.

There were other, more general but just as alarming implications. Ships could be their next victims. . .or weapons, and American ports their new targets. A desire to get a new brand of terrorist specialist in the country, and in especially around here, had alarming ramifications.

Whatever the truth behind these two curious correspondents, the intelligence community had already anticipated weaknesses in this area. The September attacks turned paranoia to our benefit, and no theoretical stone of violence was left unturned.

In late 2001 the International Chamber of Commerce reported: "It is not impossible that hijackers or terrorists could hijack ships, particularly LNG, LPG, or large tankers to undertake suicide missions for their cruise. Forged ship documents and crew travel documents can easily be obtained with the right connections."

The ICC comments were informed. They were well aware of the Malacca pirates and their "ship to order" sidelight industry. At $300,000 a head, a ship could be taken and secluded. But their comments were also prescient. Minor terrorist attacks had already been made on ships, like the USS *Cole* (October 2000).

If terrorists had not shrunk from attacking a warship, their boldness would easily be directed now at unarmed merchant ships after their 9/11 success.

Sure enough in October 2002 the ICC's worst fears were realized. The oil tanker *Limburg* was hit. This was getting too close to home. Blowing up one of these babies in a crowded port would engulf it in flames.

In November 2002 counter-terrorism agents worked quickly. Abd al-Rahim al-Nashiri was arrested. He had been identified as the operational commander for the al-Qaeda network in the Gulf of Aqaba region. Supposedly, he was their maritime operations specialist. Allegedly, Nashiri was also behind the planning end of the attacks on the *Cole* and *Limburg*. Interrogation yielded some valuable information. Al-Qaeda was interested in super-tankers, "particularly their vulnerability to suicide attacks and the economic impact of such operations." This information came from an unnamed security official who let it spill in Lebanon's *Daily Star* newspaper. He said that al-Qaeda terrorists "actually have a naval manual on this. It tells them the best places on the vessels to hit, how to employ limpet mines, fire rockets or rocket-propelled grenades from high-speed craft and turn liquefied natural gas (LNG) tankers into floating bombs. They are also shown how to use fast craft packed with explosives and the use of trawlers, or ships like that, which can be turned into bombs and detonated beside bigger ships or in ports where there are often petroleum or gas storage areas that could go up as well. They even talk of using underwater scooters for suicide attacks."

With this, of course, the Strait of Malacca raises its strategic head. Where would be the best place to strangle world commerce but at that natural choke hold on world shipping? About 50,000 ships pass through there each year. Sinking a huge oiler there, it was feared, could close or significantly restrict the channel.

But this thinking was about as narrow as the channel. Even

a huge sunken ship can be blown to pieces quickly enough to allow commerce to continue. Terrorist attacks on the area also wouldn't really add significantly to the level of danger, considering that this area was already a cash cow for the pirates.

But there was one other danger, and the presence of possible terrorists with some of the pirate attacks underscores it. Australia's government jumped on the bandwagon of fears, and I believe rightly so. Terrorists could hit the area with a dirty bomb, they feared. This would be devastating. If a general cargo ship was taken, disappeared and then a dirty bomb built aboard, it would be a powerful projectile. Sailed to the narrowest point of the Strait, its detonation would make the Strait impassible from radiation for 90 years. World traffic would have to rack up close to 1,000 miles more on their journey east and west and go through the Sunda Strait.

If this was the reason for the "dry runs" by terrorists, they faced a number of problems. The biggest was the pirates. Pirates wouldn't be inclined to let their golden goose get killed, and they far outnumber terrorists in that region. They have a world network connecting Indonesia, Africa, and the Caribbean that is probably more impressive than a terrorist network and easier to conceal. Nevertheless, there is a disturbing middleground. Pirates could teach terrorists the ins-and-outs of seizing ships, or they could even agree, for a hefty fee, to steal the ships for them. But Malacca could never be the target. The initial reporting of pirates and terrorists together was in 2002-2004, and after that there is no real record that I know of. Could it be that the infamous pirates of Malacca were initially more than happy to supply ships for a price and even train the terrorist crews? But when they found out the goal was to cripple the Strait, did they tell al-Qaeda to pip off?

There should be little surprise that terrorists and pirates should forge links. It had been suspected for a long time that some ports in Haradheere or Kismayo had been used as hideouts for pirated ships. The seclusion did not come cheap, however. The pirates paid a stiff "duty" to remain in port. When it came time that terrorists should consider ships as their next weapon, the contacts were there. For a price pirates will do anything. They can deliver ships well paid for (or for port concessions), and even train jihad crews to pilot a ship in some suicide run. But they're not going to cut their most valuable throat at Malacca and enrage the easy-going modern day Tortuga governments in the area.

What other targets could the terrorists set a secretly acquired cargo ship to? It would have to be one of no financial interest to pirates. My mind came back to the thousands of deserted keys, lagoons, and sequestered haunts, in south Florida.

In 1994 the head of Iraq's atomic program had defected. He later wrote a book and appeared on many American news shows (including the O'Reilly Factor). He alerted Americans to Iraq's growing nuclear capabilities. At the present time there was little worry of a nuclear bomb. . .but a dirty bomb is another matter. It doesn't have to be launched. It does not cause physical destruction; only radioactive contamination. It would only take about a tanker truck full and a half of dirty spent fuel to make "a really good dirty bomb."

Considering the worldwide developments that indicated terrorist interest in huge ships, and possible pirate deals, I wondered if our attacks on Iraq were not inspired by a fear that Iraq could supply the fuel needed to make a dirty bomb and give it its 90 year punch. The fear was never nuclear weapons, but dirty spent fuel. A huge tanker could be rigged as a dirty bomb, sailed into a port and then set off. Savannah, San Pedro, San Francisco would be uninhabitable for 90 years.

Attacks by ships would prove easier than getting dirty spent fuel into America barrel by barrel. The Triangle could prove an interesting cover for an approaching time-bomb ship. The vessel could masquerade as another ship heading for a Central American or South American port, then suddenly report mechanical problems and request to divert to a US port. Or if its SOS was designed to attract a hapless and passing cargo ship to come assist, a terrorist garrison aboard could clamber aboard the other ship and hold it hostage while the bomb ship proceeded in its place and name to its US port of call, there to be unsuspectingly admitted.

Cargo ships have furtively traveled thousands of miles even after suspected of being pirated. The case of the *Arctic Sea* is one in hand. On July 23, 2009, she left Finland. Off Sweden she was boarded by a dozen men claiming to be drug police. They tied up the Russian crew and ransacked the ship. . .supposedly. The incident was, amazingly, *not* reported for days. By this time *Arctic Sea* had passed the Straits of Dover. No one suspected anything despite the fact the captain of the vessel should have made contact with the Coast Guard. "And no-one, it seems," according to the British press, "tried to make contact with him." The huge cargo vessel disappeared for weeks before being located far from her port of destination.

A terrorist controlled vessel could easily switch identities around Bermuda and make a journey to a US port without being suspected.

Crippling and underhanded nuclear attacks would possibly yield one mutual benefit for terrorists and pirates alike: governments in upheaval. Fear of reprisal would cause some governments to shrink back. In 2001 some governments initially even refused to turn over to the US persons suspected of being involved in the 9/11 attacks. In this environment, governments will watch their own backdoor, not the world's oceans. The result is an ocean where commerce is on a free range to be pirated, ransomed, extorted— unrestricted avarice.

Already it is very difficult to tackle the problem pirates pose. "There is no reason not to be a pirate," said Vice Admiral William Gortney in 2008, commander of the U.S. Navy's 5th Fleet. He laid the scenario out plainly enough. "The vessel I'm trying to pirate, they won't shoot at me. I'm going to get my money. They won't arrest me because there's no place to try me." Admiral Mike Mullen, then Chairman of the Joint Chiefs of Staff, noted the same problem. "One of the challenges that we have . . .in piracy clearly is if you are intervening and you capture pirates, is there a path to prosecute them?" He also noted how profitable basic piracy can be even for the beginners. It was estimated that the hijacking the Saudi tanker *Sirius Star* cost only $25,000, an estimate that assumes that the perpetrators bought new weapons to begin with. ($450 for each an AK-47 Kalashnikov, $5,000 for an RPG 7 grenade launcher, $15,000 for a speedboat). The ransom demanded from the *Sirius Star*'s owners was a whopping $25 million.

What would the difficulties for prosecution be like in a post dirty bomb world?

One might counter this with noting that a dirty bomb set off in any port would only unite the world governments to sweep the seas clean of piracy and terrorists. Pirates would never do something that would unite the world against them. This is quite true, but it also presupposes that the pirates are quite politic in their thoughts— an attribute which is hardly dominant in brigands. From experience, one should also rightly doubt how whole-hearted some countries would join in, especially if the victim was America.

The belief that pirates could be easily defeated by a united force also doesn't suppose that the modern pirates of Malacca are well-connected. And yet world piracy has shown they are well-connected: from Malacca, Somalia, Yemen, Nigeria, Lagos, the Caribbean, and Turkey. Piracy manifests itself in old fashioned ways. But we know the intended victims are watched, selectively chosen, set up, and then pirated to order. They sail cargo for a while, then vanish. They are ransomed and earn their extortion money. But where are the masterminds of the pirates of Malacca? Where can they be found? They're not the captains and thugs boarding ships. These modern Henry

Morgans have contacts everywhere, plush offices and gentlemanly appearances. What is their influence on governments in Indochina, where they have long hidden behind the protection of sovereign states? Just where could the retaliation be directed?

Piracy is rampant already. Yet how much retaliation has it really inspired from world governments? In 2005 piracy was so bad that Lloyd's of London declared the Strait of Malacca a war zone. From 2007 on it has gotten steadily worse again.

But the reemergence has seen one comforting thing return, comforting, that is, in contrast to the above suppositions: the normal, old fashion, sword wielding piracy. Terrorists disappeared from the scenes. Perhaps the attacks on Iraq crippled any attempt to use a ship as a dirty bomb. Perhaps the pirates didn't want such huge escalation and they nixed the terrorists.

But the fear remains. Iran has nuclear capabilities, and that means dirty spent fuel. Thus the possibility remains today that a tanker or cargo ship could be used as a terrible weapon in a world facing the realities of dystopia.

Mohamed Abdullahi Mohamed, prime minister in Somalia's Mogudishu-based Transitional Federal Government, declared on March 10, 2011: "It will not surprise us if al-Qaeda's agents in Somalia start hijacking tankers in the high seas and use them as deadly weapons."

This they might indeed do, and this fear we must keep foremost in our minds. But we might take one more comfort, and this from history. It seems they toyed with this idea in 2002-2004 and really didn't get far. How much of this was due to counter-terrorism and how much was due to the power of the pirates of Malacca? Perhaps some. Perhaps very little. But the pirates have been in place decades longer than terrorists *and* counter-terrorist measures. They take the seas head on and no world government so far has made a dent in their network. We may owe our general safety more to them than our own retaliations. Terrorists had a jewel of a target in the Malacca Strait, but seemed to have forsaken it without our help. Ships haven't been pirated for dirty bombs so far, though it's been a long 10 years since 9/11. It may be that the pirates have kept the terrorists off their turf.

As a policy we may not deal with terrorists, but history has taught us that we can deal with pirates. We may find it easier, and worth perhaps some free booty, to enlist their aid in exposing al-Qaeda networks. Terrorists may be surprised to learn that things probably are little different today than when Henry Morgan reformed himself and became an English governor. . .or when pirates turned privateer under the Union Jack and earned pardons. Pirates today may be bleeding world shipping, but they do so for profit, not for ideology. The avaricious are predictable. Ideologues are not. Business can no doubt be achieved with pirates. The terrorists started encroaching into the realm of a profession thousands of years old and by comparison al-Qaeda are babes in arms with a limited monomania about getting rid of Israel and making the US pay for its support. This tambourine may have an annoying rhythm to pirates already.

It is a rough and tumble world again. It is an era of making history, not believing it is no longer being made. The world is getting larger, not smaller. The era of black and white clarity fades to the grays of expedience. Rogues will become leaders. Who indeed shall rise forth? Will the pirates of Malacca become a useful weapon for civilization? The high seas are lawless seas, but they are ironic seas. Those who command them command the highways of the world. That temptress lets them do it. The squabbles of mankind add not one whit to her. One thing is her domain. That one thing she will always covet, and nothing shall take it from her. She owns every portal to that distant horizon.

Bibliography

In addition to the sources mentioned within the body of the narrative, the author would like to call the attention of the reader to the following:.

Bryan, George S.   *Mystery Ship*,   J.P. Lippincott, 1942.

Dali, Alex   *Piracy Attacks in the Malacca Strait*,   Atlas Services, Singapore, 2001.

Debusman, Bernd   *The business case for high seas piracy*,   Reuters, April 26, 2008.

Fay, Charles Edey,   *Odyssey of an Abandoned Ship*,   Peabody Museum, 1942.

Gaddis, Vincent H.   *Invisible Horizons*,   Chilton, 1965.

Gibraltar *Chronicle*,   January 21, 1873.

Gould, Rupert T.   *The Stargazer Talks*,   Geoffrey Bles, 1943.

Hart, Jerems & Stone, William   *A Cruising Guide to the Bahamas*,   Dodd, Mead, 1976.

How to Defeat Pirate Success in Strait,   Time/World, April 22, 2009.

Lindbergh, Charles,   *Autobiography of Values*,   Harcourt Brace Jovanovich, 1978.

Marine Casualty Report:

                    Marine Sulphur Queen, disappearance of the SS *Marine Sulphur Queen* at sea on or about 4 February 1963 with the presumed loss of all persons aboard. US Coast Guard,

"   "   SS *Poet*: Disappearance in the Atlantic Ocean after departure from Cape Henlopen, Delaware, on 24 October 1980 with loss of life. US Coast Guard.

Marine Board of Investigation:

                    Disappearance of fishing vessel *Theresa A.*, with all persons aboard, off Atlantic Coast, September 1950.

"   "   Disappearance of fishing vessel *Paolina* with all persons aboard, off Atlantic Coast, February 1952.

"   "   F/V *Doris Gertrude*, foundering off New England Coast subsequent to 13 January 1955 with eleven crew members on board.

"   "   F/V *Four Sisters*, sinking of, with loss of life of crew in vicinity of Nantucket Shoal area during April, 1950.

"   "   Disappearance of fishing vessel *Gudrun* with all persons on board off Atlantic Coast, January 1951.

"   "   Disappearance of fishing vessel *Susan* off Atlantic Coast of the United States with seven persons on board December 1953.

"   "   Tug KING CO-BRA — Investigation into the disappearance of with loss of life on or about 2 January 1979.

"   "   F/V *Navigator* — Investigation into the disappearance of with subsequent loss of life on or about 1 December 1977.

"   "   F/V *Heidi Marie* —Investigation into the disappearance of with loss of life on or about 21 November 1989.

National Archives and Records Administration: Record Group 26, 59, 36, 41, 65 Re: *Mary Celeste*

"   "   Record Group 26, 59, 36, Re: *Carroll A. Deering.*

National Archives and Records Administrations: Boxes 1068-1070, Modern Military Branch Re: USS *Cyclops*.

National Transportation Safety Board Marine Accident Report: Loss of the U.S. Fishing Vessel *Amazing Grace* About 80 Nautical Miles East of Cape Henlopen, Delaware About November 14, 1984.

New York Historical Library, letter to author, 1992: Re: *Ellen Austin*.

New York *Times*, July 31, 1904.

Philadelphia *Enquirer*, July 31, 1904.

Quasar, Gian J.   *Into the Bermuda Triangle*, McGraw-Hill, 2003.

"   "   *Hell Ship*, Brodwyn, Moor & Doane, 2011.

"   "   *They Flew into Oblivion*,   Brodwyn, Moor & Doane, 2010.

Report of the investigation into the disappearance of William and Patricia Kamerer on yacht *Kalia III*— Foul Play is suspected, Nassau CID, 1980.

Ripley, Robert L., *Believe it or Not Omnibus,* Pearson, 1929,

Sigsbee, S.D., *Wrecks and Derelicts of the North Atlantic, 1887 through 1893 Inclusive.* US Hydrographic Office, 1894.

Simpson, Bland *Ghost Ship of Diamond Shoals,* University of North Carolina Press, 2002.

Snow, Edward Rowe, *Mysteries and Adventures Along the Atlantic Coast,* Dodd, Mead & Co., 1948.

Somali Islamists Could Grab Tanker for Attacks, Reuters, March 10, 2011.

The Cargo letter, issues 1998-2001, Law Offices of Countryman & McDaniel.

Tute, Warren, *Atlantic Conquest,* Little Brown, 1962.

Wellington *Evening Post,* November 13, 1913.

Wilkins, Harold T., *Strange Mysteries of Time & Space*, Citadel Press, 1959.

Winer, Richard, *The Devil's Triangle,* Bantam, 1974.

" " *The Devil's Triangle II,* Bantam, 1975.

Wraight, J.M. Letter to author, 1992, RE: *Ellen Austin*

Made in the USA
San Bernardino, CA
06 April 2016